WE SHALL NOT BE MOVED

We Shall Not Be Moved

Methodists Debate Race, Gender, and Homosexuality

JANE ELLEN NICKELL

PICKWICK *Publications* · Eugene, Oregon

WE SHALL NOT BE MOVED
Methodists Debate Race, Gender, and Homosexuality

Pickwick Publications
An Imprint of Wipf and Stock Publishers
199 W. 8th Ave., Suite 3
Eugene, OR 97401

www.wipfandstock.com

ISBN 13: 978-1-62564-484-8

Cataloguing-in-Publication data:

Nickell, Jane Ellen.

We shall not be moved : Methodists debate race, gender, and homosexuality / Jane Ellen Nickell.

xii + 192 pp. ; 23 cm. Includes bibliographical references.

ISBN 13: 978-1-62564-484-8

1. United Methodist Church (U.S.)—Doctrines. 2. Methodist Church (U.S.)—History. 3. Race relations—Religious aspects—Methodist Church—History. 4. Women in church work—Methodist Church—History. 5. Homosexuality—Religious aspects—United Methodist Church. 3. I. Title.

BX8331.3 .N53 2014

Manufactured in the U.S.A.

In memory of two gentle men:

my father, whose love for the church inspired my own,

and Otto Maduro, who taught me the key
to understanding its shortcomings.

Contents

Acknowledgments

I AM DEEPLY GRATEFUL to my colleagues at Drew University, especially Traci West, Morrey Davis, Laurel Kearns, Karen McCarthy Brown, Terry Todd, and Jody Caldwell, who helped shape this project, and to Lloyd Lewis, in whose class at Vanderbilt Divinity School this line of scholarly inquiry began. Thanks to the staff at the General Commission on Archives and at the Methodist Library at Drew University for their assistance with my research, with special thanks to Mark Shenise, who readily and rapidly replied to my email requests to check facts or citations after I moved seven hours away. I am indebted to Larry Mencotti, Bruce Stephens, Danuta Majchrowitz, Karen Nickell, and Carl Olson, who read all or parts of the manuscript at certain points and were important sounding boards, and to my friends and colleagues at Allegheny College for their encouragement. My special thanks to Brenda Armstrong for her friendship and assistance over the eight years we have worked together, six of which have been devoted to this project.

I acknowledge with gratitude the Methodist clergy and laity whose voices are captured in the transcripts cited here, knowing that these speeches cannot express the depth of commitment and the life stories that lie behind each one of them. In addition to the leaders mentioned here, there are many more who have guided the church through these difficult times. I am especially grateful to Bishop William Boyd Grove for his wise and compassionate leadership in the church, and for his interest in this project. Thank you, Bishop Grove, for reading the manuscript, providing details and background that went beyond the written record, and believing in the importance of this work.

Thank you to my family and friends, who put up with me always having my nose in a book, making libraries part of visits to their communities, and needing to write every day, even on the family vacation to the beach. To my brothers, sisters-in-law, niece and nephews, aunts, uncles, cousins, and friends who have listened to me rattle on about this topic, your apparent interest kept me going—and to all of you who actually said, "I'd like to read that," well, now you can.

My most special thanks goes to my mom, who, together with my dad, saw me through two midlife graduate programs, at times taking in me, my belongings, and one of my cats, and despite their concerns for my financial well-being, were solid rocks of support. Mom, for helping me, cheering me when things did not go well, celebrating with me when they did, and loving me no matter what, I thank you from the bottom of my heart. I couldn't have done it without you!

Abbreviations

Methodist Denominations

AMEC	The African Methodist Episcopal Church (1816–present)
AMEZC	The African Methodist Episcopal Church, Zion (1821–present)
CMEC	The Colored Methodist Episcopal Church (1870–1954); The Christian Methodist Episcopal Church (1954–present)
EA	The Evangelical Association (1807–1946)
EUBC	The Evangelical United Brethren Church (1946–1968)
MC	The Methodist Church (1939–1968)
MEC	The Methodist Episcopal Church (1784–1939)
MECS	The Methodist Episcopal Church, South (1844–1939)
MPC	The Methodist Protestant Church (1830–1939)
UBC	The United Brethren Church (1800–1946)
UMC	The United Methodist Church (1968–present)

Other Abbreviations

CIC	Commission on Interracial Cooperation
CRH	Council on Religion and the Homosexual
DCA	*Daily Christian Advocate*
ELCA	Evangelical Lutheran Church of America
IAWP	International Association of Women Preachers
MFSS	Methodist Federation for Social Service (since 1948, Methodist Federation for Social Action)
NACW	National Association of Colored Women
PCUSA	Presbyterian Church (USA)
RCP	Reconciling Congregations Program (since 2000, the Reconciling Ministries Network)
TCP	Transforming Congregations Program

Abbreviations

UMNS   United Methodist News Service
WCTU   Woman's Christian Temperance Union
WMC   Woman's Missionary Council (MECS)

Intransigent Leadership Patterns
Theory and Context

> "Prophetic discourse makes descend from heaven
> that which it projects there from earth."
>
> —PIERRE BOURDIEU

Introduction to Key Questions

IN 2011, THIRTY-SIX RETIRED bishops in The United Methodist Church (UMC) issued a statement calling on the church to remove its ban on ordaining gays and lesbians. They cited a number of reasons, among them the strain on closeted pastors, on active bishops who are forced to indict those who "come out," and on gay United Methodists who feel called to ministry but whose church gives them no acceptable options. They mentioned the loss of members, gay and straight, especially young adults who are embarrassed to invite friends to church. The bishops expressed "dismay at the unwillingness of our United Methodist Church to alter its 39-year exclusionary stance." Using the language of a contrite sinner, the bishops noted the church's shame and repentance for past prohibitions based on race, gender, and ethnicity, and wrote: "We believe the God we know in Jesus is leading us to issue this counsel and call—a call to transform our church life and our world." [1]

1. "A Statement of Counsel to the Church-2011." http://www.umc-gbcs.org/site/apps/nlnet/content.aspx?c=frLJK2PKLqF&b=6553001&ct=9110163.

Soon thereafter, Black Methodists for Church Renewal endorsed the bishops' statement at their annual meeting, and nine black clergy and scholars of the UMC issued their own statement against the bigotry and injustice that they felt the ban on gay clergy represents. These scholars named their familiarity with discrimination, even within their own church, and wrote that it was nothing new to see "imperfect humans draped in an august array of Christian doctrines uttering an allegiance to 'scriptural authority' and 'natural law.'" They admitted to being in the uncomfortable position of speaking against other African Americans who have "joined ranks with those who spew bigotry" and were now "wielding doctrine and scripture as their tools just as was done during slavery and the Jim Crow era." They went on to quote the Rev. Dr. Martin Luther King, Jr., who said in his eulogy of civil rights activist James Reeb, that "he was murdered by the irrelevancy of a church that will stand amid social evil and serve as a taillight rather than a headlight, an echo rather than a voice."[2] The scholars stated that the UMC had missed its opportunity to be a headlight for gay rights and must now catch up to the larger society.

These statements by United Methodist bishops and scholars reflect the tensions within the UMC since the church instituted language in 1972 that homosexuality[3] is "incompatible with Christian teaching," and they echo the stress that lingers from the church's historic restrictions against leadership by African Americans and women. These statements and the groups that made them raise the issues addressed in this book, namely: Who holds power in the UMC and its predecessor bodies,[4] not just to lead churches, but to decide who those leaders will be? How do changes in authority structures occur, and why is it such a long and painful process? Finally, how are the stories of marginalized groups within the church interrelated?

2. "An Endorsement Against Church Bigotry and the Injustice of ¶ 304.3." http://www.ipetitions.com/petition/pocforlgbtq.

3. The UMC uses the terms "homosexual" and "homosexuality" in its policies, so that language is reflected in church statements and debates. I also use "homosexual" and "gay" as adjectives, but use the noun forms "gay men" or "gays" and "lesbians." I do not use acronyms such as LGBTQ (lesbian, gay, bisexual, transgender, queer), as the UMC has only recently begun to address issues relating to bisexual and transgender persons, and has not considered larger issues related to queer identities in the denominational forums that this research addresses.

4. The UMC was formed in 1968 as a merger of The Methodist Church and the Evangelical United Brethren Church, both products of mergers themselves. Specific bodies will be identified throughout the text.

The United Methodist Church currently prohibits the ordination of gays and lesbians and the blessing of same-sex unions. Those who support these policies claim that scripture clearly indicates God's disapproval of homosexuality. Yet biblical scholars have pointed out that the handful of passages cited are difficult to interpret and address the issue of same-sex behavior, rather than more recent understandings of sexual orientation. By contrast, the UMC takes a moderate position on divorce and remarriage, which are likewise condemned in scripture.

A look at Methodist history reveals equally strong and persistent opposition to the ordination of women and to allowing African Americans to have leadership over white Methodists. After decades of debate and division, the institutional barriers to these two groups collapsed. But although segregation ended in 1968 and women gained full clergy rights in 1956, the ranks of the ordained in the UMC remain 86 percent white and 77 percent male.[5] Such figures suggest entrenched resistance that persists decades after authority structures were changed.

The theory of Pierre Bourdieu (1930–2002) offers insights into the ongoing resistance to religious leadership by these marginalized groups. Bourdieu explores the subtle and often unconscious dynamics of social domination, through which those in power and those outside of it are socialized to see certain groups in religious leadership—in this case white, presumably heterosexual[6] men. While this social arrangement seems natural, even inevitable, Bourdieu's theory reveals that the privileging of this group over others is not based on ability or gift but is, in fact, arbitrary. The complexity of the socialization process, as well as its subconscious nature, explains how people can be unaware of the roots of their resistance to changes in the social order and their reliance on ideologies such as religion to explain, or legitimate, it. Once a social structure is understood as God's intended plan, deviation is seen as a threat to divine order. Furthering that sense of threat, the church has confronted these issues during periods of social change, when new ways of thinking challenged traditional worldviews.

The history of American Methodism[7] parallels the history of the country, so it has confronted the leadership of these groups at the same

5. Clergy data from 2010, UMC General Commission on Finance and Administration. http://www.gcfa.org/data-services.

6. Because sexual orientation can be concealed more easily than gender or race, pastors who are not heterosexual can keep that identity hidden in order to protect their authority.

7. Division and reunion characterize Methodism in the United States, so there are a

time the nation was dealing with various rights campaigns. Indeed, it was often pressure from these external movements that forced change within the church. The church embraces theological, political, and racial diversity, and, like the United States, it decides policy through a delegated body— the General Conference. This book examines debates at these quadrennial General Conferences, which offer a window into the life of the church at various points in its history and a key to understanding the resistance of church members to changes in authority structures.

Methodism remains the second largest Protestant denomination in the country and embraces diverse theological and political perspectives. Other denominations are more homogenous, such as the right leaning Southern Baptist Convention, or have fractured over the issue of sexual orientation. The Episcopal Church is most famous for the conflict that ensued when it consecrated Gene Robinson, an openly gay bishop, in 2003, but the Evangelical Lutheran Church of America (ELCA) and Presbyterian Church (USA) (PCUSA) have also lost members over their pro-gay policies. In each case new, more conservative denominations or movements have arisen where congregations that want to maintain traditional authority patterns may affiliate.[8] That this issue is prompting a re-formation of American Protestantism indicates that it is a symptom of much deeper division. Using the lens of social theory, this look at historical conflicts over church leadership seeks to unmask and examine that division.

American Methodism

Methodism began as a renewal movement in the Church of England in the eighteenth century, led by John Wesley and his brother Charles, both Anglican priests. The brothers themselves made an unsuccessful mission trip to Georgia in 1836, but the American movement began in earnest in the 1760s. In 1784, American Methodists declared their independence from the British movement and became The Methodist Episcopal Church

check date

---

number of smaller denominations that share both structural and doctrinal similarities with the larger bodies described here. This book will use the term "Methodism" to refer primarily to the largest and most prevalent denominations in each historical period: The Methodist Episcopal Church (1784–1939) and Methodist Episcopal Church, South (1844–1939), The Methodist Church (1939–1968), and The United Methodist Church (since 1968). Specific denominations will be identified within discussions of each historic era.

8. These schisms will be compared to the United Methodist situation in chapter 4.

(MEC). Within a few decades, the church had lost many of its African American members, who formed separate denominations in 1816 (African Methodist Episcopal Church, or AMEC) and in 1821 (African Methodist Episcopal Church, Zion, AMEZC). The MEC itself split in 1844, as southern Methodists seceded to become The Methodist Episcopal Church, South (MECS), with slavery among the issues that prompted the divide. Smaller denominations broke away over conflicts with the larger bodies, including The Methodist Protestant Church (MPC) in 1828.

In the twentieth century, Methodists began talks of reunion, which required discussion of geographic differences related to racial issues. The early feminist movement overlapped with these tensions, prompting debate about women's leadership in the church. Differences were ironed out, and in 1939, the MEC, the MECS, and the MPC merged to form The Methodist Church (MC). The church grew even larger in 1968 when it merged with the Evangelical United Brethren Church (EUBC) to become the current United Methodist Church (UMC). It was following this merger that the new church began to deal with the issue of gay rights, again following the trend of the larger U.S. society.

Consistent throughout its history is the church's connectional nature, through which bishops appoint pastors to serve at local churches, as opposed to congregational polity in which churches call their own pastors. Methodist clergy "in full connection" agree to itinerancy, going wherever the church appoints them and are guaranteed an appointment to serve one or more churches, moving on to a new appointment whenever the bishop determines it is in the best interest of the congregation and/or the pastor. This connection requires sufficient agreement on leadership criteria, since a pastor could theoretically be appointed to serve anywhere within the denomination. Practically, clergy are affiliated with a geographic region, but even within such an area there is often a range of opinions on how the church should confront changing times and who should qualify for leadership.

Another aspect of Methodist connectionalism is the conference, through which polity is set. Originally comprising only clergy, Methodist conferences evolved to include both lay and clergy delegates, and today include both in equal numbers. Early American Methodism embraced the Wesleyan emphasis on Christian conferencing, which resonated with the fraternal, egalitarian spirit of the young republic. Although the word "Episcopal" in the American church's name referred to the bishops whose oversight distinguished the church from the British movement, the conference was a defining feature of the U.S. church, and over time came to rival the episcopacy in power and authority.

At first the MEC gathered all of its ordained clergy for periodic conferences, as John Wesley had in England. But as the U.S. church grew in size and expanded geographically, such meetings became unwieldy, leading to the establishment of multiple conferences. In 1792, clergy gathered for a General Conference, which would meet every four years to address denominational matters, while the clergy of a specific region would meet in annual conferences and be supervised by a bishop. Since 1792, the actions of each General Conference have been published in a book of *Doctrines and Discipline*, shortened in the twentieth century to *The Book of Discipline*. Issued every four years, the Discipline delineates church structure and relationships of authority and mutual accountability. By 1808 General Conference was a delegated body, rather than comprising all clergy, and by the end of the nineteenth century, lay representatives were included along with clergy delegates. The General Conference throughout its history has served as the primary policy-making body for the church and is the only official voice that speaks for the current United Methodist Church.

The General Conference is thus the forum for resolving conflict between those advocating change and those who affirm existing structures. As such, debate is often heated and reflects both personal and political concerns. As the leadership of African Americans, women, and gays and lesbians has been considered, General Conference delegates have often served as the spokespersons for well-organized caucus groups, as well as expresssing their personal beliefs. In this work, I use Bourdieu's theory to examine transcripts of those speeches for evidence of resistance to social change that may lie behind stated objections framed in theological or scriptural language.

Pierre Bourdieu's Theory

The son of a French provincial civil servant, Pierre Bourdieu studied and taught philosophy before being drafted into military service in Algeria. He remained there two years doing fieldwork in Kabylia, which provided the foundation of his sociological practice. Widely published, Bourdieu taught at L'Ecole Practique des Hautes Etudes en Sciences Sociales, directed the Centre de Sociologie Européene, and held the prestigious chair of sociology

The current state of thinking about the "subconscious" or the "unconscious" would be relevant.

at the College de France. His influence in the field of sociology has continued to grow since his death in 2002.

A protean thinker, Bourdieu draws on a wide range of scholarship and rejects attempts to associate him with a particular school or theorist as reductionist and pejorative.[9] Instead, he thinks both with and against other theorists, departing from their path as often as he follows it. Bourdieu incorporates existing theories, particularly the work of Max Weber, extending that work and bringing together seemingly contradictory schools of thought. By focusing on practice he seeks to escape the objective-subjective dualism he perceives in much social scientific scholarship. *what's this?* Rather than focusing exclusively on either the structure or the agent, he describes a dialectic process and looks for correspondence between social and mental structures. *Is this true now in Linguistics and Economics as well.*

For Bourdieu, the sociologist's task is to uncover buried social structures and the mechanisms that ensure their reproduction. His major works address education (*Homo Academicus* 1988) and culture (*Distinction* 1984), and he explores religion in just a few essays.[10] Nevertheless, his theoretical model offers valuable resources for examining the power dynamics in religious institutions; therefore, a brief survey of his theory is in order. He has articulated key concepts such as habitus, field, interest, and symbolic capital to describe the functioning of social systems and the practice of social agents. *defining unique terms prevent his ideas from being confused w*

In his efforts to transcend dualistic thinking, Bourdieu describes a dialectic between social structures and individual human agents. Integral to his understanding of this process is his concept of habitus, structuring mechanisms within agents that are inculcated through socialization, in other words, "socialized subjectivity."[11] The dialectic nature of habitus is evident in the circular language Bourdieu uses when discussing it, referring to it as "structured structures predisposed to function as structuring structures."[12] Through habitus, humans are socialized into a world that predisposes them to act in certain ways, yet within this set of predispositions, they remain free agents who determine their own practice. *prior ideas, a habit of academics.*

Habitus is a product of history that acts in the present to condition the future, but it is so internalized that it is unconscious, thus people are

9. Bourdieu, *In Other Words,* 27.

10. See Rey, *Bourdieu on Religion,* for an examination of Bourdieu's works on religion.

11. Bourdieu and Wacquant, *Invitation,* 126.

12. Bourdieu, *Outline,* 72.

How do we understand B.'s idea of a "dialectical process," one assumes it is an ongoing or cyclical creative process in which ideas feed off material arrangements and vice versa.

unaware of its connection to the past. The historic nature of habitus allows it to be changed; however, people tend to encounter experiences that confirm, or conserve, their habitus, so that change is generally gradual and unrecognized. Bourdieu notes that members of a particular group will have homologous rather than identical experiences, with individual dispositions that are structural variants of the larger habitus, a relationship of diversity within homogeneity.[13] He makes less frequent use of the term *collusio*, which reflects the immediate and unconscious agreement among members of the same social group. A sort of "collective habitus," *collusio* relates to the various social factors that shape a particular group, and can be especially helpful in discussing race, ethnicity, gender, and religion.[14]

Habitus is evident within fields, which Bourdieu describes as arenas of struggle for particular forms of capital, a concept inspired by Weber's description of contestation in the religious field among priests, prophets, and sorcerers. A field is a network of relationships involving those within it and the various positions they occupy; field thinking, Bourdieu writes, is relational thinking.[15] Habitus and field are interconnected, with a cognitive relationship through which habitus contributes to the meaning of a field, and a conditioning relationship through which field helps to structure a habitus.

In describing how fields function, Bourdieu uses the analogy of a game, noting that participants compete for various forms of capital, employing various strategies, trump cards, and collusion with other players.[16] He uses the term *doxa* to describe the tacit understanding that the game is worth playing and *illusio* to describe one's investment or interest in it. Field limits are fluid because they are part of what is at stake. Players develop a feel for the game, an unconscious understanding of how to play the game so that everything that takes place within the field makes sense to them.[17] The analogy ends, however, at the point of the agent's awareness that a game is an arbitrary social construct; one's investment in a social field prevents one from seeing its constructed nature.[18]

Bourdieu escapes economic reductionism by broadening his understanding of interest and capital to include social, cultural, and symbolic

13. Ibid., 88.
14. Rey, *Bourdieu on Religion*, 87–88.
15. Bourdieu and Wacquant, *Invitation*, 96.
16. Ibid., 98–99.
17. Bourdieu, *Logic*, 66.
18. Ibid., 67.

"Symbolic capital"

how do volunteers get paid?

capital, any or all of which may define agents' interests and motivate their actions, even as agents unconsciously conceal their interests (even from themselves). Bourdieu's notion of symbolic capital, a distinctive aspect of his theory, refers to the credit that accumulates from this "fiction" of disinterest, through the labor expended in concealing the true nature of an exchange.[19] Bourdieu makes clear that he is not talking about "naked self interest," but rather capital that is the misrecognized product of unconscious labor.[20] what is this?

I am inclined to believe this. That doesn't make it true.

Symbolic capital is critical to Bourdieu's understanding of how patterns of domination are reproduced. Symbolic capital masks the interest of dominant groups, making their dominance appear to be a natural rather than an arbitrary social arrangement. Habitus serves to establish and maintain these relations of domination, as even the dominated perceive social relations through the interests of the dominant. Once these relations are institutionalized, the dominant group exercises its domination by letting the system they dominate take its own course.[21] By participating in those institutions, those who are dominated perpetuate the power relations that disadvantage them. Bourdieu refers to this as symbolic violence that "extorts submission, which is not perceived as such, based on 'collective expectations' or socially inculcated beliefs,"[22] or, as he puts it elsewhere, "violence which is exercised upon a social agent with his or her complicity," albeit misrecognized.[23] Bourdieu describes masculine domination as the most pervasive example of symbolic violence—an arbitrary yet misrecognized form of domination that both men and women accept as natural.[24]

One should go through all possible examples to see if this schema is a useful one for discussing social relations among various classes or types of people. Of course, we do WANT some people to dominate others—

Bourdieu uses the term *doxa* to describe the correspondence between objective social order and the subjective principles of organizing the social and natural world that appear as self-evident, in other words, "the naturalization of its own arbitrariness."[25] *Doxa* is a field of unquestioned assumptions that are taken for granted and reinforced by the group's collective thought and practice.[26] Bourdieu distinguishes the subliminal state of

※A human-designed social order is not "arbitrary", it is just not "natural".

19. Bourdieu, *Outline*, 171. is just not "natural".
20. Bourdieu, *Logic*, 118. Generalized assumptions that
21. Bourdieu, *Outline*, 190. serve as short-cuts are really
22. Bourdieu, *Practical Reason*, 103. necessary to human
23. Bourdieu and Wacquant, *Invitation*, 167–68. thought. That
24. Bourdieu, *Masculine Domination*. said, they should
25. Bourdieu, *Outline*, 164. not remain unexamined
26. Ibid., 167. by philosophers et al.
He calls this "orthodoxy", a rational
and known set of assumptions,

properly dominated. Decisions should not be made by the stupid.

Some examples of "doxa" and orthodoxy should be collected. You see 'em in times of change.

doxa from orthodoxy, which carries an awareness that it may be opposed by heterodox beliefs.[27] *Doxa* itself may be challenged during times of crisis, as the dominated seek to expose the arbitrary nature of what has been taken for granted. In response, the dominant group imposes orthodoxy, an imperfect, conscious substitute for the innocent, unconscious state of *doxa*.

Bourdieu's discussion of the constructed nature of social life mirrors the work of social constructionists such as Peter Berger, who maintain that humans experience a taken-for-granted reality that is the product of an objectified symbolic universe that legitimates a particular social order. Like Berger, Bourdieu notes that religion is perhaps the most prevalent of such symbolic systems, which presents social structures as part of cosmic order. In order for religion to be effective, its constructed nature must be veiled, or as Bourdieu puts it, religious discourse "makes descend from heaven that which it projects there from earth."[28] *

Religious structures delineate boundaries between insiders and outsiders, and within the group, between religious leaders, or specialists, and the laity. Through ordination, certain persons are credentialed, or given credence, to perform ritual acts of transformation, such as changing bread and wine into the body and blood of Christ in the Eucharist. These acts of "social magic" create difference *ex nihilo* and turn arbitrary boundaries into sacred ones, keeping certain persons out and others inside the realm of the sacred. These rites are only effective if authorized and recognized by the entire social group. This goes beyond the symbolic in the Methodist tradition, where bishops ordain individual candidates, but the General Conference, representing the larger church, grants bishops that power and determines what groups qualify as candidates for ordination.

L. does not belong in this. certain persons are credentialed to present orthodoxy. The magic act is a symbolic enactment of this.

While religious leadership obviously carries a certain power, the arbitrary elevation of a certain group of people into that role, and their ongoing accrual of religious as well as political and economic capital, goes misrecognized by both the dominant and the dominated. Bourdieu notes that religion uses two forms of religiosity to reinforce social patterns: a dominant religiosity that justifies one group's dominance, and a religiosity of the dominated that recognizes the legitimacy of the dominant and misrecognizes the arbitrariness of the arrangement. These opposing poles

religion \ social structure relation works BOTH WAYS.

27. Ibid., 164. *A we understand God as part of the structures that we know. Jesus is King. Whatever that means.*
28. Bourdieu, "Genesis and Structure," 21.

B— we found religion or promote it in order to perpetuate disused social structures. Methodism values "Education".

within religion take on the appearance of unity through common beliefs and rituals that conceal the competing interpretations.[29]

As in other fields, competition within the religious field occurs when a prophet or prophetic movement challenges priestly power. In response, religious specialists will assert orthodoxy, as they seek to preserve the habitus that will reproduce patterns that guarantee their own privilege. What is at stake in such contests, Bourdieu writes, "is the *monopoly of the legitimate exercise of the power to modify, in a deep and lasting fashion, the practice and world-view of lay people,* by imposing on and inculcating in them a particular *religious habitus*" (emphasis in original).[30] In other words, religious leaders seek to retain social structures and processes that benefit them, even as others challenge the religious arguments used to justify their exclusive claim to power. Methodism's democratic polity generally gives rise to prophetic movements, rather than individual prophets, and often in response to social movements in the larger society. These movements disrupt the established order by igniting tensions between conservative and progressive forces. While the established order may appear static, it is the product of an ongoing history of change, through prophetic challenges that disrupt that history and reshape the future.

The dominant group misrecognizes its own interest not only because of its socialization and the religious arguments that justify their leadership, but also because the whole process lies at a deep, somatized level. Bourdieu points out the role that bodies play in the socialization process and in religious ritual. He describes habitus as an embodiment of history, an "immanent law, *lex insita,* inscribed in bodies by identical histories, which is the precondition not only for the coordination of practices but also for the practices of coordination."[31] The embodiment of a common habitus, incorporated so deeply that it seems natural, assures the smooth functioning of society, whereas bodily difference is consecrated through ritual, setting certain persons apart for special functions. The symbolic meaning of these bodily differences, especially between the sexes, are critical to the issues examined in this book. In all three cases, racialized, genderized, and/or sexualized differences are assigned religious significance for the group that is deemed unfit for leadership.

29. Ibid., 19.
30. Bourdieu, "Legitimation," 126.
31. Bourdieu, *Logic,* 59.

Bourdieu's understanding of how religion serves to legitimate arbitrary patterns of domination is central to the argument that contests over Methodist leadership are the product of a habitus that predisposes certain groups to be viewed as authority figures. When groups that are traditionally among the dominated are presented for leadership, it is perceived as a transgression of borders that have become so naturalized that they are seen as God's intended order. Bourdieu notes that such borders can only be abolished at the cost of a symbolic revolution.[32] Despite such entrenched resistance, revolutions do occur, leading to changes in religious habitus over time. Methodist leadership has changed over time, but not without great stress, which occurs most often during periods when society is already stressed by rapid social change, which these cases demonstrate.

Some examples of "Symbolic revolution" should be ID.

Methodism as a Religious Field

In his few works on religion, Bourdieu's discussion of the religious field focuses on the centralized, hierarchical order of the Roman Catholic Church, in which priests have an exclusive hold on religious capital by virtue of their control of the sacraments. Such is not the case in Methodism, for while clergy accrue religious capital through their liturgical leadership, the sacraments have a lesser role in Protestantism, where the emphasis on salvation by faith grants greater responsibility to laity. In addition, Methodist laity can access capital through their bureaucratic involvement in governing the institution and establishing criteria for leadership. Methodist authority is thus shared among religious specialists and laity, allowing various individuals and groups to use different forms of capital, such as social or political, as well as religious, to influence the Methodist decision-making process.

The history of American Methodism reveals a longstanding power struggle between bishops and the General Conference. From the initial move to a delegated body, bishops ceased to be members of the General Conference—they would preside over the proceedings but could not make motions or vote. General Conferences continued to chip away at episcopal power by making them subject to General Conference legislation and judicial appeals. With no official voice in General Conference sessions, bishops have protested their lack of authority over the body whose dictates they must enforce; one commented that they are no different from the potted

32. Ibid., 33.

"symbolic capital" = you could call this "respect" that is
present in the 'currency' of the Church.

Intransigent Leadership Patterns

palms that line the stage—"just part of the decoration."[33] Nevertheless, their presiding role grants them the power to determine which delegates are allowed to speak and to make rulings that influence the outcome of the proceedings. In addition, the collective body of bishops makes an episcopal address at General Conference, which, as we will see, can strongly influence the debate. Through this address, bishops gain symbolic capital, as they do by their ongoing leadership in the life of the church, and through statements that they make on various issues, either as an official body or unofficially, as did the retired bishops cited at the beginning of this chapter. Even within this dispersed, connectional system, bishops hold a certain standing, and their presiding role at General Conference should not be underestimated, given the public and political nature of those proceedings.

Bishops are, in essence, the public face of the denomination. General Conference may be the only official voice for the church, but its variable nature prevents the accumulation of any symbolic or religious capital. The Conference meets for two weeks, or less in recent years, and reconvenes four years later with different membership. The form and function of the General Conference have also made it subject to political forces, which coalesced in the twentieth century in the formation of caucuses. Existing both within the church and outside it, caucus groups seek to influence the election of General Conference delegates and to sway the votes of those elected. The influence of caucuses is evident in the coordinated effort to have speakers deliver carefully crafted, politicized speeches that represent their groups' interests. In the written records examined here, there is no way to tell in most cases which speeches represent a spontaneous outpouring, which ones have been crafted in advance, and which lie somewhere in between. Clear themes are stated around each issue that show evidence of effective strategizing, which are summarized in each chapter.

In addition to bishops, the General Conference, and caucuses, other groups in the Methodist tradition have gained a substantial share of authority as well. Methodist scholars and the church's many colleges, universities, and seminaries study and critique the church, in addition to training pastors, giving them indirect influence in the local church. As the church grew in size, denominational boards and agencies took on more leadership, and a Judicial Council was created to review episcopal and General Conference decisions. The UMC is undergoing a growth in global membership that has not been matched by increased income. The church has considered various

33. Kirby, *The Episcopacy*, 75.

restructuring plans, most of which would decrease the size of boards and agencies. In discussions of these plans, the political capital of each group is at stake, with the Judicial Council having the final say about the constitutionality of any plan the General Conference passes. This was illustrated at the 2012 General Conference, which is discussed in chapter 5.

As it has grown and developed over time, the Methodist "connection" is an intertwined web of responsibility and authority, unlike the hierarchical model that Bourdieu describes. Thus a distinct difference from Bourdieu's explanation of the priestly monopoly is that clergy and lay share power in the Methodist tradition, since religious authority is separate from bureaucratic authority. We find various groups and individuals using political or social capital, as well as religious, to pursue their own interests in seeking to modify the religious habitus, and thus the worldview and practice, of the membership of the church. Contests for power have sprung from challenges by different demographic groups within Methodism to define who is qualified for religious leadership as ordained clergy, as well as the closely related issue of who can serve as General Conference delegates.

Throughout American Methodism's first century, the General Conference was dominated by white, male, English-speaking clergy, who shared a "fraternal" bond. The entry of lay representatives was the first disruption of that bond, yet clergy made room for these white male brothers. Nevertheless, after lay delegates were admitted to General Conference in 1872, the MEC refused their entry into annual conferences, claiming that that body had special oversight for ministerial matters, thereby preserving the fraternal clergy group. Instead the MEC formed lay annual conferences that served as parallel bodies to the clergy annual conferences and were in existence until the 1939 merger. The inclusion of racial, gender, and language groups[34] posed more difficult challenges and prompted the white brotherhood's defense of a structure that privileged them. The debates examined here reveal the resistance of a demographic group, namely the white, presumably heterosexual men who served as clergy and as lay delegates, to sharing their authority. Because these delegates do not recognize the interest that drives them to preserve their leadership, they use theological, moral, and practical arguments to discredit other groups and legitimate the social order that benefits them.

34. In addition to the Evangelical Association and the United Brethren, German-language churches that were ancestors of the current UMC, the MEC at its 1844 General Conference established a German Missionary Conference that acknowledged the successful missionary efforts among German Americans.

While this process makes those who favor the established order appear shrewd and calculating, Bourdieu reminds us that such strategies are unconscious and are motivated by a habitus that leads both the dominant and the dominated to accept and perpetuate this relationship. This symbolic power, in fact, is possible only when both groups misrecognize the arbitrary nature of the authority structure. The dispersion of power in Methodism has allowed for various groups to challenge this system with greater success than in the more hierarchical Catholic Church.

Bourdieu also points out that such challenges tend to occur at times of crisis and change. American Methodism dealt with leadership of African Americans and women around the turn of the twentieth century, an era of change that touched all areas of American society. The economic and social changes related to abolition, immigration, industrialization, and modernism's challenges to the notion of a single religious truth all impacted the church, and Methodists responded in as many ways as the American public did. Progressive Methodists were part of the Social Gospel movement that sought to address the ills caused by urbanization and embraced expanding rights for free blacks, immigrants, and women. Conservative Methodists, on the other hand, rejected such "progress" in favor of traditional social arrangements, and many supported the Christian fundamentalist movement that arose in the 1920s. Methodist churches, which began as a movement of the lower classes, became more middle class and representative of the American mainstream. Methodists involved in the Holiness movement, many of them lower class, were uncomfortable with the formal worship and scholarly preaching that replaced the church's evangelical spirit, and many left to join new sects.

The church confronted the issue of gay rights on the heels of the 1960s, another period of rapid and complex social changes. The country and the church continued to deal with tensions around race and gender, along with issues of sexuality, war, science and technology, another wave of immigration, and economic and technological globalization. Mainline Protestant churches were dealing with a decline in both membership and social influence, although Methodism had just grown through its 1968 merger with the Evangelical United Brethren Church to form one of the largest Protestant churches in the world with eleven million members. From that point on, however, American Methodism experienced the same decline as other Protestant churches, losing U.S. membership every year, even as it increased in other parts of the world. The UMC has had to adjust not only to loss of influence in the United States, but also to its new identity as a global church.[35]

Frederick Norwood notes that the new UMC was aware that it came into being in an age of transition and allowed for theological diversity and change. In considering doctrinal standards, a special commission concluded that the times were not conducive to forming a new confession of faith, and instead offered the quadrilateral of scripture, tradition, experience, and reason as guidelines for theological interpretation in a time of transition.[36] Even with this mechanism for addressing diversity, forces on different sides of an issue tend to claim absolute authority for their perspective, using scripture and theology to legitimize their stances. This awareness of the impact of changing times was evident in discussions around homosexuality, as it was in earlier debates about leadership of women and African Americans.

At such times, Bourdieu notes, "the established order see-saws and the whole future is suspended."[37] Economic and other social changes lead to the collapse or weakening of symbolic systems that have structured a society's worldview, and life as one knows it is on shaky ground. Already destabilized by these larger social changes, the church feels especially threatened when prophetic movements emerge to challenge the social order in which white, presumably heterosexual men have held power. A tension is set up between those who see the established order as divinely ordained and unchangeable, and those who argue that it represents a human, political order that can and should change with the times.

The specific issues addressed in this book relate to authority, rather than larger social changes, because authority issues seem to be the most contentious for the church. Methodists were widely involved in the temperance movement at the turn of the last century, and there are currently

35. Some argue that the UMC is not truly global, since 98 percent of its membership clusters in the United States (63 percent) and in Africa (35 percent), with the rest in the Philippines, Europe, and Eurasia. However, the term does capture the more recent spread of the church beyond its European and North American roots (Statistics from *Vital Congregations: 2012 State of the Church Report* by the General Council on Finance and Administration and the Vital Congregations Initiative).

36. Norwood, *American Methodism*, 431. The quadrilateral provoked some controversy when articulated as an interpretive lens that was rooted in John Wesley's theological method, yet allowed for changing understandings. A restatement in 1988 affirmed scripture as primary, with tradition, reason, and experience as interpretive aids (Frank, *Polity, Practice and the Mission*, 134).

37. Bourdieu, "Genesis and Structure," 34.

anti-abortion and anti-gambling forces in the church, but none of these issues has prompted the sense of division within the church that leadership changes have. It is especially interesting to consider the case of divorce, which has equally strong scriptural condemnation as homosexuality, yet has been widely accepted in the church. Critics of gay marriage cite the threat that same-sex unions pose to heterosexual marriage and the Christian family, yet it can be argued that divorce poses a much greater threat to those institutions. From the Bourdieuan perspective, I would argue that divorce does not challenge the interests of the dominant group, and in fact may benefit men who wish to end a marriage without garnering any public stigma. By contrast, leadership of African Americans, women, and gays and lesbians poses a direct threat to their privileged status. As the dominant group, they are able to steer the discourse towards issues that preserve their interest—albeit unconsciously—thus the greater concern for changes in leadership.

While not prompting the same level of resistance, divorce contributes to an underlying sense of social disorder. Many view the family as a naturalized social arrangement, and indeed it is a primary institution for socializing persons into society, thus it serves to reproduce the social order. The breakup of families disrupts socialization and destabilizes an institution that has defined U.S. society. The ordination of women, in addition to representing a change in authority structures, likewise disrupted a familiar domestic arrangement that restricted women's work to the home. Similarly, gay marriage upsets the norm of the heterosexual family. While any changes to the family heighten the sense of social disorder, women's ordination and gay rights are more stringently opposed than divorce because they also pose direct threats to heterosexual male authority.

With this background, I address the questions posed at the beginning of this chapter, namely: Who holds power in the UMC, including the authority to determine religious leadership? How do changes in authority structures occur, and why is it such an arduous process? Finally, how are the stories of marginalized groups within the church interrelated? Using the historical records of Methodist General Conferences, I examine the arguments against leadership of three traditionally dominated groups in U.S. Methodism, looking in chapter 2 at African Americans, chapter 3 at women, and chapter 4 at gays and lesbians. My research focuses on resistance based on objectivated patterns of domination; however, it does not ignore that resistance in each of these cases is complex, including personal, ethical, theological, and/or scriptural factors. Equally valid are perspectives focusing on the empowerment of dominated groups, unlike this approach, which looks at resistance by the dominant group to such empowerment. My approach seeks to look beyond overt arguments and uncover resistance to changes in authority and social structures that is hidden even from those who perpetuate it.

Since these issues arose at different times, within different Methodist denominations, and with different manifestations, the common forum of the General Conference provides a uniform context for a comparative look at the three issues and at similar assumptions that may underlie them. For each issue, I examine the General Conference that first considered a change to the church's leadership structure, and subsequent years when significant and substantive discussion occurred and/or policy statements were revised. By referring to transcripts of General Conference delegates' speeches in these years, as recorded in *The Daily Christian Advocate*[38] and other records, I hope to cast new insights into what was said and by whom, exploring the power dynamics that exist within Methodism's process of establishing policy and leadership criteria. At the same time, I explore the distinctive social climate and differing arguments made for and against each group seeking religious leadership.

The conclusion in chapter 5 compares and contrasts the three cases and considers their distinctive features as well as their interrelation. Here I consider how these three examples of oppression overlap, most obviously through intersectionality. This chapter will also consider how these dominated groups dominate each other, through racism in the feminist movement that prompted African American "womanism," and the occurrence of heterosexism in black churches. Finally, this chapter summarizes the implications of this research for the UMC, for other religious communities as part of a larger re-formation within Christianity, and for the larger U.S. society given the growing acceptance of gay rights.

 What to in?

Bourdieu calls for reflexive sociology, in which scholars constantly monitor their own social locations for interests that might influence their

---

38. *The Daily Christian Advocate*, the official journal of the General Conference, dates back to 1848 in the MEC and 1856 in the MECS, and continues in the successor denominations. Currently in the UMC, an Advance Edition provides copies of the legislation for delegates to consider; a Daily Report is published at General Conference conveying announcements, accounts of speeches and legislative actions, and other news; and the Daily Edition publishes transcripts of the proceedings. It will be cited as *DCA* with the appropriate denominational acronym and General Conference year.

work, requiring that I acknowledge my own interests. As a product of a religious habitus that is racist, sexist, and heterosexist, I am shaped by those influences and find evidence of them in my own responses to these issues. As a United Methodist clergywoman, I have engaged in studies of all three of these issues within congregations, college and university settings, and in my academic research, in order to increase awareness of my own biases and those of others and to seek ways to address them productively. I unconsciously perpetuate resistance myself, based on the fact that racism and heterosexism place me in the dominant group. I am more aware of gender bias, through which I am among the dominated, although I perpetuated that bias as well by delaying entry into the ministry for years because my religious habitus prevented me from seeing myself in that role. My concern for a fully inclusive church leads me to support efforts to change United Methodist polity to allow full rights for all persons, regardless of their sexual identity, as well as continuing efforts for full inclusion based on gender and race. Recognizing my own conscious involvement in prophetic movements that seek change, as well as my unconscious but inevitable resistance, I hope that this work can provide new insights into these ongoing struggles in the UMC.

2

Methodist Unification and Race

"A Backward Race"

"God Almighty has drawn the color line in indelible ink."

—MECS Bishop Elijah Hoss

In 1787, just three years after The Methodist Episcopal Church (MEC) was established, African American members of St. George's MEC in Philadelphia walked out when white members directed them, in the middle of praying, to different seats in the church's newly built balcony. Richard Allen, a former slave who had been licensed to preach in 1784, recounted the incident that drove away the African American worshippers:

> We had not been long upon our knees before I heard considerable scuffling and low talking. I raised my head up and saw one of the trustees, Mr. H_ M_, having hold of the Rev. Absolom Jones, pulling him up off of his knees, and saying, "You must get up—you must not kneel here." Mr. Jones replied, "Wait till the prayer is over." Mr. H_ M_ said, "No, you must get up now, or I will call for aid and force you away." Mr. Jones said, "Wait until prayer is over, and I will get up and trouble you no more." With that he beckoned to one of the other trustees, Mr. L_ S_ to come to his assistance. He came, and went to William White to pull him up. By this time prayer was over, and we all went out of the church in a body and they were no more plagued with us in the church.[1]

1. Allen, *The Life Experiences*, 14–15.

Those who walked out formed a separate congregation that would become the African Methodist Episcopal Church (AMEC), with Allen as its first bishop.

As this famous incident illustrates, racial tension marked Methodist history in the United States from its earliest years, as southern churches contended with slavery and northern churches with the departure of African American members seeking freedom to worship and leadership opportunities. In addition to division between racial groups, slavery contributed to the church's 1844 split into northern and southern flanks, which did not reunite for nearly a century. This chapter looks at debate within The Methodist Episcopal Church, South (MECS) about the terms of that reunion, which occurred in the wake of larger social changes that included the end of the Civil War and the abolition of slavery, Reconstruction, the industrial revolution, and the First World War.

Historical Background

The history of racial division in American Methodism dates to its earliest years. Methodist founder John Wesley spoke strongly against slavery, and the Methodist mission to slaves drew many African American members, but segregation soon fractured the movement's inclusive beginning. Following the example of the AMEC, black Methodists in New York left the MEC in 1821 to form the African Methodist Episcopal Church Zion (AMEZC) in New York. These black Methodist denominations shared doctrinal and structural features with other Methodists, while offering African Americans religious space free of white control.

Other African Americans remained within the predominantly white MEC and continued to fight for leadership positions. Allowed to serve local churches, they were denied full clergy rights, which included sacramental leadership and itinerancy, and they remained under the supervision of white elders and bishops. The MEC ordained its first black pastor in 1832 and consecrated a bishop in 1858 to serve its mission in Liberia, which was considered a dangerous environment for whites.

In 1844, Methodists in the southern United States broke away to form a separate denomination, the MEC, South (MECS). While deeper issues were involved, including differing views of episcopal authority, the incident that provoked the split was an attempt by northern Methodists to remove a slave-owning southern bishop. The Emancipation Proclamation and the end of the Civil War had a dramatic effect on the church, as they did on all social institutions. Many free blacks joined the black Methodist denominations (AMEC and AMEZC), and the MEC began aggressive mission activity in the south. As a result, the MECS saw its black membership drop by almost two-thirds, from 207,766 in 1860 to 78,742 in 1866. Wary of the influence of northern Methodists on southern blacks, the MECS in 1870 gathered its remaining African American members into a new denomination, the Colored (now Christian) Methodist Episcopal Church (CMEC). Although this distinct denomination allowed black leadership, it was supervised and assisted by the white MECS.

As part of its outreach in the south following the Civil War, the MEC agreed that the time had come to grant its African American members the independence they had long sought and allowed the formation of separate black "mission conferences" served by black clergy. Located mostly in the south, these conferences remained under white episcopal supervision until 1920, when the church elected its first African American bishops to serve in the United States. Unlike other MEC bishops, however, who were required to itinerate throughout the connection, these black bishops could only serve black conferences.

Thus, by the end of the nineteenth century, a color line firmly divided American Methodism. The MECS was in effect a white denomination, with only three hundred or so black members out of a total membership of several million. In the MEC, a few black congregations existed within white conferences in the north, while in the south, two dozen black mission conferences provided the racial separation that southerners expected. Throughout both churches, African Americans were only allowed leadership over others of their race. Reginald Hildebrand describes this move from slavery to segregation as a transition from "monolithic, normative paternalism" to "differentiated, transitional paternalism"—or from official institutional domination to unofficial institutional domination under the guise of being "separate but equal," as the Supreme Court decreed in the landmark case Plessy versus Ferguson in 1896.[2]

When the MEC and MECS began serious reunion talks in the early twentieth century, both agreed that a united church would remain segregated, but debate over the nature of segregation in the new structure delayed unification for several decades.[3] Southern Methodists preferred a

2. Hildebrand, "Methodist Episcopal Policy," 141.

3. The Methodist Protestant Church (MPC) was involved in initial talks and was part

separate but affiliated black church, as the CMEC was, whereas the MEC advocated a black jurisdiction within the unified church. The south's concern was two-fold: to prevent the possibility of black bishops serving over white churches or pastors, and to restrict black representation in the General Conference. For African Americans in the MEC, losing representation at General Conference would revoke their voice in decision-making for the church, a power they had won in 1868.

A Commission on the Federation of Methodism met in 1910 and drafted a Plan of Union that included a separate jurisdiction for all African American members, as the MEC preferred. The MEC General Conference in 1912 approved the proposal, but the MECS General Conference that met in Oklahoma in 1914 insisted upon a separate but affiliated black church, after the CMEC model. Both churches affirmed their desire for union, so a Joint Commission on Unification began meeting in 1916 to work out the details and resolve the differences regarding race.[4] It would take more than twenty years for the process to yield a successful Plan of Union. This chapter looks at MECS discussions of this Plan of Union in 1914, a subsequent proposal in 1918, and the plan that was ultimately approved in 1938.

1914 General Conference: "The Great White Throne of Jesus Christ"

In 1914, the issue of segregation in a unified Methodist church was an open-and-shut case for the MECS General Conference. The Conference was preoccupied with other issues, most notably the church's official separation from Vanderbilt University. MECS Bishop Holland McTyeire had founded the University in 1874 with money from Cornelius Vanderbilt, but the school's increasingly liberal faculty was at odds with conservative MECS bishops on the Board of Trustees. This was just one of several issues that pitted conservative southerners with more progressive movements within the MECS and led to contentious General Conferences over the next three decades.

Towards the end of the 1914 General Conference session, the Committee on Church Relations presented the report on unification from the

---

of the final union in 1939. However, the church withdrew in 1912 until the MEC and MECS could resolve their differences, rejoining the process in 1928.

4. Davis, *The Methodist Unification,* offers an in-depth look at the work of the Joint Commission and the issues it raised.

Commission on Federation, along with the following recommendations: 1) that the MECS consider this tentative plan as containing the basic principles of a workable union; 2) that the MECS declare itself in favor of unification, but recommend that "the colored membership of the various Methodist bodies be formed into an independent organization holding fraternal relations with the reorganized and united Church"; and 3) that the MECS representatives to the Commission on Federation continue to serve on the new Joint Commission on Unification.[5]

In presenting the report, F. M. Thomas used religious language that reinforced both white superiority and the threat that conservatives perceived from modern currents.[6] He described Christian churches as "so many white glaciers" lying remote from each other, then continued:

> But over the great white range there is rising a Sun of Righteousness with healing in his wings. Shall we allow ourselves to be engulfed and swept away by the great avalanche of the oncoming tide of the modern world, or shall we build a great Church, a unified Church, a Church mighty enough, large enough, sublime enough for all the hopes and energies of Methodism[?][7]

He concluded with the hope that Methodists of the twentieth century would finally anchor "with redeemed souls by the million at the foot of the great white throne of Jesus Christ."[8] By depicting both Christian churches and the throne of Christ as white, Thomas justified a separate white church and implied that white leadership more nearly models that of Christ.

The 1914 General Conference met at a time when racially constructed divisions and the corresponding white privilege were perceived as being under threat. In the early decades of the twentieth century, many Anglo

---

5. *MECS General Conference Journal* 1914, 263–64. General Conference *Journals* include reports, sermons, and summaries of floor discussions for each Methodist denomination. Cited hereafter as *Journal*, with the appropriate denominational acronym and General Conference year.

6. Thomas's speech includes quotations from Joint Commission member Alpheus Wilson; "Mr. [James] Buckley," editor of the New York *Christian Advocate*, who was an unspoken critic of social change; and an unnamed Tennesseean, who Thomas describes as "one of the greatest figures Southern Methodism has produced." The transcription of the speech in the *DCA* has missing text and missing quotation marks, making it unclear whether the passage discussed here represents Thomas's own words or if he is quoting others in whole or in part.

7. *MECS DCA* 1914, 122.

8. Ibid.

Americans saw themselves as a civilized contrast to increasing numbers of immigrants from eastern and southern Europe and to African Americans who were liberated from the tightly restricted social space of slavery. Just two decades earlier, the White City at the 1893 World's Columbian Exposition in Chicago had posed a powerful symbol of Anglo-American triumph, with order and light countering the cramped and crowded disorder that was ⁎ the reality of many U.S. cities. The religious parallel was showcased in the Exposition's World's Parliament of Religions, which introduced religions from around the world, while depicting them as curiosities or side-shows ⁎ to white American Protestantism, which held center stage. Thomas's remarks assert an ongoing assumption of white, Christian superiority, which is mirrored in a common theological dualism that equates light with good and dark with evil.

At a time when racial identities and social conditions were in flux, Thomas reduced this complex racial dynamic to a white-black hierarchy, using images of whiteness to define the boundaries of his own racial group as superior. Within this southern gathering, Thomas appealed to whites' perceived threat from freed slaves encroaching on their space and privilege. Without overtly degrading or even mentioning blacks, Thomas affirmed white dominance as consistent with divine order. At the same time, he described the rapidly changing society as a tide that threatened to engulf all that was familiar, reflecting the stress created when ingrained social structures are challenged.

After Thomas spoke, Bishop Elijah Hoss, another member of the Joint Commission, addressed the subject of unification, urging patience until the time when "Almighty God will put his hand in, and this thing comes to pass."[9] Following Hoss's speech, the report was approved by unanimous vote, with no further discussion. The 1914 General Conference, it seems, was firmly behind its commissioners' recommendations for a separate church for African American Methodists as a means to preserve segregated social order.

⁎ in some sense, the ideal of suburban life might be a escape from this disfunctional miasmic urban environment, Mickey Mouse resists redefinition — he was a suburbanite.

9. Ibid.

⁑ hard to find an example in which the white Anglo-American seeks to learn about and relate to other cultures that does not depict them at least at first as a curiosity. The audience is assumed to be white because mostly it is.

1918 General Conference:
A Question that Is "Settled in the South"

When the MECS General Conference next convened in May 1918, the Joint Commission on Unification had met four times with no discernable progress in overcoming their differences regarding race. While all agreed that the color line should be maintained, the MEC delegates, including two African Americans, held out for a segregated jurisdiction with representation within the General Conference, while the southern church insisted on a separate body with no voice in General Conference. When the MECS General Conference met, the proposal currently before the Joint Commission placed all white U.S. congregations in annual conferences, with black congregations in a regional conference, similar to mission, or central, conferences that lay outside the United States. These regional conferences would have proportional representation in the General Conference, not to exceed 5 percent of the entire General Conference body.

The Joint Commission report was presented to the MECS General Conference early in its session and referred to the Committee on Church Relations. When the Committee reported back to the full body, the Majority Report expressed appreciation and continued support for the work of the Joint Commission, reaffirmed the action of the 1914 General Conference, and encouraged cooperation to "eliminate wastage of men and money in the territory in which both Churches have established themselves,"[10] namely the southern states where the MEC had made inroads following the Civil War. Judge John S. Candler, a member of the MECS Committee of Church Relations, along with nine others, submitted a more strongly worded Minority Report that made a separate affiliated black church a requirement of union, and urged no further action by the MECS until the MEC took "proper and suitable action with reference to the negro question."[11]

The Candler family wielded great influence within southern Methodism during this era. The judge's brother, Warren Aiken Candler, had been elected an MECS bishop in 1898 and served throughout the years in which unification was addressed. Another brother, Asa Griggs Candler, founded the Coca-Cola Company and provided significant financial support when the MECS established Emory University in Atlanta. Both John and Warren were staunch conservatives and defenders of southern ways. The bishop,

10. *MECS Journal* 1918, 197.
11. *MECS DCA* 1918, 86.

in fact, served as chair of the MECS delegation to the Joint Commission, although he was an outspoken opponent of unification. His silence during the 1918 debate may be due to the restricted role of bishops in General Conference sessions presided over by other bishops,[12] but his brother John argued persuasively toward the same end.

As they discussed the question of race, MECS delegates expressed concern that even a minority black voice in the new church's General Conference would allow African Americans a foot in the door that could lead to greater authority down the road. The surest way to guarantee white dominance in a unified Methodist church was to allow only white delegates in the policy-making body. Thus their primary concern was to deny African Americans the political power inherent in General Conference representation. Black religious leadership was less of an issue for these white delegates, since black clergy and bishops in the proposed unified structure would continue to be restricted to black-only conferences with no possibility of leadership over whites.

The most prevalent argument delegates made against African American delegates was that they were a backward race unfit for such leadership, an assumption that went unchallenged throughout the debate. For these southerners, white supremacy was a given. Both whites and blacks in the American south were socialized into specific identities—whites as the dominant race, and blacks as subordinate. This racial relationship marked the various arenas in which they interacted, with the church serving to reinscribe and lend divine sanction to the pattern of dominance that marked economic, educational, and other social fields.

The speeches reveal that the white delegates understood their dominance to rest on their superiority as a racial group. They referred to blacks as being less educated, less civilized, and dependent on whites to further their development. As John Candler stated in his opening speech:

> All of you people here from the South know that the Church has stood by your policies, which the best people of the South believed were the best policies for the negroes. There is not any use in talking. That question is settled in the South. It is absolutely settled in the South that, until a man is qualified by education, study, and proper preparation, he is not competent to make laws for the white people of this section.[13] *nothing being asserted about hereditary differences.*

12. Morris Davis notes that Candler contributed little to the Joint Commission conversations either (*The Methodist Unification*, 140).

13. *MECS DCA* 1918, 96.

Conservative delegates seeking to preserve existing social structures and ideology ironically appealed to the modern concept of evolution to make their case. Although they rejected biological evolution as being contrary to their understanding of scripture, here they used social evolution to justify the prevailing social structure. For many, white American progress had led to an advanced society, justifying conquests abroad and marginalization of non-whites at home. W. E. B. Du Bois describes such understandings in his 1931 *Christian Century* article, writing that "the world is a hierarchy headed by the white people, with other groups graduating down by grades of color to smaller and smaller brain power, ability, and character."[14] Teddy Roosevelt, among others, offered African Americans as evidence of social evolution, pointing out how much more advanced they were than black Africans, although not yet equal to white Americans.[15]

This is reflected in the paternalistic tone of these speeches, which Reginald Hildebrand attributes to an understanding that God had made southern whites guardians over African Americans.[16] Blacks, like women, were seen as "not quite adult," and social order required that both be under white male control. Prior to emancipation, white southern men understood slavery as "the instrument that God had chosen to place Africans 'under the Christian tutelage of Anglo-Saxon Protestants,'" and they believed that their defeat in the Civil War was God's judgment for their inability to make slavery a "truly Christian institution."[17] Hildebrand argues that this logic allowed southern white men to see the collapse of systemic domination in the form of slavery as their failure to take responsibility for the welfare of African Americans.

Such an understanding continued in 1918, when MECS delegate F. J. Prettyman claimed that whites could boast "of the great distinction of having brought up a race from Africa through slavery into a wide and cultured civilization."[18] Prettyman's speech reflected the white delegates' claim that what progress African Americans had made was due to assistance from whites. The delegates returned repeatedly to the example of the CMEC and the wisdom of its white founders in allowing space for blacks to develop, while remaining under white sponsorship. John Candler reminded del-

14. Du Bois, "Will the Church," 174.
15. Jacobson, *Barbarian Virtues*, 120–21.
16. Hildebrand, *The Times*, 9.
17. Ibid., 7.
18. *MECS DCA* 1918, 98.

egates of the success of the CMEC, "working by themselves, assisted by you" and the MECS's continuing "sacred obligation" to that church,[19] while A. F. Watkins asked his colleagues: "In the name of all that is broad and Christlike, have we in these years drifted so far from the poor, helpless, undeveloped, vicious, struggling negro that we are not willing to stand where our fathers stood in 1866 [when the CMEC was established]?"[20]

The developmental argument goes directly to the issue of leadership: being less advanced, these delegates argued, blacks were not qualified to make decisions for superior whites. Whereas John Candler cited lack of education as what precluded African Americans from making laws for white people, Prettyman, like Watkins, was more direct. After affirming the ideal of religious inclusiveness, Prettyman nevertheless claimed that,

> there is no principle of sound philosophy and no revelation of religion that would compel an advanced race, such as we represent, to put themselves under the domination, under the fear of the domination, or even fear of the balance of power in the hands of a backward race two thousand years behind ourselves in the achievement of civilization.[21]

Prettyman commended the power differential among various groups as natural and necessary for the good of all. For him, equality of numbers did not mean equality of status; democracy, as it related both to the state and Methodism, should place greater power in the hands of the superior race. He said:

> I recognize the fact . . . that we are not to be subject to a mere count of noses of anybody that comes into the Church. The men who talk of democracy, who juggle with that modern word and with a modern meaning, are forgetting that there is no such thing as a pure democracy. . . . The putting of the basis of government upon a mere count of noses puts one open to a stampede of every tide that flows and every wind that blows. . . . Let us not look upon the backward races as equal, because they may happen to be equal to us in numbers, in representation in the great lawmaking body of our Church; but look at them in their true light, by the measure of their true achievements in Christ Jesus, in the measure of what they have possessed themselves of by our ministry and by inheritance from us, treating them as a missionary enterprise,

19. Ibid., 96.
20. Ibid., 98.
21. Ibid.

29

putting them, as long as they are dependent upon us for money and leadership, where they belong. But it would be a disgrace to us in our achievement of Christian civilization if they had yet got up even with us. But if ever they catch up with us by growth or by a display of the divine Spirit of God, let them stand on the merit of their achievement as Christians, on the same basis, on the same equality in the same governing body, as we know they are traveling with us at last to the same destiny and the same throne of God.[22]

Prettyman based white domination, even within a democracy, on white cultural and spiritual superiority, while reinforcing black dependence on white missionary activity. He acknowledged the future prospect of spiritual equality, but affirmed that church structure should correspond to the social order in which whites held power.

Prettyman and other southern whites perceived their dominance not only as the natural order, but also as an arrangement that benefited black Methodists. They considered it their Christian duty to aid those less fortunate; as H. C. Morrison stated, "I believe the men who have spoken . . . desire the best for the colored people. Anything else would not be Christian. We must desire peace within our bounds, and we must desire the best for our colored people. They have been our people. We have loved them. We must wish for them the very best."[23] Morrison and others understood an arrangement in which blacks were dependent on whites to be the best way to support blacks' developmental potential.

M. M. Satterfield hinted at the benefits whites derived from a segregated structure when he noted that allowing blacks to be set apart with self-leadership would make them better workers.[24] Although slavery had been abolished, most African Americans in the south still worked for whites as tenant farmers, sharecroppers, and, as the region became more industrialized, as low-wage laborers. Racial policies effectively barred them from landownership, education, and the technical training needed for personal advancement, guaranteeing white economic control. Delegate Satterfield implied that a separate black church would provide an arena for blacks to exercise leadership, thus satisfying their desire for self-determination in a way that did not threaten white church leadership or white dominance in the economic or political fields.

22. Ibid.
23. Ibid., 99.
24. Ibid., 97.

* There is such a thing as cultural superiority. It is by no means self-evident WHICH culture is superior.

Satterfield's comment also pointed to issues of class that are insepa-rable from race. American Methodism had evolved from a rural, working class movement to a mainstream church with national clout. Lower class whites found themselves dominated by upper classes, but dominant over their fellow black laborers. Racial lines delineated the lower classes, who comprised the historical core of Methodism, and provided whites with a sense of superiority based on race, even as they found themselves domi-nated economically. The speeches at the 1918 General Conference reflected such an understanding of white dominance and responsibility, even if they were not entirely conscious of the privilege that came with their race.

John Candler's opening speech raised a related theme, namely the extent to which blacks submitted to or resisted their own domination. Bourdieu's claim that such patterns are largely misrecognized by both the dominant and subordinated groups is problematic when applied to race. It is difficult to argue that African Americans were unaware of, much less complicit in, their enslavement or their continued and often violent domi-nation after slavery was abolished. In no way can this be seen as a case of "blaming the victim," which is how some have construed Bourdieu's notion of symbolic violence. Slavery by its very nature is a system of domination, and overt violence was used throughout slavery and beyond to extract obe-dience, even against compliant slaves. This system of domination was visible to all concerned, and surviving slave narratives reflect ongoing resistance.

Whites could not easily ignore the fact that this social pattern advanced their interest, nor blacks that they were disadvantaged by it. However, what went misrecognized was the arbitrary nature of white dominance. In American racism, the white/black binary is white domination over black, but despite what these white Methodists argued, they were not inherently superior to blacks. Over time, the ongoing process of socialization shaped both blacks and whites to see white supremacy as inevitable, or as "the way things are." W. E. B. Du Bois noted the church's role in legitimating this domination, claiming that in the United States alone during the time of slavery, some ten million sermons were preached on the text "Servants, obey your masters, for this is well pleasing in the sight of the Lord."[25]

John Candler distinguished more compliant southern blacks from northern blacks, who were portrayed as troublemakers, and claimed that by not specifically addressing the question of race, the Majority Report

25. Du Bois, "Will the Church," 175. Such passages are found throughout the Christian epistles, including Ephesians 6:5, Colossians 3:22, Titus 2:9, and 1 Peter 2:18.

sought to "'keep the nigger in the woodpile,' still covered up." He said: "I am not ashamed of him, and, between you and me, I love those who stayed down here with us and have been with us all the time better than I do those fellows who ran away up North."[26] Candler and others spoke affectionately of former slaves who appeared to accept subordinate status, or at least did not overtly challenge it.

These southern whites reinforced the sense of their custodial relationship to blacks through the language in their speeches, using possessive terms ("our negroes," "our people") and singular references such as "the negro" or "the brother in black" that depersonalized African Americans. Thus the language in these speeches is steeped in a long history and embodies power relationships between white and black southerners. While not aimed directly at African Americans, since they were not present, the speeches served to reinforce the white delegates' understanding that blacks were under their charge and required their caretaking.

The policies under discussion clearly affected black Methodists, and again, their absence is striking. The power of words relates to the delegated power of these spokespersons, whose speech reflects the accumulated symbolic capital of their social group and is given additional authority by their position within the institution. Indeed, this was the very issue at stake: whether blacks merited a share of the institutional authority that pertained to General Conference delegates of a unified church. For white southerners, the answer clearly was "no."

In contrast to those seeking authority in the church, the MECS delegates repeatedly affirmed CMEC members, who outwardly accepted subordinate status. Delegates were especially protective of the CMEC, with which the MECS had a paternalistic relationship. Even as they disparaged northern blacks, these speeches may reflect that whites felt greater pressure from southern blacks who had joined the MEC after it spread to the south, where nineteen out of the twenty-one black MEC conferences were located. This movement to a church that granted them a voice and vote in General Conference suggests that southern blacks were, to some extent, both aware of and discontent with their dominated status in southern Methodism, despite white delegates' assertions to the contrary.

With this in mind, H. H. White expressed concern that allowing blacks to have any authority in the united church would lead to a "negro aristocracy" that would set them apart from other black Methodists. An

26. *MECS DCA* 1918, 96.

assumption of white superiority underlay White's contention that giving blacks an equal voice to whites, as in the "Northern Church," would raise their social status above those in all-black denominations. He affirmed the MECS insistence that a separate black organization be formed, one that might eventually unite with the AMEC, AMEZC, and CMEC churches, so that there would be "one unified white Church in America and one unified negro Church in America."[27] Such an arrangement would draw even more firmly the color line that divided American Methodism.

Many of the speeches reflected a longing for the past, when the relationship between blacks and whites seemed more clearly defined and few blacks challenged their domination. Watkins spoke directly of antebellum days, lamenting that the current generation lacked the ties of affection that existed between "those old masters and those old slaves."[28] The delegates reaffirmed white responsibility for blacks as a virtue that was being lost in the current era, which had been altered by emancipation and other social changes. The recent world war likewise threatened to upset racial relations, as H. C. Morrison noted:

> We are coming into a new era in the history of these United States. We are going to have come back to us before long a great number of young colored men who have gone out and stood shoulder to shoulder in this tremendous war. Germany did try to raise Japan and Mexico and the colored people of this country against us. Whatever we do, we must keep in close, sympathetic touch with our colored brethren. We must wield an influence over them that will keep a strong bond of sympathy between us.[29]

As whites resisted changes to social relations, some asserted that southern blacks were equally distressed by changes to familiar social structures. Southern whites claimed that they were not seeking to preserve their own privilege, but rather fulfilling their benevolent duty to a less developed race. Watkins specifically rejected the notion of white benefit from a separate black church when he said: "It may be, however, that lying back in your mind there is a question, as there is in mine, whether or not in so deciding we are not rather consulting our own convenience, pleasure and privilege than our duty to the negro."[30] He noted that just as Methodist

27. Ibid., 99.
28. Ibid., 98.
29. Ibid., 99.
30. Ibid., 98.

preaching prevented slave revolts, white benevolence could help prescribe social relations in the current time of change. Despite his protestations, the public nature of these sessions suggests that political motivation was clearly involved, whether consciously or not.

Just as the white delegates did not acknowledge their own interest in white supremacy, they also failed to recognize their resistance to change as an obstacle to unification. The Minority Report required the MECS to hold firm until the MEC moved closer to the southern position on the place of African American members in the united church. Commenting on that report, John Candler said: "Until our Northern brethren can make some proper (as they may consider and as we must finally determine) arrangement with their colored membership, there is nothing more to be said between us. That is their trouble, not ours. It is not up to us to settle the rock wall that they have run against."[31] Candler clearly did not see himself as part of that "rock wall" of entrenched social relations. He commented that the 1914 MECS statement went "just as far as decent, self-respecting southern Methodists can go," which was echoed by J. O. Willson's claim that "plain, good, Methodist people, man-loving and God-fearing people, have a fixed opinion that you dare not go against."[32]

These speeches by Candler and Willson also spoke to boundaries, an aspect of field structure that are always subject to contestation. The MECS delegates considered themselves part of southern white Protestantism, which could be seen as a sub-field of the larger religious field. References to similar struggles in the Presbyterian Church[33] suggest a closer alliance with other white southerners than with northern white Methodists, and certainly than with black Methodists. While they were willing to align with northern white Methodists, extending their boundaries to include black Methodists stretched southern whites beyond acceptable limits.

In preserving the geographic boundaries of white southern Protestantism, the delegates were also preserving social boundaries. Allowing African Americans to have authority in the church would legitimate their authority in other social arenas, raising the specter of "social equality," an idea that Morris Davis refers to as the "bogey" of the Joint Commission proceedings.[34] Davis writes that the color line preserved white privilege

31. Ibid., 96.
32. Ibid., 97.
33. See *MECS DCA* 1918 for speeches by Willson, 97, and Satterfield, 98.
34. Davis, *The Methodist Unification*, 84.

and power, thus social equality was viewed as a threat to "the place where race would be undone: sex and reproduction."[35] A. F. Watkins, a ministerial representative to the Joint Commission and president of Millsaps College, gave voice to the fear that other delegates skirted when he advocated maintenance of a strict color line, saying: "We want to get closer to these people, but who would not repudiate social equality? . . . Can we not put our hands upon these people for their education and their spiritual uplift without being contaminated or without any danger of social equality?" The sexual nature of Watkins's fears was made explicit in an anecdote he told about a man from Boston who would rather see his beloved granddaughter "dead than married to a negro."[36]

Watkins's use of contamination language reflects the extent to which arbitrary social boundaries become naturalized and even sacralized. The northern church, in calling for black representation in the General Conference, challenged racial boundaries to a point, but even they maintained a strict line between black and white Methodists. Watkins drew on hyper-sexualized stereotypes of black men and the perceived threat they posed to white women, a stereotype rooted in fear that served to preserve social distinctions. After abolition, such depictions had replaced the stereotype of the lazy, shuffling slave, while locating both whites and blacks in the new social order.[37]

Some white southerners used this stereotype of black men seeking to rape white women as justification for lynchings, the most violent form of social control. Although nowhere near the numbers of the 1890s, lynchings were on the rise following World War I and again at the beginning of the Great Depression, as an already stressed society confronted new crises. Both sexualized stereotypes and lynchings represent whites asserting social control and even violence over blacks, while confirming the embodied nature of habitus. As Cornel West writes, "White supremacist ideology is based first and foremost on the degradation of black bodies in order to control them."[38] Exerting their power as the dominant group, whites could portray black bodies as dangerously sexual, which justified keeping a strict

35. Davis draws on the work of Donald G. Mathews, who describes white southerners' concern with racial authenticity and purity in "'Christianizing the South'" and other works (Davis, *The Methodist Unification*, 85).

36. *MECS DCA* 1918, 98.

37. Myers, *Racetalk*, 48.

38. West, *Race Matters*, 85.

social distance, while black bodies were subjected to violence to demonstrate the consequences for transgressing social boundaries.

While southern Methodists officially denounced lynchings, they weakened their stance at times by expressing suspicions about the lynching victims and sympathy for the lynchers. Bishop Warren Candler illustrated that posture in a 1921 article, in which he admitted that lynchings were "unspeakably wrong and ineffably shameful" and could not be condoned or defended. He went on to defend them, however, as he compared lynchings to the murder rate in northern cities and urged northerners to get their own house in order before condemning the south for its lynchings, which he described as "generally speaking an outburst of passionate indignation against an unspeakable crime." Northern contract killings, on the other hand, were "cold blooded murders and assassinations apparently under the vile impulse of inhuman greed." He further noted that northerners "have not had the temptations to lynchings which met the people of the South."[39]

While the prevailing Methodist discourse advocated segregation but condemned violence, the bishop's article reflects a persistent drive for racial purity that motivated the Ku Klux Klan, which included Methodists among it members. Candler wrote: "In the South there is the purest type of Anglo-Saxon American to be found in any other section of the country. Most of us can pronounce one another's names without the help of a dictionary." Southern religion, he wrote, represented "the purest form of evangelical Christianity." Bishop Candler also expressed the idea that African Americans were less than human, when he wrote, "If a man has a brutal origin and a beastly end, the offense of maiming or killing him is no greater crime than that of cruelty to animals."[40]

Such rhetoric was part of the rationale behind the wide acceptance of lynchings in the south and indicates the permanence with which Methodists invested racial boundaries. These boundaries inscribed every aspect of Southern life, which helps to answer the question that many ask when looking back at this period, namely, how could southern white Methodists reconcile such violence with their professed religious beliefs that dictate love of God and love of neighbor? A Bourdieuan analysis suggests that they could perpetuate racial domination, even through violence, because it was what they knew, it benefited them, and they were socialized to see it as God's order. The argument that African Americans were less developed allowed

39. *Alabama Christian Advocate*, February 3, 1921, 13.
40. Ibid.

whites to treat them with less concern than they did other humans—they did not see social equality as acceptable or appropriate. While not all resorted to violence, many people found justification within their worldview, including religion, for self-serving actions at the expense of others.

To keep black Methodists in their place, A. F. Watkins and other delegates hinted at the troubling prospects that could result from black political power in a united church. More moderate voices claimed that such fears were unwarranted; as Morrison said, concerns that "the next General Conference, four years hence, would be flooded with a large representation of colored people . . . [are] most improbable."[41] Even so, moderates such as Morrison did not argue in favor of black representation, but in favor of the Majority Report, whose language still affirmed the southern position against black representation—a position, Morrison noted, that was as safe in the commissions' hands in the future as it had been in the past.[42] Thus white moderates appeared to be equally concerned that even a small number of black General Conference delegates could open the door for blacks to move toward a position of equality within the church.

While the MECS delegates' speeches reflected concerns about losing racial dominance over blacks, they also expressed anxiety about being dominated by the larger, more powerful MEC in the proposed merger. The north had triumphed over the south militarily in the Civil War, ideologically in the abolition movement, and economically as northern-based industrialism outpaced the rebuilding south. John Candler, speaking once again for southern resistance, chastised nineteen southern members of the Joint Commission who had voted for compromise at the Savannah meeting. He linked their acquiescence to the "boasted unity that we all love to talk about when we get up and wave the flag, and cry 'Hallelujah,' 'Glory,' and talk about the Stars and Stripes and all that,"[43] reflecting cynicism toward the forced unity that followed the southern defeat in the Civil War. Having made sacrifices for national unity, white southern delegates stubbornly resisted doing the same for the sake of a unified Methodist church. H. M. Smith spoke directly to southern concern for "states' rights" and self-determination, saying, "I do not believe that our Southern ideals are in any danger." He suggested a broad General Conference with a bond that was

[handwritten margin note: well, assassinating Abe Lincoln was a bad idea.]

41. *MECS DCA* 1918, 99.

42. Ibid.

43. Ibid., 96.

"as light as possible," allowing regional conferences to legislate matters that were "distinctly local."[44]

In looking for religious legitimation of the delegates' positions, we find that distinctly religious language was used sparsely, most clearly in appeals to "peace in Zion" that were employed to justify a conservative approach to union, caring for blacks out of Christian love, and achieving a union that would merit divine approval.[45] The only use of scripture was a delegate claiming, "We are all baptized by one spirit into one body"[46] as he argued for a sense of Methodist unity that would transcend a separate black Methodist structure, as well as for a weak General Conference that allowed greater local authority. Religious concepts were not directly used to explain black inferiority; however, they were brought up to deny ecclesiastical or political authority to black Methodists and continued white leadership understood as Christian benevolence. Delegates also appealed to religious ideals to promote a sense of unity that transcended political and social order.

Thus these white delegates sought to keep the black church separate and dependent on them, thereby safeguarding their own interests, while understanding themselves to be fulfilling their Christian duty. As Bourdieu notes, dominant groups must legitimate both aspects of their dominance: justifying their own privilege, or the "theodicy of their good fortune," while concealing from others the arbitrariness of their domination.[47] MECS delegates advocated continued division, even as their appeals to Christian unity and common Methodist heritage maintained an outward appearance of oneness.

Through their speeches, all the speakers reflected resistance to allowing African Americans a place in the reunited church, and thus its General Conference; the only debate was whether to adopt the Majority Report or the more strongly worded Minority Report, both of which guaranteed racial segregation. Once the authors of the Minority Report were assured that the church was in agreement on these matters, Candler withdrew it, and the Majority Report passed. As in 1914, southern white delegates were unified in their insistence that blacks should be denied any authority over white Methodists and, more importantly, any voice in the decision-making

44. Ibid., 100–101.

45. See *MECS DCA* 1918 for speeches by Willson, 97; Morrison, 99; and Alderson, 97.

46. Smith, *MECS DCA* 1918, 101. A paraphrase of 1 Cor 12:13.

47. Bourdieu, "Genesis and Structure," 16.

body of the General Conference. White supremacist control of the MECS and its General Conference guaranteed that within that body, at least, little challenge was made to the social structure that privileged them.

1938 General Conference: A Union Defined by Racial Division

Following the 1918 General Conference, talks of union continued off and on, and the Joint Commission ended its meetings in 1920. Discussion in the early 1920s led to a Plan of Union with separate jurisdictions for MEC and MECS congregations. The plan passed the MEC General Conference in 1924, and the MECS called a special General Conference that year, which also approved the plan. As the plan was submitted to the MECS annual conferences for approval, Bishop Warren Candler helped to form the Association to Preserve Southern Methodism, an anti-union caucus, which was balanced by the Friends of Unification, a pro-union group. As senior bishop in the MECS, Candler not only used his symbolic capital through frequent articles and speeches, but in presiding over annual conference sessions, he was also accused of making questionable rulings that may have impacted close vote counts. MECS bishops traditionally held greater authority than their northern counterparts, who were more clearly accountable to the General Conference, and bishops on both sides of this issue used that authority to lobby for their cause. In the end, the plan was approved by just over half of MECS members, short of the required two-thirds majority.

Finally, a 1934 Plan of Union proposed a separate Central Jurisdiction for African American churches, with bishops restricted to serve only in the jurisdictions that elected them. Although there was no cap on General Conference representation, the small African American membership of the unified church (4.2 percent) would serve to limit their influence. In 1936 the General and annual conferences of the MEC and the MPC approved the plan, despite opposition from African Americans, who were less willing to accept a segregated structure than they had been in 1918.[48] The MECS, eager to act on the proposed plan, submitted it to annual conferences in 1937, where it passed all but one and was approved by a total margin of almost 86 percent.

---

48. Of forty-seven African American delegates to the MEC 1936 General Conference, thirty-six voted against the Plan of Union, and eleven abstained (Thomas, *Methodism's Racial Dilemma*, 43).

Even so, the Plan of Union generated a day of debate at the 1938 MECS General Conference before being approved. In the two decades since the 1918 discussion, the MECS had dropped its insistence on a separate institution and was willing to accept the all-black Central Jurisdiction, which was consistent with southern Jim Crow laws. As the first speaker in favor of union noted, the current plan gave the south the segregated structure it had wanted all along.[49] Pro-union delegates also seemed satisfied with the issue of General Conference representation, and their speeches affirmed forward movement and the spiritual possibilities offered by a unified Methodist Church (MC).

Opponents focused on legal questions, which were eventually dismissed by a Judicial Council ruling,[50] but speeches revealed continuing fears of northern domination and accommodation of modern trends that threatened southern ways. The few mentions of race reflected the same concerns that the 1918 delegates voiced, namely that the segregated structure was not permanent and would allow a mingling of races along with an ongoing need to assist African Americans.[51]

Delegates expressed resistance to change as a longing for the past, opposition to radical secular movements such as socialism and communism, and fears that the distinctive southern church would be swallowed up by the larger MEC. Charlton DuRant noted that when southern youth had attended an event in the north, they experienced interracial fellowship and "they adopted resolutions favoring communism, or socialism, or some other kind of 'ism' that we haven't got in South Carolina, thank God!"[52] Jere Wells read a letter from John M. Slayton, former Governor of Georgia, expressing concern that such movements would overwhelm the ideals of the southern church:

> The leaders of those churches by which we are to be absorbed entertain views exactly contrary to my own, and I have loved the Southern Methodist Church all my life. No more will we hear preached from its pulpit Christ in Him crucified but a conglomeration of political, sociological and interracial questions.

49. Stuckey, *MECS DCA* 1938, 6.

50. Opponents argued that because the Plan had failed to pass one annual conference, North Mississippi, it had not met the required approval of all annual conferences. The Judicial Council overruled the appeal, claiming that the 86 percent approval margin met the required 75 percent vote for passage.

51. See *MECS DCA* 1938 for speeches by Curtis, 9, and DuRant, 16.

52. *MECS DCA* 1938, 16.

(Laughter) If this unification be perfected, the saintly traditions and memories of the past will have been abandoned so far as our churches are concerned.[53]

For a nation on the brink of another world war, "godless" communism and socialism prompted genuine concern. The delegates made specific mention of the MEC's Methodist Federation for Social Service (MFSS), part of the Social Gospel movement that advocated reform and, in the eyes of some southerners, introduced communist and socialist influences into the church.[54] During the Depression years, the MFSS advocated social changes to address the inequities of a profit-based economy. Southern labor markets had, if anything, become more segregated following World War I; therefore, such equalizing principles as the MFSS proposed would threaten white economic control in the south, reinforcing southern resistance to merging with the larger, and in their eyes more radical, MEC.

The 1938 discussion reflected additional concern about clergy dominance over laity. Opponents of union claimed that MECS clergy were pushing through the Plan of Union without the southern laity understanding or approving of it. The lay-clergy division on the issue was evident in the status of the delegates who spoke to the plan: nine lay delegates and one clergy spoke against union, while the pro-union speeches were evenly divided among five lay and five clergy.[55] Because clergy and lay share institutional, political authority in Methodism through their election as delegates to conferences, all of the southern delegates faced a potential decrease in power by becoming a minority voice in the unified church. Clergy's religious leadership would preserve their authority over laity, which may explain why lay delegates spoke in larger numbers against the merger.

Retired bishop Warren Candler made use of his symbolic authority to argue against the plan when he and fellow retired bishop Collins Denny took the unprecedented step of issuing a statement in opposition to the Episcopal Address, which had commended the Plan of Union to the General Conference. Candler and Denny's statement summed up arguments against the plan made by delegates from the floor. While they cited the unconstitutionality of the plan as their major objection, they expressed

53. Ibid., 13.

54. Durant, *MECS DCA 1938*, 16.

55. Many delegates identify themselves as lay or clergy, while the status of others can be deduced from references within their speeches. Three speeches could not be so identified, two against (Harrison and Kyle) and one for union (Purcell).

the same resistance to changing social structures and concerns about loss of power that the delegates did. In speaking of northern domination, the retired bishops wrote:

> Suffice it to say that in our opinion this proposed Plan will be ruinous to effective Methodism in the South. Already in important and vital respects it has become abundantly clear that the North places one interpretation on the Plan and that the South places another. It is equally clear that the Northern interpretation will prevail and that the future will not hold for us peace and harmony, but strife and discord.[56]

Denny and Candler feared that southern ways would be engulfed by the larger and more powerful northern church, echoing the concerns of other delegates.

Unlike the tone of forward movement found in the Episcopal Address and in speeches by pro-union delegates, Denny and Candler looked backward, claiming to know "that it is no longer popular to refer to the past, but we likewise know that the past holds many lessons which may well be a sure guide to the future." Their perspective affirmed MECS structures, which were threatened by "this new, novel, and dangerous arrangement."[57]

Denny and Candler also criticized clergy power and defended the voice of the laity when they wrote: "Is it not significant that during the recent weeks from the Gulf to the Potomac a spontaneous uprising of the man in the pew has taken place in opposition to this Plan?"[58] In shifting the focus to lay resistance, the bishops advocated a traditional perspective, since many considered laity to be more conservative than clergy. The early twentieth century saw an increase in the number of clergy trained in seminaries, where theological liberalism was centered, and the split with Vanderbilt University in 1914 indicates the extent to which many southerners distrusted liberal education. Without mentioning race, Denny, Candler, and other conservatives argued for traditional (segregated) structures, and against a unified church that would weaken laity's political power.

56. *MECS DCA* April 29, 1938, 15–16. The bishops' speech appeared in the version of the *DCA* that was issued daily at General Conference.

57. Ibid., 16.

58. Ibid. Collins Denny Jr., a layman and the bishop's son, joined the fight on this issue as the legal chair for the Laymen's Organization for the Preservation of the Southern Methodist Church. Not being a member of the General Conference, he was not permitted to address the body.

T. D. Ellis, the Joint Commission member who presented the Plan of Union, summarized the pro-union position and refuted the arguments against it. Ellis spoke directly to "the Negro question," maintaining that white Methodists had a Christian duty to help "this race that needs us still." He noted that the plan granted the Negro a degree of autonomy but "in a way that will never embarrass him,"[59] a reference perhaps to the limited African American voice in the General Conference, which in essence put black Methodists under white control on all but jurisdictional matters. Ellis reassured MECS delegates that jurisdictional lines would never be altered nor a black bishop assigned to a white jurisdiction, unless that jurisdiction asked for such a change. Ellis also argued against disenfranchisement of laity and the prospect of northern domination.

In making the case for union, Ellis cited the common origin and doctrine of the three churches and the need to unite against new challenges, rather than being guided by old prejudices. The church should move beyond "old dead issues" and "meet the [new] issues like men of God."[60] Ellis and other pro-union speakers looked forward and asserted the potential influence that the MC could have against secular forces. These speakers advocated broadening their perspective beyond southern white Protestantism and looking toward a Methodist body that extended further than regional boundaries—boundaries that were not only geographic but also circumscribed different social patterns and relationships.

By confronting the race issue and rejecting old prejudices, Ellis sought to move the church toward a new age when global challenges required a larger, more powerful church. Like the 1918 delegates, though, Ellis did not argue in favor of an integrated church or increased power for African Americans. Instead he assured MECS delegates that the plan addressed such concerns by keeping African Americans segregated and by limiting their influence on the larger church. Therefore, racial prejudice should not derail unification and the potential role that a unified Methodist Church could play on the national and international fronts. Racial prejudice had not been overcome, but was accommodated within the Plan of Union.

Scriptural language was more prevalent in this debate than in 1918, most often in support of union. One delegate cited Peter's vision of clean

59. *MECS DCA* 1938, 62.
60. Ibid., 63.

and unclean animals,[61] which helped him "overcome his prejudices,"[62] while another quoted John 17:21: "I pray that they all may be one, as thou, Father, art in me, and I in thee; that they also may be one in us."[63] The most stirring religious rhetoric was from Harry Denman, a lay delegate, who offered a sermonic appeal that drew on scripture, Methodist history, and the indwelling of the Holy Spirit. Citing the need for a spiritual awakening in the nation, Denman envisioned the evangelistic potential of a unified Methodist Church:

> I am a layman, but I want to see my church, to which I have given my life, be a spiritual power in the life of this nation. I want that church to drive the forces of unrighteousness from America. I want that church to send its missionaries by the thousands around the world. I want that church to stand in our pulpits, our great city pulpits, and preach the Gospel of Christ. I want that church to go out into the rural life of America and proclaim our Christ. I want that church to go down into the city slums and heal lame humanity. I want that church to help bring God's Kingdom to earth.[64]

For Denman and others, the potential for the new MC to be a spiritual and political force outweighed any concerns about racial equality. Religious ideals, rather than the defense of existing social structures, were used to envision a more inclusive future that brought together long divided Methodist bodies, while, ironically, continuing to divide the church racially.

Race, in fact, was the defining characteristic of the reunited church. In its earliest days, Methodism opposed slavery and was an egalitarian movement with blacks, women, and people of differing economic classes providing local leadership. Increasingly, though, leadership was restricted to white men, and social divisions that marked the larger society took hold in Methodism as well. By the time of church union in 1939, racial division so defined American Christianity that the newly reunited MC, as the largest and most powerful Protestant church in the nation, embraced that division as being central to its own identity.[65] White dominance, which

---

61. In Acts 10, Peter, while on the rooftop, sees a vision of both clean and unclean animals, which God orders him to kill and eat. Peter interprets this as a sign that Gentiles and Jews need not keep separate from each other within the new Christian movement.

62. Newby, *MECS DCA* 1938, 11.

63. Dobes, *MECS DCA* 1938, 21.

64. *MECS DCA* 1938, 20.

65. Davis, *The Methodist Unification*, 9.

pervaded American society, would also pervade the new MC, which thus relinquished the opportunity to stand against racial injustice.

When put to a vote, the Plan of Union was approved by 95 percent of the MECS General Conference delegates (434–26), an even larger margin than the annual conference vote. White southern delegates were satisfied that their racial authority was secure and that the prospect of being overpowered by the north was balanced by the increased power the unified church could wield in the larger society. Geographic jurisdictions afforded white southerners some degree of control over their own affairs, and ensured leadership by pastors and bishops from that region. In the end, arguments for unity and inclusiveness carried the day—yet unity was related to the overall structure of the new denomination, which nevertheless incorporated a new form of internal division in its geographic and racial jurisdictions, and inclusiveness referred to token numbers of black delegates, while white men still comprised the vast majority of General Conference delegates and could direct the course of the new church according to their interests.

A few disgruntled holdouts formed the Southern Methodist Church, which grew out of the remnants of the Laymen's Organization for the Preservation of the Southern Methodist Church. Inspired by Bishop Candler and led by Bishop Collins Denny, the Laymen's Organization was founded in 1937 as a last-ditch effort to stave off union. The denomination lost legal battles that prevented them from using the MECS name or retaining any property, but it continues today with 5,000 members in over 100 congregations throughout the southeast.[66]

The Church and the Color Line

It is easy to look back from the twenty-first century and see these early twentieth-century discussions as blatant statements of racism, understood now as systemic oppression based on socially constructed differences. The speeches examined here sound degrading to African Americans, and make white southerners appear narrow, paternalistic, and self-interested. They reflect an understanding at that time of social evolution that lay behind many reactions we would describe now as racist and xenophobic. Bourdieu's theories suggest a more complex situation, in which white resistance

66. Southern Methodist Church website: http://www.southernmethodistchurch .com.

to black authority is the result of social conditioning that leads one group to dominate another and both groups to see that arbitrary structure as inevitable.

Southern white Methodists reflect three centuries of socialization rooted in an economic arrangement that relied on the enslavement of African people. Supporting this socialization process were cultural and religious understandings of the superiority of white European Christian civilization, and the need for other peoples to "progress" or evolve in that direction. Over time, white dominance over African Americans came to appear increasingly natural and required less conscious effort to reinforce and inscribe in successive generations. Lacking the social or political power to oppose their domination, African Americans were perceived to tolerate, or even accept it.

Looking at these dynamics through the lens of Bourdieu's theory, race becomes part of a habitus that preconditions the way social agents understand themselves and others, offering a model that bridges essentialist theories focusing on biological differences with theories that dismiss race as a social construct.[67] Bourdieu acknowledges the constructed nature of social relations such as racial differences, while recognizing that, once objectivated, they are perceived as reality that has real consequences for human relationships.

Bourdieu's focus on the dominant group resonates with more recent scholarship on whiteness. Here race, and specifically whiteness, is a form of social or cultural capital that accrues privileges of which the beneficiaries are largely unaware. Whiteness becomes the norm, and both whites and people of color are shaped by language and other symbolic systems, including religion, that communicate a hierarchical set of social relations. White dominance is invisible to whites because it resonates with their habitus, and until disrupted, everyday behavior and language continue to reinforce symbolic or cultural meanings that perpetuate those power structures.

Religion is one of the symbolic systems that has served that purpose, as W. E. B. Du Bois (1868–1963), who lived through the period addressed here, was quick to point out. Du Bois implicated the U.S. Christian church in racial oppression, writing in his 1903 book *The Souls of Black Folk* of the "doctrines of passive submission" embodied in the Christianity taught to

---

67. Smaje, "Not Just."

slaves,[68] and pointing out in *The Negro in the South* (1907) Christianity's complicity in slavery, as part of southern economic history.[69]

More than two decades later, he wrote in *The Christian Century* (1931), that he believed the church would be "found consistently on the wrong side" of the issue of race.[70] People of color were enslaved, he wrote, "under the aegis and protection of the religion of the Prince of Peace,"[71] and their domination continued after abolition in the form of a "color caste."[72] Du Bois exposed the church's legitimation of racial oppression as a product of human material interest rather than the divine mission it claimed. In asserting that religion sanctions racial domination, Du Bois noted that white Americans inculcated in people of color images of a white God and a white salvation figure in Jesus, promising that African Americans would be rewarded for their earthly trials when they reached heaven, which was accessible to them through obedience and suffering.

A distinctive African American Christianity emerged as a form of resistance to the oppression slaves associated with their slave owners' church. Religiously sanctioned domination and generations of socialization failed to convince blacks that slavery represented God's divine order, and they found within the Christian tradition stories of liberation that spoke powerfully to their situation. Born in the secret space of "hush harbors" on plantations, black churches became important social centers for newly emancipated slaves and a space that was free of white control. Preaching and music centered on freedom and empowerment, rather than submission and domination at the hands of others.

Despite there being two independent black Methodist denominations, a number of African Americans remained under white leadership in the MEC and the CMEC, allowing white members of those churches to think these black Methodists accepted their dominated status. The southern white Methodists examined here did not see themselves as oppressors, but instead felt bound by Christian duty to assist those they perceived as less advanced and incapable of self-sufficiency.

In the twenty-five year period examined here, southern resistance to Methodist reunification reflects such understandings of white superiority,

68. Du Bois, "Of the Faith," 52.
69. Du Bois, "Religion in the South," 69–70.
70. Du Bois, "Will the Church," 174.
71. Ibid.
72. Ibid., 176.

even as the delegates changed their strategies to adapt to changing social situations. From more straightforward concerns about black authority and "social equality" in 1918, delegates in 1938 spoke of the need to unite with other Methodists against external movements such as socialism, fascism, and communism. Throughout the period, the delegates expressed concern about losing southern culture and social relations that included white dominance. Racial segregation and white privilege defined the various social fields that Methodists inhabited, and the MECS understood itself to have a particular role in protecting this arrangement as part of God's intended order; as MECS Bishop Elijah Hoss once proclaimed: "God Almighty has drawn the color line in indelible ink."[73] This color line was codified in the segregated structure of the MC that emerged from these discussions in 1939.

Robert Sledge argues that during the last two and a half decades of its existence, the MECS saw a transition from conservative dominance to more progressive leadership, a process that facilitated union with the north. His book *Hands on the Ark: The Struggle for Change in the Methodist Episcopal Church, South, 1914–1939* covers the same period examined here, which was marked by prohibition, immigration restrictions, and an economic depression. The MECS faced internal transitions during this period as well, including the rise of religious fundamentalism in response to liberalism, changes in mission structure and supervision, and democratizing movements to grant more lay power and limit episcopal control. In this unsettled time, southerners resisted additional changes that would come with church union related to racial relationships and liberal agendas in the north.[74]

In mounting a reform movement, southern progressives had to overcome the idea that the MECS was a hallowed institution and that to change its structure was to "lay unclean hands upon the sacred ark of God, upon the vessel of salvation."[75] Sledge attributes the eventual changes in the MECS to the success of several efforts in the 1930s that brought Methodists together, a change in the power base from a group of conservative bishops with tight control to more progressive and diffuse leadership, and a shift from looking backward to looking forward. Even so, American notions of progress

73. Mariner, "The Negro's Place," 161.

74. Sledge, *Hands*.

75. Ibid., 7. The imagery refers to the story in 2 Samuel 6, in which an Israelite named Uzzah puts out his hand to steady the Ark of the Covenant while it is being transported, only to be struck dead on the spot. MECS leaders used the image in 1906 and 1920 as a cautionary tale for General Conferences that were facing contentious issues.

in the early twentieth century had a distinctly racial tone, with whiteness depicted as the pinnacle of civilization and morality; thus, Methodists saw white dominance in the new church as entirely appropriate, even necessary.

Nevertheless, delegates in 1938 were open to allowing black Methodists a place in the united church and a voice in General Conference, albeit a marginal one—a move away from the strict institutional separation that marked their relationship with the CMEC and that the 1914 and 1918 delegates required. This slight broadening of ecclesiastical borders entailed a less restrictive understanding of racial relationships for the south, cracking open the possibility of greater institutional change down the road. As Bourdieu suggests, periods of social change bring both prophetic challenges and greater resistance from the status quo, raising the possibility of changing power structures, but not without a battle.

In the end, MECS members allowed the power and influence that a unified Methodist Church could have on the national stage to overcome their resistance to their own loss of dominance. Even if they were swallowed up by the larger MEC, they would be part of the largest Protestant denomination in the United States at the time, which could better prevail against such modern movements as socialism and communism. Lay delegate Harry Denman expressed the ecumenical spirit that carried the day when he claimed that these churches, "consummated into American Methodism, and known as the Methodist Church, committed unto God, and possessing a heart-warming experience can, under the leadership of the Holy Spirit, bring to this nation a great spiritual revival."[76]

Change was also facilitated by the passage of time since talks of union began, which progressive Bishop John M. Moore claims had "dissolved many issues, softened many attitudes, and altered many viewpoints."[77] Some resistant leaders had died, while others, such as Bishops Candler and Denny, had retired and been replaced by leaders who were more receptive to change. A new generation of leaders saw that their authority could more effectively be used defending against secular and modern trends that they perceived as threats to Christianity, rather than preserving a racial dominance that did not seem to be in immediate danger. Thus southern Methodists renegotiated their authority in various areas, while retaining white dominance and continuing to relate to African Americans with an attitude of charity and support.

76. *MECS DCA* 1938, 19.
77. Quoted in Sledge, *Hands*, 241.

Institutional segregation that restricted black authority persisted in the MC until it merged with the Evangelical United Brethren in 1968 to form The United Methodist Church (UMC). Although this merger dissolved the Central Jurisdiction, which included all black Methodists, United Methodist congregations continue to be largely segregated,[78] and many white churches still today resist the appointment of black clergy. Although institutional barriers have collapsed and language that overtly affirms white superiority is no longer acceptable in most social circles, a racist habitus continues to shape much of American society, including the UMC, where racial integration and equality are largely resisted, suggesting the durability of domination patterns.

78. According to 2001 statistics from the Department of Statistics, UMC General Council on Finance and Administration, 1.3 percent of United Methodist churches could be considered multiracial congregations, which the Multiracial Congregations Project at Hartford Seminary defines as having no more than 80 percent of members from one racial group. hirr.hartsem.edu/cong/research_multiracl.html.

3

Resistance to Women's Ordination

"The Time Is Not Ripe"

"If God wants women to preach the Gospel,
he will call them so loudly that the Church will hear."

—REV. DR. H. GRAHAM

IN 1895, ELIZABETH CADY Stanton and a group of women published *The Woman's Bible*, which challenged the peripheral role of women as portrayed in scripture and the implications of the church's reliance on that text as the inerrant word of God. These forerunners of later feminist theologians pointed to the connection between gender roles and religion that underlies Western thought. Emerging out of patriarchal contexts, the Bible affirms the masculine domination that Stanton and others perceived in the church and the larger society. The women's movement in the mid-nineteenth century arose out of that religious context. The case for women's rights, along with abolition, was preached by revivalists and championed by Quakers such as Lucretia Mott, who argued for rights on moral grounds. The Seneca Falls Convention in 1848, which featured Mott and Stanton as speakers, was held in Wesleyan Methodist Chapel in Seneca Falls, New York. After encountering resistance from the religious community, however, the movement became more secular. Still, Methodist women such as Anna Howard Shaw, Frances Willard, and Madeline Southard supported the larger women's movement, while advocating for women's rights within the church. This chapter traces efforts to gain women's ordination, along with the related issue of lay delegation to General Conference, in The Methodist Episcopal Church (MEC) and later The Methodist Church (MC).

Over the decades that it took for Methodism to grant women full clergy rights, the church struggled, as did U.S. society in general, with reluctance to acknowledge women's equality. Rather than casting women as inferior to men, however, many in the church outwardly affirmed women's abilities by promoting the roles of wife and mother as superior to church leadership. In addition they cited practical problems as reasons to delay granting them full clergy rights. This curious rhetoric that claimed to affirm women's abilities masks an understanding of male superiority and domination that restricts the use of those abilities to the home where it poses no real threat to men in the public sphere. It also reflects resistance based more on a changing social climate and challenges to existing power structures than on religious prohibitions.

Historical Background

The course of women's ordination in Methodism is not easily traced, because women gained varying degrees of leadership in the different Methodist denominations over nearly two centuries. In the late eighteenth century, John Wesley himself allowed a few women to serve as lay preachers, acknowledging that they had an extraordinary call, and in isolated cases, women provided leadership throughout the movement's history in America. There was a similar pattern in other churches in this country, with no concerted appeal for women's ordination until the late nineteenth century when Methodists such as Anna Howard Shaw and Frances Willard joined others in fighting for ordination, along with the larger cause of gender equality.

The denominational bodies associated with American Methodism took various approaches to the question of women's leadership over their history.[1] Some licensed laywomen as preachers, and a few isolated ordinations occurred, but these moves involved no change to the churches' *Books of Discipline* that would guarantee continuation of such rights. The United Brethren Church (UBC), an ancestor to the current United Methodist Church (UMC), licensed women as early as 1849 and gave Sarah Dickey

1. While American Methodism fragmented into numerous denominations after its founding in 1784, this analysis focuses on the denominations that are ancestors of the current United Methodist Church.

full clergy rights in 1894, while The Methodist Protestant Church (MPC) ordained Anna Howard Shaw in 1880. However, the UBC rescinded women's licenses in 1857 and the MPC ruled Shaw's ordination out of order in 1884. Mergers of these smaller denominations with larger Methodist bodies in the twentieth century always resulted in women's rights being curtailed. When the UBC merged with the Evangelical Association (EA) to form the Evangelical United Brethren Church (EUBC) in 1946, women lost all clergy rights. Methodist Protestant women also lost full clergy rights in the 1939 merger with the MEC and the Methodist Episcopal Church, South (MECS) to form the MC.[2] In the larger ecclesial bodies reviewed in this book, we see resistance to women's leadership, both lay or clergy, from women's first appeal for ordination to the MEC General Conference in 1880 to the granting of full clergy rights by the MC more than seventy-five years later.

Methodist women in the late nineteenth century were engaged in several movements that advanced their visibility and leadership within the church and outside it. In an effort to have a direct impact on the lives of women overseas, Methodist women formed mission societies to raise and direct funds independent of male-controlled mission boards—in the MEC in 1869 and the MECS in 1910. Many of the missionaries themselves were single women, who carried the gospel to women in countries where social restrictions would prevent interaction with male missionaries. Methodists were also leaders in the deaconess movement, through which women ministered in urban and rural low-income areas in this country. Rooted in German Methodism, deaconesses were found in the MEC, as well as both the UBC and the EA, predecessor groups to today's UMC. Like mission societies, this "separatist" movement granted women control of a sphere of ministry outside of male supervision.

The mission society and deaconess movements supported the campaigns for lay representation and for clergy rights, as women sought a voice in decision-making and to fulfill their call to preach. This chapter looks at the 1880 MEC General Conference, when those issues were first addressed; the extensive debate in 1888 over whether women could serve as lay delegates; MEC discussions of women's ordination in 1920 and 1924; and the resolution of the debate at the 1956 MC General Conference.

---

2. This accommodation of more conservative positions regarding women's rights mirrors the accommodation of southern resistance to an integrated church that marked the 1939 merger of the MEC, MECS, and MPC (see chapter 2).

1880 General Conference: An Open-and-Shut Case

In 1869, the MEC licensed its first woman preacher, the powerful evangelist Maggie Van Cott of New York, amid ongoing controversy. Several other women were licensed, and in March 1880, Anna Oliver and Anna Howard Shaw came before the New England Annual Conference requesting ordination. Although both women had earned theology degrees from Boston University and were recommended for ordination by the Annual Conference, Bishop Edward G. Andrews ruled them ineligible. Shaw took the bishop's advice and left the MEC to be ordained in another denomination (the MPC), but Oliver took her case to the 1880 MEC General Conference, which considered ordination of women an open-and-shut case that merited no debate on the floor.[3] Petitions on Oliver's behalf were referred to the committees on Itinerancy and the Judiciary. The Judiciary Committee supported Bishop Andrews's ruling as being "in accordance with the Discipline of the Church as it is."[4]

The Committee on Itinerancy made two reports on the issue. Its Report No. IX found that the Willoughby Avenue MEC, which Oliver served and which petitioned on her behalf, was not connected with the MEC and therefore had no official connection to the General Conference. The original handwritten petition bears the penciled notation: "Subcommittee—return this paper as having no legitimate place in the General Conference." While this abrupt dismissal presumably related to the congregation's lack of affiliation, it could also reflect the lack of legitimacy with which women's ordination was regarded in 1880.

The Committee's Report No. X, which addressed several other petitions regarding Oliver's ordination, ruled that in relation to "the licensing of women as exhorters and local preachers, their ordination, admission to the traveling connection, and eligibility to all offices in the Church," women were "accorded all the privileges which are necessary to their usefulness."[5] Thus, not only was Shaw's request for ordination rejected, but the MEC eliminated the licensing of women as local lay preachers, as per the Discipline. While no discussion from the committee or the General Conference floor was recorded, a change in the handwritten ruling may reflect the tone

3. No discussion is recorded in the published *Journal*, the *DCA*, or in the manuscript minutes in the Methodist Archives at Drew University.

4. *MEC Journal* 1880, 353.

5. *MEC DCA* 1880, 90.

of any discussion that transpired. The phrase "in their [the committee's] judgment" was struck, and in its place was added: "by general consent of the church," suggesting an attempt to make this a more forceful ruling that represented universal opinion and not that of the committee members alone.

The lack of debate offers no material for analyzing the nature of the resistance to women's ordination—a lack that suggests that there was little, if any, opposition to rejecting Oliver's petition. The message to Anna Oliver and other women who might consider ordination was clear: the MEC was not ready for this step. In this first appeal for women's ordination, masculine domination went unchallenged, as the all-male General Conference reaffirmed the all-male nature of MEC ministry. Eight years later, however, the question of laywomen serving as delegates to General Conference provoked a substantive discussion of women's authority within the church.

1888 General Conference: What to Do with Five Female Delegates

The cause of women's rights overlapped with a movement to increase the rights of laity in Methodist conferences. A constitutional change in 1872 allowed lay delegates into the MEC General Conference, which to that point had included only clergy. Sixteen years later, when the 1888 General Conference met in New York, five women were sent as delegates from their annual conferences. Among them was Frances Willard, by some accounts the most famous Methodist of her day, male or female.[6]

A champion of women's rights, Frances Willard devoted her life to helping them achieve spiritual fulfillment lived out in moral lives and service to others, the hallmark of Willard's own Methodist faith. She saw women's potential as unlimited, claiming that "Woman will bless and brighten every place she enters and she *will* enter *every* place!"[7] Her fervor stemmed, perhaps, from a pledge to "be a Christian girl" if God let her survive a bout of typhoid fever at age nineteen,[8] and her autobiography and many years of journals chronicle her life-long effort to make good on that vow. Willard taught and served as president of Northwestern University's Ladies College,

6. Introduction by Carolyn De Swarte Gifford to 1987 reprinting of Frances Willard's 1889 *Defense of Women's Rights to Ordination in the Methodist Episcopal Church*, n.p.

7. Gifford, "My Own Methodist," 89.

8. Ibid., 83.

before joining the temperance movement, where she quickly established herself as a major player. She served as national president of the Women's Christian Temperance Union (WCTU) from 1879 until her death in 1898, and under her leadership it became the largest women's organization of its time. She was involved in the suffrage movement as well, but unlike other feminists who rejected the Christian church as too patriarchal, Willard saw a reformed church as the path to women's freedom.

Willard had attempted to speak at the 1880 General Conference on behalf of the WCTU, but met with resistance. She wrote in her autobiography, "In our simplicity, we thought it the most natural thing imaginable thus to bring the work we loved back to the church that had nurtured us and given us our inspiration. . . . One would have thought, however, that something revolutionary had been proposed."[9] The delegates spent more than two hours debating the issue, and when the question was carried over to the next day, Willard, preferring to "settle the matter peacefully," sent a note removing her request, claiming that "never having attended a General Conference before, I had no idea of the strong opposition that would be manifested, or I would not have listened to the generous friends who urged the matter on your attention."[10]

The "strong opposition" prompted by that request was nothing compared to the firestorm that erupted when Willard and the other females elected as lay delegates arrived at the 1888 General Conference in New York. The Chair of the Committee on Arrangements urged Willard to show up and take her seat with the rest of her delegation when the Conference began; however, Willard returned home to Illinois where her mother was seriously ill and remained there for the duration of the Conference. The other four women stayed in New York, but the men kept them waiting for a week while they debated whether to seat them as delegates.

The primary issue under debate was whether women qualified as delegates under the 1872 legislation. Women's advocates argued that the language did not specifically exclude women, and in fact the word "male" had been struck from the legislation, so that women would be allowed to vote in the church-wide referendum required for a constitutional amendment. Because women comprised two-thirds of the church membership, advocates argued, it was largely their vote that approved lay delegation, and their right to vote carried with it the right to be elected. The General

9. Willard, *Glimpses*, 615.
10. Ibid., 617.

Conference had further ruled that for matters related to the election of delegates, the word "laymen" included "all the members of the Church who are not [clergy] members of the Annual Conferences." In other instances the General Conference had ordered that male pronouns were used generically and included women.

Opponents countered that delegates in 1872 did not intend to include women; that the intent in defining "laymen" was to include lay preachers, not women; and that the inclusion of women in male pronouns related to only a few specific local offices. Advocates, they argued, could not read into the law sixteen years later something that went beyond the intent of its framers. The only solution was to submit the idea of women delegates to another church-wide vote, so that the question would be settled once and for all. Arguments in favor of seating the women reflected the notion of gender equality that prompted the women's rights debate in the late nineteenth century, while the opposition reflected a sense of masculine domination that was so deeply ingrained that male pronouns as applied to church leadership could not possibly be gender inclusive.

While these arguments formed the main architecture of the debate, the speeches also reveal tensions about the authority of various bodies within Methodism, ideological differences, and discussion of women's fitness for leadership. Those who would seat the female delegates asserted the authority of the General Conference, whose broad 1872 ruling, they claimed, was sufficient to justify including women. These delegates saw no need for another church-wide vote, and some chastised the bishops for over-reaching their authority in their opening address that discouraged the seating of women.

On the other side, delegates argued that the General Conference would tend toward despotism if it enacted such a radical decision without a vote of the membership. Several delegates spoke of the need for a separate judicial body, since the MEC General Conference at that time ruled on the constitutionality of its own legislation. As compared to the MECS, the MEC continued to vest more authority in the General Conference than in the episcopacy, but the debate reflected power struggles between General and annual conferences.

Embedded in these arguments were ongoing tensions between laity and clergy. Several clergy delegates cautioned that admitting women would weaken the pool of laity, which was intended to bring to General Conference the expertise of men in secular professions. As Rev. J. R. Day warned:

> For every woman admitted you displace a man, and you weaken
> the lay element—you weaken the man element. . . . We have not
> enough lawyers, we have not enough senators, we have not enough
> governors, we have not enough judges and business men now in
> this body. We do not want to lose one of those we have by even the
> substitution of ministers or women.[11]

The laymen, although the ones who would suffer such displacement, spoke and voted in favor of admitting women in larger numbers than did the clergy. Of the thirty-nine speeches made on the issue, twice as many lay members spoke in favor of women (six speeches for and three against), while more clergy spoke against the action (eleven for and nineteen against). The final vote to refer the issue to annual conferences was determined by clergy (159 for referral to 122 against), since the lay vote was essentially even (75–76).

While it would seem that the laity stood to lose more power by admitting women, it is also possible that as a marginalized group that had recently gained new authority, laity used that authority to advocate for extending power to another group on the margins. Male clergy, on the other hand, while still outnumbering lay delegates,[12] had seen one incursion into their legislative power and were reluctant to agree to another. Clergy delegates spoke specifically to the rights of the annual conferences, which remained exclusively clergy, versus the General Conference. Rev. Dr. James M. Buckley, known for his rhetorical gifts, remarked on the "usurpation of the powers that belong to the whole body of elders . . . [who] sit supreme in the sublime prerogatives given them by the fathers above any and all General Conferences."[13]

Clergy delegate John Wilson compared arguments against women delegates to those made against black delegates[14] and laity, and he urged delegates who were part of those marginalized groups to stand up for women:

> How much like the arguments for the exclusion of colored men
> and male laymen are these for the exclusion of female laymen.

11. *MEC DCA* 1888, 35.

12. Each annual conference was allowed to send only two lay delegates, in addition to a larger clergy delegation determined by the relative size of the annual conference.

13. *MEC DCA* 1888, 54.

14. Black delegates had been admitted to the MEC General Conference just twenty years earlier in 1868.

Brothers in black, Brother laymen, help to prevent from these women that wrong which a too-slow conservatism would have inflicted upon you. As ye would that men should do unto you so do ye unto these women.[15]

The only delegate identified as African American, however, Rev. Dr. A. E. P. Albert, spoke against extending lay rights to women and was one of the few who challenged their fitness for leadership. In the following comments, Albert appeared to recognize the irony that as a member of a marginalized group himself, he did not support the rights of another marginalized group:

> I know you will give me the credit of an honest difference of opinion when I tell you through what mental struggles I have labored to reach the point where I could allow myself to occupy opposite grounds with such bold defenders of human rights as have espoused the cause of the admission of women in this General Conference. But, after a careful and prayerful deliberation of the matter, I feel that I would be unfaithful to the dictates of my own conscience to the Church of my choice, and the Conference that has honored me with their confidence, were I, for any reason to fail to express my conviction in this presence.[16]

Former Indiana Governor Will Cumback, a lay delegate, addressed that same irony when he said, "I had a sense of pain in my heart when my colored brother stood here and construed all the doubts against women, and restricted them in the full enjoyment of their rights in this Conference."[17] Dr. J. Lanahan, on the other hand, was appalled that a black delegate would be chastised so publicly,[18] while Rev. Dr. Arthur Edwards defended "the only colored delegate who has spoken in this debate," saying: "Brother Albert, you are a freeman. If your liberty of speech is not perfect, we must do our work over again. Speak with the greatest liberty, for you are a man among men."[19]

As these comments indicate, racial tension was still very much alive in the MEC General Conference, even as it addressed tension over gender. Albert began his remarks with an apology, saying, "Mr. President, it seems to be the most stupendous presumption on my part to arrest your attention,

15. *MEC DCA* 1888, 27.

16. Ibid., 61.

17. Ibid., 54.

18. Ibid., 62.

19. Ibid., 50b.

when so many men of recognized authority and wisdom are claiming your attention."[20] It is unclear whether Albert's humility was sincere or was calculated to soften the impact of his speaking at all, much less in opposition to including another marginalized group. The white delegates who responded to Albert revealed equal discomfort, as Cumback, who supported women's rights spoke against the only vocal African American, while Lanahan and Edwards, who opposed seating the women, were able to support inclusion by defending Albert's right to express his view.

Racial dynamics were also evident in those who equated the quest for women's rights with the MEC's stance against slavery, noting that New York had also been the site of the 1844 General Conference, when the MECS split off from the MEC in large part over slavery. Lay delegate Leslie Shaw, a lawyer and self-professed conservative, spoke with pride that in 1844 the MEC "took advanced ground on the question of slavery." He went on:

> In less than forty-four years from now when, if we read the times aright, woman shall have become eligible to all places of public trust, let it not be said that, in this year of grace 1888, the constitutional law of this Church had to be amended to admit women to its chief councils. I do not like the thought of going home and facing the record that the Church I love above all others, the Church for which my prayers ascend and to which my toils are given, was so conservative and so prejudiced in the last quarter of this nineteenth century as to vote to exclude women from her seats [sic] with no law or precedent to support its decision.[21]

Yet for all its talk of human freedom and its pride in standing against slavery in 1844, the MEC in 1888 remained a segregated institution. While African Americans were included in the General Conference, they were a distinct minority, and black clergy were restricted to serving black churches under the supervision of white bishops. As we saw in chapter 2, the issue of African American leadership would continue to plague the church in the next few decades as it approached reunification with the MECS and dealt with the ongoing changes that marked the larger society. Consideration of women's rights only compounded the wave of change both within and outside the church.

Reactions to social change framed ideological differences between those favoring women delegates under the current Constitution and those

20. Ibid., 61.
21. Ibid., 53.

who would refer the matter for a church-wide vote. Advocates for the women spoke of progress and the need for the church to keep up with the spirit of the age. They supported their stance with such scriptures as Galatians 3:28 ("There is no longer Jew or Greek, there is no longer slave or free, there is no longer male and female, for all of you are one in Christ Jesus") and Joel 2:28 ("I will pour out my spirit on all flesh; your sons and your daughters shall prophesy," also cited in Acts 2:17).

Opponents of seating the women referred less overtly to scripture, with one of the only references being Jacob Rothweiler's claim that "God himself ordained the Church government" in the Mosaic covenant and in Jesus' selection of the apostles, both of which excluded women.[22] These delegates urged caution, with Rev. Dr. Wheeler claiming, "the only safe course for us to pursue is to pursue the wise, careful, judicious, and conservative— I mean every word—and conservative course we have heretofore pursued through all our history."[23] Rev. Albert said that he failed to see "a single scriptural warrant granting [women] the right of Church government," and urged those clinging to the "orthodox teachings of the Church" to hold fast, even if depicted as "hide-bound and antiquated bigots." Like Rothweiler, Albert asserted that his view represented God's will, saying: "I am quite willing to be so classed, if my antiquated ideas are grounded in the word of God, and are nurtured by the sunshine and influences of divine sanction."[24]

Progressive and conservative delegates reflected different reactions to the unsettling feelings that accompany social changes, which several speakers addressed directly. Said professor and lay delegate John Clark Ridpath: "For the moment we feel, while shaking in the blast, the pangs of transformation." Even so, he noted, they could not turn women away "without a denial of the manifest tendencies and purposes of our age."[25] Clergy delegate H. H. Moore echoed that sentiment, saying: "My brethren and friends, it is coming. It is useless for us to try to seize the crest of this rolling wave and double it back. It is coming. It will come."[26]

Clergy delegate Jacob Rothweiler urged just the opposite response to this tide of change:

22. Ibid., 35.

23. Ibid., 28. There were two clergy delegates named Wheeler, and the record is not clear whether Rev. Alfred or Rev. Bert E. delivered this address.

24. Ibid., 61.

25. Ibid., 62.

26. Ibid., 50.

> We should not be swept to and from by the imagination of the rationalistic notions of the time. The great strength of Christianity is its stability, its unchangeableness, and its firm adhesion to the law and the Gospel. If we take any action here, let that action be in harmony with the word of God, and in harmony with what is established by Protestantism.[27]

Summarizing these differences and the inevitability of change, Rev. W. N. McElroy said:

> There is and has always been, however, a steady battle between conservatism and progress along this line, in Methodism as well as elsewhere. It was so in the slavery agitation, and the Church today is ashamed of much of her history and record upon that subject. It was so in reference to the introduction of lay representation. It was rent in twain over it, and only realized after a contest extending over a score of years. It is not so [sic] in this question. But the upward ground swell of truth and righteousness swept away that conservatism that stood in the way of the Church's progress, and so it will this.[28]

McElroy also addressed women's fitness for leadership by describing them as Methodism's "most spiritual and loyal half" whose presence could only benefit the General Conference: "We need woman's intelligence and ready forethought, and wise counsels in the legislation of the Church. Let us welcome them, then, to our chief councils. Nor say them nay. They will do us good and not harm."[29] Others acknowledged women's leadership in their own mission organizations and in the temperance movement, as well as their service to the local church.[30]

Even most of those who opposed seating these five women as delegates did not outwardly question their merit. This tone was set by the bishops in their opening address; although they urged the need for a constitutional amendment to settle the question of women delegates, they said: "Happily no question of competency or worthiness is involved in the question of their eligibility as delegates."[31] However, it is not uncommon for churches to give verbal support to the idea of gender equality while denying women

27. Ibid., 35.
28. Ibid., 55.
29. Ibid.
30. See *MEC DCA* 1888 for speeches by Fisk, 45, and Wilson, 27.
31. *MEC Journal* 1888, 52.

leadership over men. At least one delegate used this "equal but different" argument,[32] but most MEC delegates relied on the lack of clarity surrounding the admission of lay delegates to affirm their support for women and their role in the church, while denying them a place in General Conference.

Only a few delegates directly challenged women's fitness for leadership. One of these was Rev. Dr. James M. Buckley, a prominent opponent of both lay and women's rights who had tremendous influence as editor of the New York *Christian Advocate* and as a delegate to eleven consecutive General Conferences during this pivotal era, from 1872 to 1912. A master of rhetoric, Buckley spoke up for "the holy cause of women" and women's own right to speak to this matter in a church-wide vote, nevertheless implying that many of them would vote against their admission to General Conference. He further asserted that two of the women elected were "as competent to sit in judgment on this question as any man on this floor," even as he opposed their admission by stating that not a single church in the world admitted women to its law-making body. He affirmed the importance of male leadership with the comment: "Every time you put a woman in, you put a man out."[33] Buckley made this point more explicitly in an editorial following the 1888 General Conference, when he wrote: "All objections to the admission of women into the General Conference come at last to this—that they are *women* and not men." (emphasis in original) [34]

Rev. Dr. J. R. Day likewise affirmed his admiration for women and their devotion to the church, but claimed that lawmaking is a matter of the head and not the heart, reflecting a dualistic stereotype that associates men with rationality and women with emotions, making them less fit for leadership. Day remarked: "Law is not to be made by gifts, by sacrifices, by tears, by devotion. Eligibility to a place in the law-making body of this great Church is not to be established by the devotion of these godly women. It is altogether another question, a question which lodges up here [pointing to forehead] and dwells here."[35]

African American delegate A. E. P. Albert explicitly rejected women's leadership in the church. In claiming that nothing in scripture, church history, or Methodism supported the leadership of women, he asserted that the issue questioned "the very foundation of Church authority." He was one

32. Moore, *MEC DCA* 1888, 50.

33. *MEC DCA* 1888, 27.

34. "'The Rights' of Women and Others," quoted in Schmidt, *Grace Sufficient*, 221.

35. *MEC DCA* 1888, 35.

of only two delegates who mentioned the prospect of women's ordination, which, having been raised at the 1880 General Conference, no doubt contributed to resistance to women delegates eight years later. As Albert noted:

> Admit once that women may become members of the General Conference, and I defy any authority to keep them from being successively licensed to preach, ordained to orders, and finally occupying a place on this platform as General Superintendents [bishops] in the Church—an idea which never even suggested itself to the Church when lay delegation were adopted.[36]

The other delegate to mention women's ordination was Rev. Dr. H. Graham, who spoke in favor of a church-wide referendum to discern God's intention for the church. In his remarks, Graham equated the will of God with the will of the church, with no admission of the human interests that influence church politics:

> It has been my conviction that if God wants women to preach the Gospel, he will call them so loudly that the Church will hear. And if God calls them the Church will recognize that call, and every obstacle will be taken out of the way. . . . And if God wants women in our General Conferences, they will be there in spite of all opposition, and be there by the consent and wish of the Church. I am prepared to accept the wish of the Church as the voice of God in this matter.[37]

While not directly related to women's ordination, the discussion of whether women could serve as lay delegates to General Conference offers a window into how Methodism viewed the larger issue of women's rights at this pivotal time. This discussion reveals ongoing tensions between conservative forces that would maintain traditional leadership structures and delegates who argued for greater inclusion—tensions that were complicated by the continuing dynamics of racial inclusion, as liberal white delegates found themselves opposing the more conservative view of the only black delegate to speak, capturing the complex nature of such transitional times. The delegates who advocated for opening the doors of General Conference to women represent the prophetic voice that can emerge at such periods and admit the possibility of change in the existing power structure. While there had been no recorded discussion of women's ordination in 1880, by

36. Ibid., 61.
37. Ibid., 36.

1888 there was significant support for allowing women to serve as lay delegates. This could relate to the growth of the secular women's movement over that time, and/or the fact that lay delegation was a less direct threat to men's—especially clergymen's—leadership than ordination was.

The focus on the constitutional issue of lay delegation reflected continuing power struggles between various Methodist bodies. At the same time, it allowed much to go unspoken that could have clarified the nature of both support for and resistance to women's rights. Those on both sides of the debate acknowledged that women outnumbered men two-to-one in denominational membership, and they commended women's leadership at the local level and nationally in their mission organizations. Women's advocates cited these facts as support for admitting them as delegates, while others saw such limited roles as an appropriate level of leadership for women.

Preventing women from serving as delegates continued their exclusion from the body that made decisions regarding ordination and other matters that would affect them, affirming Bourdieu's contention that "women are excluded from all the public spaces, such as the assembly or the market, where the games ordinarily considered the most serious ones of human existence, such as the games of honor, are played out."[38] With no voice in General Conference, Methodist women relied on the advocacy of those male delegates who had been persuaded of women's leadership ability in the larger religious field and in secular society.

The 1888 General Conference sent home the five women selected as delegates that year and voted to put the question of women's eligibility as lay delegates to a church-wide vote, where it achieved a majority but not the three-fourths needed for a constitutional amendment. Women delegates were finally approved by the 1900 General Conference, and the first female delegates took their seats four years later.

Willard wrote in her autobiography of her dismay in learning that the very lay delegates that the women's vote had secured now voted to exclude women, and that the bishops had "left us lamenting." Despite her disappointment, she took an optimistic view of the whole ordeal:

> I lost no sleep and wasted no tears over the curious transaction, and I confidently predict that we five women, whose election was thus disavowed, will have more enviable places in history than any who opposed us on those memorable days. Of them it will be

---

38. Bourdieu, *Masculine Domination*, 49.

written, while doubtless they did not so intend, that they committed an injustice; of us, only that in silence we endured it.[39]

1920 and 1924 General Conferences:
Clergywomen and "Embarrassing Difficulties"

The MEC General Conference did not consider women's rights again until
1920, when the issue of women's ordination resurfaced, and again it mirrored progress in the larger women's movement. As the General Conference
met, the country was in the process of ratifying the Nineteenth Amendment to the Constitution, granting women the right to vote. And as some
opponents of admitting female delegates in 1888 had feared, women lay
delegates were prominent champions of women's ordination.

Presenting the resolution was Madeline Southard, an evangelist and
activist who had preached since her teens, lectured on temperance, written on women's rights, and served as a foreign missionary. Like Willard,
Southard was a journaler, keeping a diary until her death at age 90, and she
selected a scripture passage to guide her each year. Her passage for 1919
was Revelation 21:7: "Those who conquer will inherit these things, and I
will be their God and they will be my children." Thus inspired, Southard
was propelled into leadership at the 1920 General Conference by achievements in the previous year, which included founding and leading the International Association of Women Preachers (IAWP), publishing her article
"Woman and Ministry" in *Methodist Review*, and completing a master's
thesis in theology at Northwestern University entitled "Jesus' Attitude Toward Women."[40]

Southard's new visibility led to her being tapped to draft a petition to
General Conference urging clergy rights for women, which read:

> Whereas, Today the principle of equality of opportunity for wom-
> en is being recognized in all fields of activity; and
>   Whereas, This General Conference has gone on record as urg-
> ing political equality for women by requesting the Delaware house
> of representatives [sic] to sign the Susan B. Anthony amendment;
> therefore be it

39. Willard, *Glimpses*, 621.

40. Southard's thesis was published in 1927 by the George H. Doran Company as
The Attitude of Jesus Toward Woman and is still in print.

Resolved, That the General Conference approve ecclesiastical equality for women, that it remove all restrictions and limitations upon women in the service of the church, and that it instruct the proper committee to make any changes in the Discipline necessary to accomplish this end.[41]

In presenting the resolution, Southard appealed to women's growing rights in mainsream society and to the leadership of Frances Willard and other Methodist women in the recently ratified Eighteenth Amendment (prohibition). She claimed that the church had misinterpreted Paul's instructions for women to keep silent (1 Corinthians 14:34–35), urged the need for progress, and pointed to the clergy shortage following World War I, commenting: "Now I can hardly believe that any of the brethren are consciously saying, 'We would rather not have the gospel preached and men brought to Christ than to have the work done by women.' I do not think any men have consciously taken that position, and I trust it will not be done unconsciously."[42]

After brief discussion, the resolution was referred to the Committee on Itinerancy, which returned two weeks later with a recommendation that women be licensed as local preachers and that a commission be appointed to study and report back to General Conference in 1924 on the questions of ordination and annual conference membership, or "full connection," which would carry a vote in the proceedings and guaranteed appointment to a church. George Elliott, editor of *Methodist Review*, offered an amendment to ordain women, leaving only the question of conference membership, but the amendment was defeated. Southard, having made the same amendment in committee and seen it defeated there, had voted for the compromise that the report represented, as at least a step forward for women.

As in previous debates, speakers either urged progress or caution in the wake of changing times. Those supporting women's ordination cited the history of Methodist women's leadership, their personal experience of capable women pastors, and women's expanding rights. Opponents insisted that the church not rush such an important decision, but rather let it to unfold in its own time. M. C. Singh, a delegate from India, noted that in overseas churches that are "not so far advanced in the liberty of the women," such a change would be "a great stumbling-block for the cause of Christ."[43]

41. *MEC DCA* 1920, 190.
42. Ibid., 191.
43. Ibid.

Elliott and Southard addressed concerns about the proper role of women that were part of the larger debate, although unspoken on the plenary floor. Elliott commented that fears of great numbers of women entering ordained ministry were exaggerated, since most would continue to choose marriage and motherhood. He thus affirmed women's traditional place in the home, while advocating full clergy rights for those few called to ministry to fill a need or as a fall-back position if they were unable to have children:

> As long as June days come, with roses and moonshine, women are going to fall in love, and the great majority of them will become wives and mothers, the embodiment of eternal, supreme womanhood. But there is no reason why, in the need of the church, for filling vacancies and special services, we should not utilize these women to whom God has denied that privilege, but has made their motherhood a wider motherhood, and given them an even greater task.[44]

Southard addressed fears that a woman might rise to the level of bishop, echoing qualms that allowing women to vote could lead to a woman president. Even as she cited Queen Victoria's leadership as evidence that women could rule effectively, she did not affirm women's ability to serve as bishops, but instead maintained that Methodist women were making a more modest request: "I have all confidence in the Methodist ministry and laity, and I believe that when they understand the real situation, what it is we want, they will not be afraid to give us all we ask."[45]

All of the women who spoke and some men favored full rights, while those urging caution were all male. Only one layman spoke, along with several laywomen, which could relate to their comparatively small numbers relative to clergy delegates. In a remarkably brief speech, Lizelia Moorer, an African American woman from South Carolina, made several key points. She used the idea that women are equal but different to advocate for their inclusion, saying, "while men are largely spurred to action by brain power, women are spurred to action by heart power. When the two are blended they make for the highest efficiency." Thus, she argued, the fact that women are less rational than men did not represent a deficit but offered important balance. In calling for a spirit of inclusion, she referenced a bishop's speech

44. *MEC DCA* 1920, 565.
45. Ibid.

on "the divine impartiality of God" and Peter's dream of clean and unclean animals in Acts 10,[46] along with the MEC's own history on slavery:

> The thought comes to me that it is about time for the pillars of Methodism to go up again on the housetop, and get another vision which tells them that God is no respecter of persons; and while the vision tarries, may they not learn the lesson that that applies with as much force to the sexes as to the races.[47]

The General Conference was persuaded by the conservative forces to license women and await the commission's report on ordination and annual conference membership four years later. The discussion continued in 1924 when that commission recommended local ordination for women but not annual conference membership, which would have guaranteed an appointment, along with voice and vote. While acknowledging the need for "an effective sacramental ministry on the part of women," especially in the mission field, the commission concluded that conference membership would have both social and spiritual implications, that it would introduce "peculiar and embarrassing difficulties" in Methodism's connectional polity, and that there was "no imperative demand" for conference membership at that time.[48]

As the ensuing discussion revealed, the "embarrassing difficulties" introduced by conference membership would relate to finding guaranteed appointments for clergywomen, when most congregations resisted female leadership. Excluding women from conference membership not only denied them voice and vote in their annual conference, but also made them ineligible as delegates to General Conference as either lay or clergy. Women would have to choose between the religious capital of ordination, albeit limited to local congregations, or the possibility of serving as lay delegates to General Conference, where they could fight for greater rights for women.

Indeed, conference membership was the main point of contention, with no real resistance expressed to women's ordination, as long as it was restricted to a local congregation. As we saw with African American leadership, the connectional nature of Methodism was a key piece of the resistance, since congregations do not choose their pastors. Racial segregation allowed for the partitioning of black pastors and congregations into a separate body,

46. This story was also cited in support of union between the MEC and MECS (see note 99).

47. *MEC DCA* 1920, 565.

48. Ibid., 195.

as they were in the CMEC and would be upon the merger of north and south churches in 1939; thus, unwilling congregations were not forced to accept black leadership. The resistance to women's leadership, however, was not so easily accommodated. Since segregating women and the churches that would welcome them was not feasible, "local ordination" offered a way to rhetorically support women's equality while denying them conference membership would limit their service to accepting congregations.

Delegates did not voice these implications for women's authority, but focused their arguments primarily on changes in the domestic sphere. Speaking for the commission, Joseph Gray listed the various difficulties for married clergywomen. Clergy couples might find their family life disrupted if they were appointed separately, he said, but marriage to laymen raised "even more embarrassment" by breaking up the honored tradition of the Methodist parsonage:

> We dare not deny to women the high privilege of maternity, in which the preachers' wives have been heretofore so honored and so great. But the question of pastoral efficiency which would en-sue must be frankly faced; the delicate and difficult social situation which might be so easily created must be frankly faced also.[49]

With this implication of the difficulties raised by pregnant clergywomen, Gray was among those who construed itinerancy as a burden that women could escape if they remained at home, content to serve the "large and splendid functions" the church already allowed for them.[50]

As did some of the speakers in 1920, Gray reflected the extent to which the church esteemed home and motherhood following the Victorian era. Beverly Harrison writes that in the face of the women's rights move-ment, women's subjugation was masked by romanticizing the home as a "'beatific' arena" that was "maintained largely by a dualism of gender role expectations, values, and norms that was . . . deeply unfair to women."[51] This elevation of domestic roles veiled restrictions on women's entry into the public (predominately male) sphere of activity, in much the same way that religious arguments are used to justify social structures and relation-ships that privilege those in power. Thus raising the status of "the home" served to reinforce traditional gender roles and authority structures and to convince women that no calling in the wider public world could surpass

49. Ibid., 211.

50. Taylor, *MEC DCA* 1920, 234.

51. Harrison, *Making the Connections*, 27.

their role in the private sphere of the home, a rhetorical pattern Harrison calls "pedestalism."[52] Harrison also notes that the Protestant church became a champion of this "cult of true womanhood" as a "last-gasp cultural barricade" against social change.[53]

The speech of one female delegate threatened to peel back this veneer of adoration and expose the degradation of women as impure that lay beneath it. Winnie Gabrielson, a missionary to India, argued that finding appointments for women would be no more embarrassing than situations she had observed in India. She recalled times "when my Indian sisters, because of age-long customs, have felt a cringing when a man's hand touched them in baptism, yet I have stood and have been impotent to do anything." She went on: "My hand has not been pure or clean enough to administer that sacrament, according to the statutes of our Church!"[54] In contrast to the moral elevation of women that framed many delegates' remarks, Gabrielson exposed the notion that women are morally inferior.

For the most part, however, MEC delegates consistently praised women's place in the home and the privilege of giving birth to sons who might grow up to be preachers or even bishops. Several referred to Bishop Fred B. Fisher's mother, who was introduced to the Conference just before this debate and reported that she had prayed at her son's birth that he might grow up to be a Methodist preacher.[55] Commission member W. E. Shaw compared that "glory" to the "mere privilege of belonging to any annual conference."[56] Similarly, George H. McClung imagined what fate would have befallen Methodism had Susannah Wesley gone into the ministry instead of giving birth to Methodist founders John and Charles Wesley.[57] While rhetorically elevating the status of women as mothers, these men revealed an assumed male superiority by asserting that a son who may (or may not) become a preacher was more valuable to the church than any woman who sought that role.

McClung was one of the few who questioned women's qualifications and contended that God's natural order did not include women's religious leadership: "I doubt very seriously whether the work of the stated pastorate

52. Harrison, "Misogyny," 7.
53. Harrison, *Making the Connections*, 204.
54. *MEC DCA* 1924, 255.
55. Ibid., 243.
56. Ibid., 254.
57. Ibid., 256.

71

is a part of the work that the Almighty intended for women to do." He assumed a God-given division of labor that excluded many of the public roles women were assuming at that time. Speaking to a substitute motion that would extend conference membership to women, he said: "There is a serious question in my mind whether or not women would be qualified for membership in the Annual Conference, but granting that she is, and that it is a part of the work that God intended that she should do, I do not believe that the time is ripe for the adoption of this substitute." [58]

Advocates of full clergy rights for women relied on gender equality and argued against McClung and others that indeed the time *was* ripe. Women and men alike argued gender equality, and claimed that women's work in mission organizations demonstrated their leadership abilities. As George H. Spencer remarked: "The whole movement of the modern world is to grant to women an equality with men." He continued: "I believe . . . it is pusillanimous to go half way and give them a crust when they are asking for bread, to admit them into the vestibule when they want to come to the altar of the temple, to hold them outside the fellowship when they want to get in and have a full part." [59]

Labeling an unvoiced fear he sensed in some delegates, A. S. Watkins said, "I am not afraid of the women . . . (who) are harmless in the annual conference as well as in the home." In the following speech, he compared the current discussion to the 1888 resistance to women delegates, summed up the social changes of recent decades, and advocated for change by reinterpreting the argument that women should remain "at home":

> There was a time within the memory of many who are in this body when it was common American sentiment that there was only one place designed by the Lord for a woman and that was in the home. That sentiment is in perfect accord with the sentiment in America 250 years ago and is in perfect harmony with the sentiment of the cave men long before the American Indian's time. . . . I want you to remember that in these modern times the home is broader than it used to be in the days when all the cooking and spinning and weaving was done under the roof close by the brother who worked in the field. The home was a narrow institution geographically. Now when the various members of the home go out to various

58. Ibid., 255.
59. Ibid., 212.

occupations, the home has wonderfully broadened and stretches from the dwelling place to the ballot box for women today.[60]

Mrs. Mary Northrup, a field secretary for the Women's Home Missionary Society, affirmed women's equality but spoke in favor of the report's limitation on their power, claiming that the church was not ready to accept them as pastors. Women would be the ones to suffer, she said: "If admitted to that membership perhaps they will be sent to where no brother wants to go." She concluded: "Brothers and sisters, we must face the condition as it exists today. I do not believe the time is ripe for the ordination of women and for their admission to the annual conferences of our great church."[61]

An exchange between J. M. M. Gray (clergy) and J. N. Dryden (lay) considered the ordination of women in light of the feminization of teaching that had occurred in American public education. Men had dominated the teaching profession in the colonial era, but the supply and demand for female teachers increased in the nineteenth century, as more females gained literacy, and as the move from one-room to graded schools increased the need for teachers. With few other employment options, women would work for one-third to one-half the salary that men would, and as increased teaching credentials required summer training, men who taught part-time left for more lucrative full-time work elsewhere. The men who continued to work in public education fell into specific roles: they taught upper grades, where they were needed for discipline or as mentors to older male students; they used teaching as a stepping stone into ministry, law, or other male-dominated professions; or they became administrators in the increasingly bureaucratic educational system, in which female teachers were placed under male authority.

Gray pointed out that the presence of women in public schools had led to "the almost entire elimination of male teachers in the grade and high schools, and among the boys' schools where male teachers are most necessary." He also blamed the prevalence of female teachers for the proliferation of private (mostly Catholic) schools, "with all that is involved of antagonism to our American ideals and principles."[62] As a clergyman, Gray may have feared that a feminized ministry would suffer the same devaluation as teaching had, not only in salary but also in status.

60. Ibid., 257.
61. Ibid., 256.
62. Ibid., 211.

Susan B. Anthony had spoken to such fears when she addressed a group of schoolmasters in 1853, as they considered why teachers no longer commanded the same respect as lawyers, ministers, or doctors:

> Do you not see that so long as society says a woman is incompetent to be lawyer, minister, or doctor, but has ample ability to be a teacher, that every man of you who chooses that profession tacitly acknowledges that he has no more brains than a woman? And this, too, is the reason that teaching is a less lucrative profession, as here men must compete with the cheap labor of woman. Would you exalt your profession, exalt those who labor with you. Would you make it more lucrative, increase the salaries of the women engaged in the noble work of educating our future Presidents, Senators, and Congressmen.[63]

Whereas Anthony's remarks were aimed at raising the status of women, however, Gray seemed concerned that acknowledging women's competence to serve as clergy would reduce the status of that profession, along with men like him who answered that calling. In addition, with the family, school, and church being the primary sites of socialization, men had a stake in preserving male leadership within these institutions.

Speaking in favor of ordaining women, John N. Dryden, a layman, refuted Gray's assertion that women's presence in public schools had led to the increase in private schools, calling on the body to disclaim any libel against "those noble women." As a longtime member of the Board of Education, Dryden affirmed that women "were more highly qualified as teachers than the men," adding, however, that in hiring women, "we were able to save a good deal of taxes by keeping the salaries down." Assuming that clergywomen would be unmarried, Dryden noted that the church could see even further savings by not having to support clergy families or widows.[64] He thus affirmed women's equality, or even superiority, as teachers, while confirming Anthony's assertion that they were "cheap labor," so the church could benefit on two counts.

Opponents of women's full clergy rights used the potential reunification with the MECS to bolster their view and enlist the support of moderates, reflecting the idea that church members who resist women's ordination have more influence than their numbers suggest because others in the

63. Stanton et. al., *History*, 514.
64. *MEC DCA* 1924, 255.

church accommodate their resistance in order to keep peace.[65] Accordingly, MEC members argued that a change in policy regarding women's ordination might derail the process of reunification with the MECS. The MEC had just days earlier approved the current plan for reunion.[66] Delegates argued that making a change in the terms of annual conference membership would "imperil the whole matter of unification," which was "the most important thing before us."[67] Assuming more conservative views among southern Methodists,[68] delegates were willing to delay full rights for women so as to not jeopardize the reunification process.

As in previous years, the expressed arguments regarding full clergy rights for women followed non-religious ideology related to either tradition or progress. As Spencer, Watkins, and others urged the church to keep up with the times, delegates such as McClung and Shaw urged caution. Most admitted that women would inevitably be given full rights, and, Ray Allen argued, "if eventually, why not now?" Allen used the cause of unification to urge a progressive position, saying:

> We do not yet know the temper of this Conference, other than that it means to be fair. Two days ago we saw it was ready to be progressive, when it joined with such unanimity in the movement for union with the Church, South. Now we are to understand whether or not it means to be progressive in what it does today concerning women.[69]

Gray, along with others who opposed annual conference membership, claimed that local ordination would give women more opportunities in the church than ever before.[70] The current report, Gray noted, would accommodate the need for women missionaries to perform sacraments and would "grant to women every possible right, status, and authority granted

---

65. Lehman, *Women Clergy*, 285.

66. This plan, which entailed separate jurisdictions for the MEC and MECS, passed both General Conferences but failed to earn the required two-thirds vote of MECS annual conferences (see chapter 2).

67. Lockwood, *MEC DCA 1924*, 256; see also Shaw, 243, and Gray, 258.

68. Both Chaves (*Ordaining Women*, 135) and Zikmund ("The Protestant," 143) note greater resistance to female clergy in the south, and indeed, the MECS did not seat its first women delegates until 1922, and at the time of reunification in 1939, had not yet granted women the right to be licensed or ordained.

69. *MEC DCA 1924*, 254.

70. Ibid., 210.

to any other ordained minister in the Church."[71] Gray failed to mention the very points of contention, namely that women would not have the right to a guaranteed appointment, the status of annual conference membership, or the authority that comes with a voice and vote in the church's governing bodies. Summing up the position of those who urged caution, McClung quoted an unnamed bishop who said, "If you don't know what to do, don't do it."[72]

The MEC General Conference in the 1920s included strong forces both for and against women's rights. Emboldened by winning the vote and entry into secular professions, albeit positions with lower status and pay, women took their case to the church and sought the right to preach. Women and men alike argued gender equality, and claimed that women's work in mission organizations, temperance, suffrage, and other social movements demonstrated their leadership abilities. There was little expressed resistance to women's religious leadership, or even to them having authority over men in local congregations. Instead, resistance was framed positively, through the promotion of their loftier domestic gifts and calling. Although some spoke of God's natural ordering of the sexes, no delegates cited scriptural passages that prohibit women's leadership, except Southard's claim that such passages had been misinterpreted. Women may have avoided such concerns by making modest claims, deflecting any suggestion that they sought higher authority as district superintendents or bishops.

Rather than a theological argument against women's leadership, resistance was rooted in an underlying sense of male leadership as natural and appropriate, and the threat that the women's movement posed to that social order. The main sticking point was not ordination, but itinerancy and annual conference membership, distinctive aspects of Methodism's connectional nature. Delegates urged that resistance to women's leadership should be accommodated, sparing bishops and district superintendents the difficulty of finding them appointments. With women advancing in the state through voting rights and in the educational system as teachers and as students in colleges and seminaries, MEC delegates in the 1920s defended the church against such change by limiting their access to power and encouraging them instead to remain in the home, where their presence would serve to maintain traditional sex roles. Delegates used theology in the form of natural law to justify this position, claiming that women clergy were not

71. Ibid., 258.
72. Ibid., 256.

part of God's division of labor and that mothering was "the noblest capability God has committed to human creatures."[73]

All the women who spoke affirmed women's equality, although one voted against full rights because women would suffer from the church's lack of acceptance (Northrup); however, men took various positions on the issue. While some affirmed traditional social structures, others set aside their own interest and advocated for women's rights, including twenty men who signed a substitute motion that would grant women the same rights and privileges as men. As in 1920, all the men who spoke except one were clergy, reflecting their continued dominance in the General Conference.

The single layman who spoke, J. N. Dryden, reminded the body that men would still hold the majority of power and could control the entry of women into the field. He noted reassuringly that even if women were allowed to be ordained, all candidates must pass through the Quarterly Conference, and "most of us being men, we are likely to be very sound in our discrimination." Men still held power to decide who was ordained, so it was "wholly immaterial how many women . . . shall enter the portals."[74] Even with such reassurance, delegates opted to limit women to local ordination, denying them conference membership and the possibility of election as bishops or General Conference delegates, where they would have broader authority over men.

1956 General Conference: A Process Still Controlled by Men

During the 1930s, American Methodism was preoccupied with north-south reunification, but throughout the 1940s, the Women's Division of the Board of Missions petitioned the newly merged MC to grant women full clergy rights. At the 1952 General Conference, the matter was raised and dismissed quickly, amid considerable laughter, and women were determined to convince the 1956 General Conference that this was no laughing matter.[75] They flooded the General Conference that year with some two thousand petitions on the issue.

---

73. Taylor, *MEC DCA* 1924, 234.
74. *MEC DCA* 1924, 255.
75. Troxell, "Ordination of Women," 125.

Delegates to the 1956 General Conference made the same arguments that were made three decades earlier, raising concerns that women remain at home with children, and that congregations not be forced to accept a female pastor they did not want. Those delegates supporting full clergy rights for women appealed to the idea of progress and eradicating discrimination.

The discussion began with the report of the Subcommittee on Full Clergy Rights for Women, under the Committee on the Ministry, which proposed that the church allow "unmarried women and widows" to apply for the traveling ministry, or itinerancy.[76] Presenting the majority report, James Chubb noted that in principle no one could object to extending full rights to women, but that district superintendents had spoken to the committee "very persuasively" of the practical problems involved.[77] Dewey Muir presented a minority report that would continue the current policy that closed itinerancy to all women.[78] Amendments were offered to allow all women to apply but gave district superintendents the option of leaving them without an appointment, to strike the restriction to unmarried women, and to allow the inclusion of married women through a three-fourths vote of the annual conference.[79] The minority report and all amendments failed before William Alderson proposed amending the majority report to allow all women to apply to the traveling ministry, putting everyone on "equal basis,"[80] which was approved by a show of hands. Thus the General Conference offered women the same access to the ordination process as men had, and granting successful female candidates full clergy rights.

As in previous years, delegates favoring full rights argued the need to keep up with the times. James Chubb, speaking against the minority report, said, "We have said for several quadrenniums now, 'Some day we will do it.' The time has come to do it now!"[81] A delegate from India spoke of the irony that someone from the "back woods of Bengal" would have to champion the cause of the "all-powerful American woman."[82] Mrs. Edwin Anderson spoke with pride of the MC's ability to "adapt itself to change" and urged

76. *MC DCA* 1956, 192.

77. Ibid., 521.

78. Ibid., 522.

79. See *MC DCA* 1956 for speeches by Slutz, 522; Davis, 525; and Boyd, 530.

80. *MC DCA* 1956, 531.

81. Ibid., 529.

82. Singh, *MC DCA* 1956, 526.

that it "set an example in granting equal rights and opportunities of service to all its members, regardless of sex."[83]

Opponents did not overtly defend a cautious or conservative position as they had in previous years, but pointed to the practical problems itinerancy would create in the home and in the appointive system. The heart of the problem, one delegate argued, was the matter of "women rearing a family."[84] In offering his amendment that would open the door to all women with the safety valve of leaving them without an appointment, Leonard Slutz expressed a bias against single women when he said, "I feel that a married woman with a normal family life is on the average better fitted to lead our church than is a single woman."[85] Concerns about finding appointments for women were dismissed as being "hypothetical and . . . magnified out of all proportion to their importance,"[86] and Chubb noted, "We can't solve the practical problems until we have the opportunity to do so."[87] Extending full rights to women was no longer the groundbreaking move it would have been in 1924, and many in 1956 realized that it was a step whose time had come.

In this decade when the Civil Rights movement addressed racial discrimination, the language of discrimination was more prevalent than in previous years. Even as he expressed an attitude of discrimination against single women, Slutz argued that the majority report discriminated against married women,[88] while C. Anderson Davis noted that the majority report discriminated against married women without children.[89] Countering arguments about discrimination against women, Farris Moorer claimed that the exclusion of men from the category of deaconess was a form of discrimination,[90] although the category was created in the first place to address gender discrimination in ordained ministry. Mrs. Henry Ebner insisted that as a local preacher she had never felt any sense of discrimination,[91]

83. *MC DCA* 1956, 528.

84. Duncan, *MC DCA* 1956, 524.

85. *MC DCA* 1956, 522.

86. Anderson, *MC DCA* 1956, 528.

87. *MC DCA* 1956, 529.

88. Ibid., 522.

89. Ibid., 525.

90. Ibid., 526.

91. Ibid., 528.

but Mrs. Edwin Anderson no doubt reflected the feelings of other locally ordained women when she said:

> They are permitted to perform all the services that men ministers perform, and they are required to attend the sessions of annual conference. Each woman minister brings her lay delegate. The lay delegate is permitted to sit within the bower of the church and has the privilege of the floor: the woman minister has no privileges.[92]

When offering the amendment that would finally pass, Alderson noted that it would "solve the problem of discrimination" and insure that "both men and women are on an equal basis, when they come before the Annual Conference for admission."[93] Ralph Taylor Alton drew laughter from the house when he characterized the amendment as "discriminatory legislation in favor of women."[94]

In presenting the minority report that sought to preserve the restriction on conference membership due to administrative difficulties, Dewey Muir claimed to "share in the sentiment" that "no privilege should be granted one sex which is denied to the other." The problem lay with congregations' continued resistance to women clergy and not with women's fitness for leadership: "The ability to preach and to give leadership in the church is not in any sense determined by sex. . . . That some women have done excellent and outstanding work and service is recognized." He concluded: "I trust that the General Conference, not out of any spirit of division, not out of any spirit of ill-will, but only with a sense of the importance of the problem of administration, will see fit to adopt the substitute report."[95]

Even as they appealed for a greater voice in the business of the church, women allowed men to make that case for them. In 1920 three out of four speakers advocating full rights for women were women, and in 1924 half of the supporters were female. In 1956, by contrast, only two of the dozen or so proponents of full rights were female. Georgia Harkness, the first woman to teach at a Protestant seminary in the United States and an advocate of full rights for clergywomen, wrote that during the 1956 debate, "I purposely sat in silence, for there were able and discerning men to carry the issue, and I had long before learned that this is often the surest way to get something

92. Ibid.
93. Ibid., 531.
94. Ibid., 533.
95. Ibid., 522.

passed."[96] By 1956, a sufficient number of men were willing to use their power as the dominant group to grant women full clergy rights.

In addition to the two women who supported full clergy rights, one woman spoke in favor of the minority report that would continue to restrict women from conference membership, illustrating Bourdieu's notion that dominated groups are complicit in their own domination. Having claimed not to feel any discrimination from the church, Mrs. Henry Ebner simultaneously asserted that the church was not ready to accept women's full ordination and its implications:

> But before we vote on this question, those of us who might be tempted to vote to change our "Discipline" would have to answer yes to three very important questions, and I submit them in all seriousness.
>
> First of all, if I voted yes, I would be able to say to my district superintendent, "Yes, send me a woman pastor."
>
> Secondly, the ministers as well as the laymen would have to say, "I am willing to serve under a woman district superintendent," for if this goes through, we are not going to discriminate. (Applause)
>
> I do not like even to use the word "discrimination" because in my mind it has always been connected with unhappiness and discontent. I have never felt that I needed as a woman to fight for equal rights with men. I feel I have far more rights than the men will ever have. (Applause)
>
> Furthermore, Bishop, my last question that I believe the delegates of this Conference would have to answer in the affirmative if they vote yes, would be this: We are willing to elect a woman bishop. Now, you may think that is rather exaggerated, but believe me, it is not. You have had reference to the power of womanhood. I leave that to your own thinking.[97]

In addition to three women who spoke, only two other lay delegates (Slutz and Singh) took part in the discussion, compared to seventeen clergy, although the MC General Conference comprised an equal number of lay and clergy delegates at this point. Only one African American delegate spoke (Davis); Bishop Willis J. King of the Central Jurisdiction presided over the decisive session, but had no vote. Although the two laymen and the one African American who spoke all advocated broader rights

96. Harkness, *Women in Church and Society*, 30, quoted in Troxell, "Ordination of Women," 125.

97. *MC DCA* 1956, 528.

for women, such small numbers make it difficult to characterize any clear distinctions between clergy and lay, or between black and white Methodists on this issue. What is clear is that white male clergy dominated both sides of the discussion, and it was the influence and votes of male delegates that finally opened the doors fully to women.

The only delegate to use religious language to any extent was Dewey Muir, who expressed the hope that the General Conference would, to the best of its ability and judgment, "fulfill the will of God as it relates to the ministry of The Methodist Church." Although the body was divided on the issue, Muir declared: "Yet I am sure that those who are for this or for that are all of them trying to be motivated and guided by a spirit of love and spirit of our Christ." Rather than claiming to know the will of God in this matter, Muir expressed an openness to discerning the divine will as he summed up his speech:

> We leave it to your hands and for your decision, and I have faith to believe that that which we propose and do shall be done only with the thought in all our minds that we are instruments in the hands of God trying to work out here not that which serves any special group, male or female, but that which serves the best interests of the church and on-going Kingdom of our God.[98]

Other than Muir's speech, the rhetoric focused on social order more than religious ideals.

The conference session in which the deciding vote was taken opened with a hymn ("Dear Lord and Father of Mankind") and a prayer ("if any man lack wisdom, let him ask of God, who giveth to all men liberally";)[99] that reflect the continued prevalence of masculine language in Christianity. Feminist theologians point out that such language perpetuates the implication that men are not only dominant but are also closer to God. As Mary Daly puts it, "if God is male, then the male is God."[100] Similarly, a picture in the issue of the *Daily Christian Advocate* that records this debate[101] shows two women, with Cornelia Russell at the Lost and Found desk thanking Mrs. M. F. Peterson for finding her lost earring. Women were thus visibly present at General Conference, but Russell, the Executive Secretary of Town and Country Work of the Woman's Division of Christian Service, was

98. Ibid., 529.
99. Ibid., 523.
100. Daly, *Beyond God*, 19.
101. *MC DCA*, 1956, 521.

pictured not in any official capacity, but in the less significant act of retriev-
ing a lost earring.[102] Women sought equal rights in the face of continuing
language and imagery that affirmed male dominance and slighted women's
fitness for leadership.

It is interesting to note that during the debate, Davis's amendment to
strike the phrase "only unmarried women and widows may apply" for traveling ministry[103] was defeated, although it would have had the same effect
as the ultimately successful amendment by William Alderson. Alderson
framed his amendment not as an open door for women, but as empower-
ing annual conferences to decide whom to ordain. In this way he satisfied
proponents of full clergy rights for women, but also tapped into ongoing
tensions between annual and General Conference authority. Other amendments seeking to curtail the influx of clergywomen had failed, but Alderson presented his in a way that satisfied those seeking such a safeguard, as
well as those seeking full rights. As Dryden had pointed out in 1924, the
ordination process was and would for some time be controlled by men,
giving them ultimate authority over which and how many women would
be admitted to conference membership.

Masculine Domination and the Church

Bourdieu depicts masculine domination as the most prevalent form of social domination, and one that even its victims perpetuate. Through a long
process of collective labor across cultures, masculine domination has been
naturalized and eternalized to the extent that both male and female bodies, as well as social time and space, reflect this ordering, which appears to
most people as natural, logical, and inevitable. This social order is durable
and pervasive, serving as a homologous quality of fields across social space
and throughout history, including the religious field. For Bourdieu, the
patriarchal values and anti-feminist view of women in the Roman Catholic Church was given divine mandate and reinforced through teaching,
example, and ritual.[104] Speeches by some Methodist delegates reflect the

---

102. Pictures of men in the same issue included one of the choir from Garrett Biblical
Institute singing during a session (524), and one of two U.S. bishops greeting a delegate
from Liberia (531).

103. *MC DCA* 1956, 527.

104. Bourdieu, *Masculine Domination*, 84–85.

same assumptions about a divine ordering of gender roles and the need for church structure to adhere to that order.

Judith Butler argues that dominated groups have more power than Bourdieu grants them, and that they can in effect shift their field position and gain some degree of authority through performative speech acts, even to the point of appropriating derogatory terms such as "black" and "queer" to dilute their oppressive power.[105] While women can indeed exercise linguistic challenges to male dominance, the continued use of generic terms such as "man" and "mankind" both within the church and in the U.S. culture at large indicates the persistence of the male norm. Bourdieu has little hope that challenging such norms, as Butler and other feminists call for, can overcome this deeply entrenched pattern;[106] what is needed is collective action in the form of a symbolic revolution that questions the foundation of social production and reproduction.[107] The church, as both an institution that perpetuates masculine domination and one that operates in the symbolic realm, can play a large role in either resisting or facilitating such a revolution.

Arguments against ordaining women are rooted in the Christian narrative, including readings of the Jewish-Christian creation story (Genesis 2:21–22) to explain that woman was derived from man and is therefore secondary, traditional readings of the "fall" in Genesis 3 that blame woman's disobedience for humanity's sinful state, and passages that mandate women's submission (Ephesians 5:24) or their silence in public worship (1 Corinthians 14:34). Based on these readings, women have been constructed on the underside of a dualism that associates men with rationality, the transcendent mind, and godliness and women with embodiment, sexuality, and sin. Within strongly sacramental traditions, most notably the Roman Catholic Church, these associations reinforce resistance that relates the efficacy of the sacrament to the male priest's resemblance to Christ. Such arguments were not verbalized in the Methodist discussions, yet even the idealization of the Victorian woman could not erase centuries of association with sin and impurity, which provided the subtext for arguments against female religious leadership, although spoken objections focused, for the most part, on larger currents of change and gender roles.

105. Butler, "Performativity," 123–24.

106. Bourdieu, *Masculine Domination*, 102–4; see also Bourdieu and Wacquant, *Invitation*, 171–72.

107. Bourdieu, "Genesis and Structure," 33.

In the seventy–six years from the time women first petitioned General Conference for ordination until full clergy rights were granted in 1956, the nation and the church underwent significant changes, and both external and internal factors related to those changes affected the course of women's place in the church. Among the social changes involved in moving from an agricultural to an industrial economy was an elevation of middle class women's roles as homemakers and mothers, especially by the church as it sought to preserve traditional family structures. Two world wars led to a shortage of men entering ministry, as in other professions, and prompted consideration of women to fill those pulpits. Debates about gender overlapped with racial tensions, as the larger society struggled with the place of free blacks following emancipation, and American Methodism sought to heal its own racial division.

The most significant external factor affecting women's campaign for ordination was the women's movement, in which women gained the right to vote and many left the private sphere of the home for the public workplace. Methodist women such as Anna Howard Shaw, Frances Willard, and Madeline Southard were involved in this larger movement, as well as fighting for women's ordination within the church. The women's movement promoted the ethic of gender equality, and few General Conference delegates argued against such a notion, urging instead the equal or even superior calling of motherhood and the traditional structures it represented. This affirmation of maternity reflects resistance to the women's movement and the ideological changes that contributed to a sense of unrest during these transitional decades. For some, women's ordination no doubt represented accommodation to the modern and increasingly secular world, and thus a rejection of traditional sex roles that they saw affirmed in scripture and God's natural law.

The Methodist debate turned on the sexual division of labor, and specifically matters of human reproduction, a factor that Terry Lovell insists both feminist theorists and sociologists such as Bourdieu fail to take into account, along with the ways that such division is codified in social relations and institutions.[108] Delegates touted motherhood as the highest possible achievement for women, thereby making a positive argument affirming the social structures related to reproduction rather than using a negative rhetoric that degraded women's leadership in public arenas. As we saw with the MECS arguments to keep black Methodists dependent on

108. Lovell, "Bourdieu, Class, and Gender," 52.

them, delegates denied women leadership while asserting that it was for their own good. This argument allowed male delegates to affirm women, albeit in traditional roles, while advocating a power structure that preserved their own dominance in the public and ecclesiastical fields. As male "heads of household," as school principals and superintendents, and as clergy, men remained in control of the primary institutions through which new generations would be socialized into existing power structures; thus, women's ordination had implications beyond the church.

Whether a female preacher had children was a principal concern, even more than her marital status. As the 1956 discussion considered restricting traveling ministry to single women and widows, one delegate indicated that such a policy would discriminate against married women with no children—although, curiously, no one made the corresponding argument that the proposal could include widows *with* children, presumably because it was inconceivable that a single mother would "abandon" home and children for public ministry. This differentiation between women with and without children bears out Lovell's point that women are differentiated not only by race, socio-economic class, and sexuality, but also "by those who become, willy nilly or by choice, the mothers of children and those that do not."[109] Women's role as mothers and as primary childcare providers is reinforced by the persistence of this discussion, as well as the fact that no such questions are raised about *male* clergy with children. Motherhood thus includes issues of identity for women and practical issues for clergy-women such as dealing with pregnancy and childcare. As feminist theorists remind us, including women's experience in considering this and other male-dominated roles may also bring insights that can broaden and enrich men's work as ministers.[110]

Even as they remained at home with children, women in the late nineteenth century took on new leadership roles in the church. An influential aspect of the women's movement within the church and one of the strongest factors leading to women's ordination was the formation of independent women's mission organizations. Through such organizations, women gained leadership experience, accrued power within the church, and raised

---

109. Ibid.

110. Similarly, sociologist Meredith McGuire ("New-Old Directions," 201–5) discusses how her own motherhood allowed her to connect with the mothers who were her research subjects in a way that provided mutual insights.

awareness of their abilities. In addition to her work with the WCTU, Frances Willard was a leader in the MEC mission society as well.

In 1956, the Women's Division of the Methodist Board of Mission was largely responsible for prompting a flood of more than two thousand General Conference petitions regarding clergy rights for women. The successful vote that year was more likely due to pressure from denominational leaders and women's organizations than from large numbers of women seeking ordination.[111] Delegates were assured that there would be no great influx of women to the itinerancy, and that male-dominated annual conferences would control the ordination process. Deaconess Mary Lou Barnwell noted that of the church's five hundred deaconesses, only twenty-seven might consider ordained ministry, mostly to serve rural areas that suffered a shortage of trained clergy.[112] Such reassurances were borne out in the small number of women who entered ministry from 1956 until the second wave of feminism in the 1970s;[113] women still comprised just 21 percent of ordained elders in the UMC in 2010.[114]

Denominational decentralization, or the level of congregational autonomy, is another internal factor that influences decisions about women's ordination,[115] and throughout these debates, the connectional nature of Methodism was one of the chief obstacles. Because Methodist congregations do not call their own pastors, they have little control over whether they receive a female pastor. Delegates consistently argued how difficult it would be for district superintendents to find congregations that would

---

111. Chaves and Cavendish, "Recent Changes," 578–79.

112. *MC DCA* 1956, 529.

113. Chaves cites U.S. census figures that show an increase in female clergy from 3 percent in 1970 to 10 percent by 1990 (*Ordaining Women*, 1).

114. In 1996, the UMC added a new category of ministry, the ordained deacon, to replace the lay category of diaconal minister. Deacons are ordained into ministries of service, whereas elders are ordained to the sacraments and leadership of the church's communal life. Women comprise 76 percent of ordained deacons, raising the total number of ordained women in the UMC to 23 percent, with 21 of elders being female (2010 figures from UMC General Commission on Finance and Administration, http://www.gcfa.org/data-services). Only 7 percent of lead pastors of churches with one thousand or more members are women (from UMC General Commission on the Status and Role of Women, http://www.gcsrw.org/Research.aspx). Although the category of deacon elevates those in service ministries to ordained status, there continues to be a division by gender role ideology, with women dominating service ministry and remaining a distinct minority in positions of authority.

115. Chaves, *Ordaining Women*, 140.

accept a clergywoman. Even as they expressed confidence in women's preaching and leadership, delegates accommodated the resistance they presumed they would find among congregations, rather than granting women opportunities to use their ministerial gifts. Similarly the MEC in 1924 urged caution so as not to jeopardize reunification with the more resistant MECS. Contact with female pastors can reduce such resistance, and indeed delegates cited their personal experience with women pastors in advocating for their full rights. For many, though, male leadership was the norm and seemed to both men and women the natural, even divinely mandated, pattern that should continue.

In her study of Church of England clergy and their wives, Nancy Nason-Clark concludes that factors related to social order, namely sex role ideology, carry more weight than religious belief in determining views on women's ordination.[116] Nason-Clark echoes Bourdieu's claim that theological and biblical arguments are used to legitimate socially constructed relations of power. The lack of such justification in these Methodist discussions could indicate, as Nason-Clark finds, that religious rationales carried less weight than the perpetuation of familiar social patterns and authority structures. The omission of theological and biblical arguments suggests that masculine domination was so deeply inscribed in social relations that for many it seemed self-evident and required no justification.

While delegates made little appeal to scripture or theology in arguing either for or against women's rights in the church, a few spoke of divinely ordered sex roles, and one speaker flirted with women's connection to Eve and temptation, warning delegates to not get swept away by "very clever speeches . . . from the lips of these women."[117] And while none of the opponents quoted scriptural mandates that women must keep silent and submit to male authority, or suggested that there were purity issues at stake, women delegates refuted these claims in their own speeches (Southard in 1920 and Gabrielson in 1924). Proponents of women's ordination used biblical support to make the case for equality (Joel 2, Galatians 3), but even those tactics waned over time, so that the only spiritual appeal in the 1956 debate was Muir's call for Christian charity in resolving their differences.

Language did play a role, though, in the prevalence of masculine terms and imagery that has contributed to male domination in the church. Women's absence from Methodist seats of power is not surprising given the

116. Nason-Clark, "Ordaining Women," 271.

117. Eckman, *MEC DCA* 1920, 565.

lack of female imagery or terminology related to God and to religious leaders, which serves to re-inscribe the idea of male leadership as consistent with divine design.[118] The 1888 discussion of lay delegates turned on such language, with proponents of women's rights arguing that the word "layman" and male pronouns included both genders, and resistant delegates claiming that while this was the case in some instances, it was unthinkable that women were included in these terms as they referred to General Conference delegates, a role with significant power to determine church policy.

The use of inclusive language continues to be an issue in many Christian churches, where many men and women find comfort in familiar images of God as father, king, and lord, unaware that such language reinforces male leadership. Such language is understandable, perhaps, as is the use of male pronouns for the divine, where the alternatives are female imagery or pronouns, which stretch many beyond their comfort zone, or a depersonalized, neutered God. The continued use of "man" and "mankind" when acceptable terminology such as "human," "humanity," "person" and "people" is available demonstrates the entrenched nature of masculine domination. More than fifty years after women won full clergy rights, the habitus of the church is still socializing individuals to see men as the norm and as more nearly resembling God, therefore more fit for leadership.

In the end, women's voice and vote did not win the cause of women's ordination, but men argued for and approved the change. While this demonstrates that deeply inscribed power structures can be changed, it simultaneously reinforces the notion that it is members of the dominant group within that structure who have the power to change it. The change itself challenges the critique of Butler and others that Bourdieu's theory of habitus is rigidly deterministic. However, while they claim that the *dominated* have the power to disrupt habitus through their own speech acts, in these debates it was the dominant group of men who finally granted the change. The exclusively male General Conference of 1900 voted to admit women as lay delegates, and women were still a distinct minority in the General Conference bodies that granted them local ordination in 1924 and full clergy rights in 1956.

Women did speak to the issue once they were admitted as delegates, but they were present in small numbers and often had difficulty being heard. The *Western Christian Advocate* described Madeline Southard storming to

118. Barbara Troxell notes that the *MC Book of Discipline* continued to use male pronouns to refer to clergy until 1964 ("Ordination of Women," 125).

the front of the room during the 1924 General Conference and demanding the floor, after several unsuccessful attempts to gain it from her seat in the rear.[119] While women spoke to the issue and demonstrated leadership abilities in their various roles in the church, gaining full rights depended on their ability to persuade male delegates to their cause. Ruth Wallace, who has documented women's rights within the Roman Catholic Church, notes the importance of women's lay leadership and of male allies to advocate for increasing their authority. She warns, however, that women should expect resistance, because men do not give up rights and privileges easily.[120] The history of Methodism illustrates just such resistance to women's leadership, but also the role of male allies who eventually voted to relinquish a portion of their own power and privilege in granting women full clergy rights.

After the turn of the century, very few delegates argued against the principle of women's ordination, and thus of gender equality, but instead suggested that the time was not ripe for such a change, or "yes but not yet"—an ambivalent position that frustrates both those who support and those who oppose women's ordination.[121] This emphasis suggests again that resistance related more to the pace of social change and less to absolute scriptural or theological positions prohibiting women's leadership. In the midst of the social changes that marked the turn of the twentieth century, the church was reluctant to grant women ordination rights beyond the local congregation. This step essentially created a congregational policy at odds with the denomination's connectional nature, allowing congregations to "call" female preachers if they desired one. At the same time, it served to preclude women's authority in the church's governing body or over any congregation that did not welcome them.

Some have suggested that the MC, along with the Presbyterian Church, finally granted women full clergy rights in 1956—between the early women's movement and the second wave in the 1970s—because by mid-century, the principle of gender equality had become formalized,[122] yet there were few women seeking ordination.[123] I would argue that the timing also coincided with a more stable period in American history and

119. *Western Christian Advocate*, May 15, 1924, 8, cited in Noll, "A Welcome in the Ministry," 98.

120. Wallace, "Bringing Women In," 301–2.

121. Nason-Clark, "Ordaining Women," 263.

122. Chaves, *Ordaining Women*, 82.

123. Chaves and Cavendish, "Recent Changes," 582.

in the life of mainline Protestant churches, when such a change was not compounded by other social transformations and could be more easily accommodated. Prophetic voices for women's ordination did emerge at a time of social change; but in this case, the "time was not ripe," and the change was not fully accomplished until the church and society arrived on more stable ground.

4

Emergence of Anti-Gay Policy
"Incompatible with Christian Teaching"

"...the church believes that homosexuality is not the norm
which God has intended for human beings."
—WILLIAM A. MCCARTNEY (DCA 1984, 462)

IN THE 1970S, ANITA Bryant, a singer, beauty queen, orange-juice spokesperson, and evangelical Christian, led an anti-gay campaign against an
ordinance in Dade County, Florida, that prohibited discrimination on
the basis of sexual orientation. The campaign mobilized religious groups
around the country, as evangelicals like Jerry Falwell joined the cause, and
gay rights activists soon mounted a response. The gay rights movement
had hit the national stage in 1969 with riots following a police raid on the
Stonewall Inn, a well-known gay bar in New York City. The movement was
fueled by the 1978 murder of Harvey Milk, an openly gay city supervisor in
San Francisco. On the heels of the turbulent 1960s, the 1970s brought more
layers of challenge and change to familiar social patterns.

Bryant voiced the concerns of many religious people by claiming that
homosexuality was a chosen lifestyle that was against God's natural order,
and that gays could change if they desired: "I know a homosexual can be
liberated from these hideous chains."[1] As the head of a religious group
at the time, I opposed this opinion as being unscientific.

1. Williams, "Homosexuals," 39.

92

at the time I saw this as controversial promoted among naive people.

called Save Our Children, Inc., Bryant warned that homosexuals posed a threat to children, whom they were out to molest or recruit. Asked about her personal feelings towards gays and lesbians, Bryant articulated a common Christian posture when she replied, "God loves them. I love them. I love them enough to tell them the truth—that homosexuality is wrong, not by my standards but by God's standards."[2] Yet she vowed to continue the fight against their rights: "Before I yield to this insidious attack on God and His laws, I will lead such a crusade to stop it as this country has not seen before."[3]

As this battle played out in demonstrations in major cities and in the national press, the newly formed United Methodist Church (UMC) was considering its social statement and leadership criteria. As was the case with leadership by African Americans and women, the church was divided on the ordination of gays and lesbians, with strong advocates both for and against the move, and the debate continues four decades later. Both advocates and opponents of the ordination of gay and lesbian persons root their arguments more clearly in religion than in the case of race or sex. Opponents echo Bryant in using the language of sin to construct gays and lesbians as morally unfit for leadership, while proponents of their ordination call upon biblical messages of diversity and inclusion.

Historical Background

Open debate about sexual orientation in American Methodism has a much shorter history than discussions of gender and race, having been rarely addressed in any churches before the 1960s. The National Council of Churches, Episcopal churches, and the United Church of Christ took steps in the 1960s to include gays and lesbians in their ministries; however, most churches remained silent. One exception was Glide Memorial Methodist Church in San Francisco, which, in the early 1960s, included gays and lesbians in their outreach to marginalized populations in that city. With gay rights groups, the church formed a Council on Religion and the Homosexual (CRH) in 1964, providing a forum for the two communities to come together. Funded in part by The Methodist Church (MC), the group sought to improve understandings of homosexuality, pastoral care for gay persons, and advocacy of gay rights. CRH chapters formed around the country and,

2. McCombs and Feinstein, "Anita Bryant Visit," C1.
3. Williams, "Homosexuals," 39.

for its ten years of existence, provided a major forum for conversations on religion and homosexuality.

The gay rights movement sparked by the Stonewall incident in 1969 affected many institutions, including the UMC, which had come into being just one year earlier though the merger of the Evangelical United Brethren Church (EUBC) and the MC. In 1969, *motive*, the UMC's student magazine, created controversy when it published an issue on women's rights that included a discussion of lesbianism. United Methodist congregations and individuals threatened to withhold their apportionment dollars, and the denomination's Board of Education, which published the magazine, withdrew its support. Without institutional funding, *motive* ceased publication, devoting its final two issues to gay rights.

From 1968 to 1972, the UMC was also in the process of considering a set of social principles for the newly formed denomination. The MEC had adopted a social creed in 1908, which reflected the Social Gospel concerns of the time. Statements from other Methodist denominations soon followed, and the EUBC crafted a social statement when that denomination formed in 1946. Neither the EUBC nor the MC addressed homosexuality in their social statements before 1972: the EUBC made no mention of human sexuality, while the MC affirmed sexual relations within marriage and condemned the sexual freedoms of the time, stating: "The outrageous exploitation of the strong forces underlying sexual experience is a destructive element of our culture. It not only distorts the meaning of sex experience but constitutes a blasphemous disregard of God's purpose for men and women."[4]

The 1972 General Conference of the UMC discussed possible language about homosexuality and about gay and lesbian persons that might be part of the new denomination's Social Principles. This chapter looks at the statement that emerged, and more specific language about ordination of gays and lesbians that was passed in 1980 and 1984, along with the actions of the General Conference session in 2012.

---

4. *MC Book of Discipline* 1964, par. 1820.III.C.6. Hereafter cited as *Discipline*, with the appropriate denominational acronym and General Conference year.

1972 General Conference: A Fearful Time

When the UMC met for its first General Conference in 1972, delegates went over the proposed Social Principles with "meticulous order"[5] in lengthy and emotional sessions that dealt with the issues of the day, from environmental concerns and space exploration, to conscientious objection and the war in Vietnam. Among the most contentious debates were those dealing with human sexuality, including abortion, marriage and the family, birth and death, and homosexuality. On the last issue, the Social Principles Study Commission presented the plenary body with a two-sentence statement that read:

> Homosexuals no less than heterosexuals are persons of sacred worth, who need the ministry and guidance of the church in their struggles for human fulfillment, as well as the spiritual and emotional support of a fellowship which enables reconciling relationships with God, with others and with themselves. Further we insist that homosexuals are entitled to have their human and civil rights insured.[6]

The statement was intended to guide the church in pastoral care of this newly visible minority, following the model of Glide Memorial and the CRH. In response to this statement, several approaches to homosexuality emerged among the General Conference delegates. Only a few advocated full acceptance and rights for gays and lesbians without condemnation, as the proposed statement encouraged. Others condemned same-sex sexual activity, or "homosexual practice,"[7] while affirming the worth of homosexual persons.

The dominant voices, however, echoed the rhetoric of Anita Bryant and other anti-gay activists at the time in depicting gay men as abnormal, immoral, perverted, and a threat to boys and young men. All the delegates to speak to this issue were male, except one (Wilcox), indicating that men still dominated the General Conference body, and the conversation fixated on gay men, largely ignoring lesbians. The fearful tone of the debate, while aimed at the protection of young boys, may suggest that male delegates saw

---

5. *UMC DCA* 1972, 593.

6. *UMC Journal* 1972, 1057.

7. Although those in the LGBT community resist the bifurcation of gay identity and same-sex sexual activity, that division is a key aspect of the UMC conversations examined here.

gay men as a threat to their own male identity, a reversal of a traditional gender order that privileged them, and a further erosion of their ecclesial power, having admitted women into full leadership just sixteen years earlier.

When the Study Commission presented its proposal, Russell Kibler immediately moved to delete the sentence protecting gay rights, claiming that such a statement licensed gay men to "continue in their activities of preying upon the young men of our community and of your school, and I want [the statement] eliminated."[8] Carlton Dodge echoed those concerns, and associated homosexuality with the permissiveness of the times: "I feel that on this subject of homosexuals we are pointing up just one problem area so far as abnormal behavior is concerned. . . . If we are going to cover this area of abnormal sexual behavior then we must include other forms of perversion as well." Dodge quoted a letter that his Eastern Pennsylvania delegation had received, which suggested that the proposed legislation "sounds more like an expression of a drug-oriented commune than of a responsible church committee." The letter writer claimed to have seen "too many youth, including small children, victimized by homosexuals and by persons practicing various so called life styles."[9]

Delegates depicted gay men as sexual predators, citing the rape and murder of a young boy,[10] and claiming that gay men were unsuitable to work as Boy Scout leaders or church school teachers.[11] Among those promoting such portrayals were a prosecutor (Cooper) and a physician (Shipps), who rooted their comments in their professional experience and understandings. On the other hand, Katherine Wilcox, a clinical psychologist and the only female voice in this debate, relied on her professional expertise to refute such portrayals, noting that she had worked with far more heterosexual criminals than homosexual ones.[12]

Other delegates did not construe gay men as dangerous, but viewed their behavior as abnormal, even as they considered legislation that acknowledged their worth as persons. To the committee's statement affirming the rights of all persons, Don Hand moved the addition of the line: "though we do not condone the practice of homosexuality and consider this practice

---

8. *UMC DCA* 1972, 706.

9. Ibid.

10. Kibler, *UMC DCA* 1972, 705–6.

11. Shipps, *UMC DCA* 1972, 712.

12. *UMC DCA* 1972, 707.

incompatible with Christian doctrine."[13] Hammel Shipps promptly offered as a substitute a more specific resolution that read:

> We, The United Methodist Church, resolve first, to stand firm in the belief that the Bible condemns the practice of homosexuality and gives no basis for approving it as an acceptable way of life. Second, to extend the healing ministries of our churches to the homosexual in his desperate need of God's love. And third, to call upon all appropriate agencies within the church and Christian community to expand the study relating to the cause and cure of homosexuality.[14]

Speaking to his resolution, Shipps, a physician, maintained that homosexuality was a "reversion to Paganism. It is frowned upon by respectable society and condemned in the Bible. By many, it is looked upon as a disease. Homosexuals are notably promiscuous and a causative part of the alarming spread of veneral [*sic*] disease in this country." Given that understanding, Shipps called his resolution a "conciliatory stand" that took seriously the spiritual nature of the "problem" and affirmed that "Christ died for the homosexual as well as for any other sinner. His grace can redeem and change the homosexual."[15]

While the Shipps resolution failed, the Hand amendment passed, thus adding condemnatory language to the more affirming statement proposed by the committee. A later motion changed the word "doctrine" to "teachings," under the rationale that "there is no Christian doctrine on homosexuality."[16] The resulting two-sentence statement read:

> Homosexuals no less than heterosexuals are persons of sacred worth, who need the ministry and guidance of the church in their struggles for human fulfillment, as well as the spiritual and emotional care of a fellowship which enables reconciling relationships with God, with others and with themselves. Further we insist that all persons are entitled to have their human and civil rights insured, though we do not condone the practice of homosexuality and consider this practice incompatible with Christian teaching.[17]

---

13. Ibid., 712. This statement, as eventually revised, has become known as the "incompatibility clause" and will be so referenced in this paper.

14. *UMC DCA* 1972, 712.

15. Ibid.

16. Moon, *UMC DCA* 1972, 718.

17. *UMC Discipline* 1972, par. 72.C.

The overall tone of the General Conference discussion in 1972 was fearful, reflecting not only fear of gay men as sexually dangerous, but also fear of change. In their Episcopal Address to the 1972 General Conference, the bishops spoke to the changing times and their effect on religious and moral understandings. Addressing scientific change, they stated that, "the body of basic truth about the universe is constantly changing" and had altered more in their lifetimes than in the previous 500 years. Scientific change begat social change in such areas as health and urbanization, which in turn encouraged a secularization of society that threatened the church with irrelevance. Suggesting that "man does not seem to need God any more," the bishops noted:

> Even many of the time-honored offices of religion are preempted by Science: we don't seem to need salvation when we have psychiatry; we don't need priests to bless the fields at the time of planting, to ensure their fertility, we have tractors; and what is the use of prayer for health when you have penicillin? Why aspire to heaven when so many heavenly goods are available on earth? Worldly success has cut the cords of dependence which leads to the heart of religion.[18]

The bishops cut to the heart of many delegates' concerns when they acknowledged that such change makes religious beliefs and morals relative instead of absolute:

> There are "points of view" in religion but no knowledge. Hence, confusion reigns in the moral realm, and no religious faith that is confused as to its values can be aggressive. In wide areas of contemporary human experience the Christian ethic is frankly regarded as obsolete. Moral relativism is in the saddle, and there are few value-guides for earnest and aspiring men in our day.[19]

In this address, delivered the week before the plenary discussion of homosexuality, the bishops foreshadowed the fearful note in that debate when they referred to science that "threatens to become our Nemesis," change as an "insidious adversary for religion," and the "perilous" nature of modern life. Their speech encouraged a conservative posture by casting moral relativism as a "prejudice against the past" and affirming the unchanging nature of Christian truth and the value of its historicity.[20] In this first UMC

18. *UMC Journal* 1972, 208.
19. Ibid., 208–9.
20. Ibid., 207–10.

General Conference, in which delegates would determine "what things are changeable, what are relative to time and place, and what things are stable,"[21] the bishops' role as presiders with no vote was not insignificant.

At the heart of the debate on homosexuality was disagreement among delegates over exactly what *was* changeable and what was not. One delegate expressed concern about the changing nature of the church, asking, "Where are we headed in this work?" and noting the danger in wanting to "take everybody in."[22] Another feared that Methodists would defect to Baptist churches if the UMC failed to take a clear stance on the issue.[23] But other delegates, such as Leigh Roberts, a psychiatrist, urged the necessity of the church changing with the times:

> We do live in a time of change as has been noted many times before this body. Part of that change is an attitudinal change by our society towards sexuality including changes in laws and changes in social attitudes that move toward an acceptance of discreet, consenting adult homosexual behavior, and not discriminating against them for their attitudes or their behavior. Homosexuality, *qua* homosexuality, should be no deterrent to effective professional work as position [*sic*], teacher, clergyman, attorney, Sunday School teacher, or Church layperson.[24]

Acknowledging that both the church and the larger U.S. society had much to discern on this complex topic, Walter Muelder appealed for "compassion and justice" rather than approving statements that would "prejudge all future thinking and reflection in our church on its social principles."[25] Others sought to dissuade specific fears of homosexuals as sexually violent and cautioned against basing church policy on the fearful rhetoric of the times.[26]

Robert Moon, speaking for the Study Committee that presented the original statement of support for gay and lesbian persons, reminded delegates that far more young girls were victimized by heterosexual men[27] and that, statistically, heterosexual persons were more dangerous than ho-

21. Ibid., 209
22. Cooper, *UMC DCA* 1972, 706.
23. Vaughan, *UMC DCA* 1972, 711.
24. *UMC DCA* 1972, 708.
25. Ibid., 710.
26. White, *UMC DCA* 1972, 706.
27. *UMC DCA* 1972, 709.

mosexuals.[28] Moon noted that "this General Conference has come a long way and so has our society in recent years in understanding the nature of sexuality in ourselves and in others. It seems to us as we have surveyed the situation that this is exactly the kind of statement that the General Conference ought to be making at this time." The statement, he said, was not a plea from within the gay community, but represented the "honest concern of well informed people."[29]

The discussion centered on gay rights in general, and the specific question of ordaining gays and lesbians was not addressed, except for Roberts's comment above that homosexuality should not preclude a person from holding any position, including "clergyman." A delegate from the Philippines raised the issue of same-sex marriage.[30] Discussion revealed concerns about changes to the institutions of marriage and family,[31] and the body approved Vinluan's motion to add to its Social Principles, "We do not recommend marriage between two persons of the same sex."[32]

The power dynamics embedded in language were evident in the way delegates objectified gays and lesbians by referring to them as "these people" and as "the homosexual." These generic references recalled the way earlier Methodists had objectified African Americans, denying them individual personhood and referring to them as a category or a stereotype. Few of the delegates used scripture or religious ideals to support their statements, with the exception of Hammell Shipps, who cited 1 Corinthians, Jude, and Romans to condemn homosexual practice, and Katherine Wilcox, who claimed that gays and lesbians are "Children of God" who have a "right to be a part of the reconciling fellowship of the Christian church."

1972

The breakdown of comments by lay and clergy delegates supports James Wood's findings that lay delegates are more conservative than clergy on this issue.[33] Of those advocating acceptance of gays and lesbians or urging more time to consider the issue, five were clergy and three were lay

---

28. Ibid., 713.

29. Ibid., 709.

30. Vinluan, *UMC DCA* 1972, 710.

31. Borger, *UMC DCA* 1972, 711.

32. *UMC Discipline* 1972, par. 72.B. This statement went through various amendments in subsequent General Conferences, and in 1996, the church passed legislation stating that "Ceremonies that celebrate homosexual unions shall not be conducted by our ministers and shall not be conducted in our churches" (*UMC Discipline* 2012, par. 341.6).

33. Wood, *Where the Spirit Leads*, 65.

delegates. Of the three laity, one was female (Wilcox) and another (Hoover) was young enough to be confused for a youth delegate, which affirms findings that women and young people are more accepting of homosexuality.[34] Delegates who argued against gay rights and in favor of language that condemned "homosexual practice" were overwhelmingly laity—seven lay delegates to one clergy. The sole clergy voice arguing this point was from the Philippines (Vinluan), and while surveys by Wood and others focused on U.S. attitudes, a split between North American United Methodists and those from overseas churches would become increasingly evident in General Conference discussions over the next decades.

The delegates to the 1972 General Conference revealed an array of opinions about homosexuality. Delegates expressed fear of gay men as sexual predators; resistance to same-sex marriage as an erosion of traditional values and morality; support for the rights of gay and lesbian persons from those who disapproved of their sexual behavior; affirmation of both gay identity and same-sex sexual acts; and general confusion over the causes and effects of homosexuality and the nature of sexuality in general. Some saw homosexuality as an immoral choice, while others understood it as a sinful proclivity to be resisted, and a smaller group claimed it as a normal sexual variant.

These perspectives mirrored those in the larger U.S. society regarding this complex issue, which had only recently become a matter of wide public concern, and they also reflected the church's fear of becoming irrelevant in these changing times. The final statement in the new UMC's Social Principles followed what many considered to be a middle path, affirming the sacred worth of homosexual persons while declaring their practice to be "incompatible with Christian teaching." Victor Paul Furnish, notes, however, that the "incompatibility clause" added on the 1972 General Conference floor changed a statement advocating pastoral care into a moral judgment,

> without the benefit of any kind of study, either of homosexuality itself or of "Christian teaching" about it. What had started out to be solely an expression of pastoral concern for homosexual persons ended up including a clause which appeared to give theological warrant to a widespread opinion that all homosexuality is "sinful" and that homosexual persons are dangerous both to themselves and to society.[35]

34. Ibid., 86; See also Loftus, "America's Liberalization," 764.
35. Furnish, "United Methodist Experience," 180.

The statement on homosexuality that the 1972 General Conference approved for its Social Principles would continue to shape the denomination's approach for decades.

1980 General Conference:
The Need for a "Statement that Protects Us"

Over the next decade, homosexuality became an increasingly prevalent issue for the UMC and other religious bodies. The inclusion of disapproving language in the UMC Social Principles prompted the organization of a gay caucus group in 1975, which took the name Affirmation: United Methodists for Gay and Lesbian Concerns.[36] Activities of this group and of seminaries and agencies seeking to explore sexuality more fully led the 1976 General Conference to pass a prohibition on any UMC funds supporting a "'gay' caucus" or being used to "promote the acceptance of homosexuality,"[37] effectively shutting down any denominational efforts to resolve conflict on the issue through study and dialogue. Although it received more than five thousand petitions on the subject and delegates raised motions to both strengthen and soften the church's position, the 1976 General Conference took no further action.

In 1978, a gay pastor in the New York Annual Conference came out and was found to be not appointable by the bishop and cabinet of that conference, who were overruled by its Board of Ordained Ministry and clergy session, based on the pastor's overall effectiveness as a minister. This controversy set the stage for the 1980 General Conference to address the ordination of gays and lesbians. The explicit stereotype of gay men as dangerous predators was largely gone, although the Conference rejected language that would have distinguished "homosexual practice" from "the abuse of homosexual practice"[38] that was so feared in 1972. In 1980, the discussion largely took place at the level of morality and involved more specific references to scripture and theology than had the earlier debate.

36. The group was formed in 1975 as the United Methodist Gay Caucus, was later renamed Gay United Methodists (GUM), and became Affirmation after the 1976 General Conference.

37. *UMC Discipline* 1976, par. 906.13; this is stated twice in the *UMC Discipline* 2012, in par. 613.19, and in par. 806.1 b) (3) *e)* 9.

38. *UMC Journal* 1980, 280.

In reviewing the statement in the Social Principles, the General Conference entertained a motion by William Walker to delete the "incompatibility clause." Walker suggested that the church's preoccupation with this issue resembled idolatry in singling out one aspect of human activity that was beyond God's redemptive grace. He urged that persons be judged on faith rather than actions, "so that we might be in unity out of our diversity, one loved by God and redeemed for graceful living and not redeemed by works or nonworks." [39] Speaking in support of the amendment, Donald Carver noted that neither scripture nor the psychiatric community were clear about the nature or morality of homosexuality. With no clear authority on the issue, Carver argued, the Social Principles should allow for individual conscience. [40]

Opponents of the amendment claimed that in fact there was clear authority in both scriptural commandments and in the majority opinion in the UMC. Not only did the majority of United Methodists condemn homosexual practice, but one delegate, June Goldman, quoted a gay friend who favored retention of the statement when he said: "I want the church that I love to affirm me, but I do not want my church to accommodate me." Goldman added that "there may well be many who are like Ron, who spoke to me pleading that the church remain true and consistent, even though it was not expedient or easy for him personally." [41] Such comments support Amanda Udis-Kessler's contention that many United Methodists view the issue as one of institutional survival and integrity, rather than affirmation of personal beliefs or relationships. [42]

Speaking in favor of retaining the "incompatibility clause," L. E Crowson appealed to the doctrine of grace and claimed its availability for all, along with the human tendency to exercise free will and reject God's grace because of "fury, anger, murder, or homosexuality, or any other sort of aberrant condition within ourselves." Rather than relying on biblical passages condemning homosexual behavior, Crowson drew support from a wider base of scripture. He cited the creation of humans as male and female to claim a heterosexual, procreative norm, and the necessity of such commandments in order to save us "from the doctrine of antinomianism," [43]

39. Ibid., 275.
40. Ibid., 276–77.
41. Goldman, *UMC Journal* 1980, 276.
42. Udis-Kessler, *Queer Inclusion*, 158.
43. Ibid., 277–78.

demonstrating continuing concern about the permissiveness of the times and the lack of clear moral authority.

Acknowledging the changing times, Arthur Melius noted that the church should take a prophetic stance, rather than deciding such issues on majority vote. If the church made decisions based on what was popular, he said, it might still have slaves or be fighting in Vietnam.[44] Melius failed to acknowledge, of course, that the structure of American Methodism does rely on majority vote, and issues such as slavery and racism were painful and divisive for decades. The majority voted against Melius in this case, 255 to 729, and against removal of the "incompatibility clause" from the Social Principles.

The General Conference also considered a report from the Committee on Higher Education and Ministry that reaffirmed the high moral expectations of candidates for ordination, citing the Social Principles' statement about homosexuality, while not specifically prohibiting ordination of gays and lesbians. Reporting on the numerous petitions received on the subject, Committee Chair Paul Hardin said the committee had chosen to be consistent with the way they dealt with other aspects of moral character, that is, in a footnote referencing the UMC's position on that issue. The Committee also recommended nonconcurrence with five different reports that represented petitions to either prohibit or permit ordination of homosexuals.

Unlike 1972, discussion of the Committee's report focused not on the rights or dangers of homosexual persons, but on the impact of its recommendations on the larger church. Those supporting the Committee's recommendation spoke to the integrity of the ordination process and the need to trust the Boards of Ordained Ministry to evaluate each individual candidate. These delegates argued that morality cannot be legislated, and that adding specific prohibitions would "[vitiate] the spirit and integrity" of the *Book of Discipline*[45] and would resemble the legalism of the Pharisees more than the Gospel of Jesus Christ.[46] William Walker considered the impact that prohibitive legislation would have on individual pastors by forcing some to "live openly dishonest lives," and he urged the need for the church to struggle together on sexuality in general and on this issue in particular.[47]

---

44. Ibid., 277.

45. King, *UMC DCA* 1980, 579.

46. Birch, *UMC DCA* 1980, 578.

47. *UMC DCA* 1980, 578.

Those who opposed the ordination of homosexuals claimed that this very struggle for clarity was the problem, and was not the process through which to resolve the conflict. Admitting that the issue was "agonizing" for the whole church, A. Jason Shirah attributed that agony to "the confusion of the indefinite." Many in the general church were "expecting a definite word," he claimed, "and it was unfair for the larger body of the General Conference to leave the decision to the homosexual," to ordination boards, and to the appointive system.[48] Shirah moved to add to the Committee's report the statement: "No self-avowed, practicing homosexual therefore shall be ordained or appointed in the United Methodist Church." Harold Karls supported Shirah's amendment and shared his concern about "agi- tation in the church and the disturbance among the laity because of this issue." He said: "I think we should settle this and in doing it we make it uniform. Otherwise, it may be something that will bother us again"[49] prescient words, given the conflict that continues to arise on this issue at every General Conference. *well here's an attitude toward the laity. # what stories? subjects?*

Delegates were concerned that the Committee's recommendation would leave the door open for gays and lesbians to be ordained, and they asked specifically about that possibility,[50] and whether the recommended footnote would have the force of law.[51] Presiding Bishop Roy Nichols replied that such decisions would rest with the Judicial Council. With no clear response to these concerns, L. E. Crowson reminded the delegates of the UMC's connectional structure, and that "if a homosexual is serving in another conference, he might serve my church."[52] Crowson's unease about that possibility, along with his use of masculine pronouns, may suggest lingering fears about gay men being sexually dangerous. Another delegate expressed concern about how the recommendation would affect the larger moral issues of "Christian marriage, family, and the home."[53]

Although such concerns were not put to rest, the delegates defeated the specific language in these amendments and approved the Committee's report that referred to the Social Principles for guidance on questions of morality. They likewise upheld the committee's rejection of all petitions

48. Ibid., 577.

49. Ibid., 578.

50. Patterson, *UMC DCA* 1980, 580–81.

51. Smith, *UMC DCA* 1980, 579.

52. *UMC DCA* 1980, 581.

53. King, *UMC DCA* 1980, 580.

recommending explicit language to either permit or prohibit the ordination of homosexuals. The General Conference thus affirmed the ordination process and placed their trust in the covenantal relationship of the UMC.

In considering demographics of those addressing the issue, the division between lay and clergy delegates was less clear than in 1972, with three lay and three clergy arguing against ordination of homosexuals or same-sex marriage. Clergy still advocated more liberal positions than lay delegates did, with ten clergy and two lay delegates urging removal of such bans or introduction of less precise language that could allow for individual conscience on the issue. Men again dominated the discussion, with nineteen men and two women speaking in virtually equal numbers for and against the various proposals.

In 1980, the body did not debate the extent to which homosexuality is a chosen lifestyle versus an inherent disposition, but focused on the morality of homosexual behavior. Camps were clearly drawn between those who affirmed faithful, same-sex relationships and supported the ordination of gays and lesbians, and those who favored their explicit exclusion from marriage or ordination. The debate centered on how much control the General Conference should exert on this specific moral issue and how much to trust the Methodist connectional process. More evident than in 1972 was concern about how the church could best address the ambiguity surrounding the issue. While some advocated explicit prohibition and others spoke for removal of all such bans, many urged less specific language that paralleled references to other moral concerns and could allow room for discussion and discernment in individual cases. James Lawson, for one, asked: "Why do we not put out a laundry list of all of the sexual things that we think are sinful? Why do we list only one matter as primary?"[54]

Concern for heterosexual marriage and family reflected continuing unease about changing social mores and structures. Voices that supported specific legislation addressing homosexuality reflected ongoing discomfort with the moral ambiguity of the times and the desire for the church to make a clear ethical statement condemning homosexuality. David Seamands said: "We have come from viewing homosexuality as a sin to be repented of or a sickness to be treated—to a lifestyle to be affirmed, and now as a relationship to be applauded, and even blessed by the sanctity of a marriage covenant." In the face of such transitions, he claimed, the church needed "some kind of a statement that protects us."[55]

54. *UMC Journal* 1980, 284.
55. Ibid., 283.

Seamands and others relied on social and ethical arguments to justify specific moral guidelines, and it was delegates such as James Lawson who appealed to religious values in arguing for openness to difference. Lawson referred to the church's focus on this specific issue as "a grotesque misunderstanding of the gospel" and urged the church to listen "to the Spirit of Christ and His concern for all humankind."[56] Lee Moorehead similarly pleaded that the widespread discussion of homosexuality had "poisoned and inflamed" the local church with "vile and vicious attitudes . . . [that were] incompatible with Christian teaching."[57] Noting that Christians had "plundered and ransacked the Bible to try to get support for all of these views," Moorehead reminded his colleagues that they were called to be pastors of all people, just as Christ had died for all. He concluded:

> In the precious time left to me to be a pastor and a preacher, I am not going to be intimidated. I do not need the Good News movement or the "bad news" movement or Anita Bryant or Rex Humbard[58] to tell me how to treat human souls. There is no room for distinction between Greek and Jews, between circumcised and uncircumcised, between barbarian and Scythians, slave and free. There is only Christ and He is everything and He is in everything.[59]

Those opposed to acceptance of "homosexual practice" succeeded in retaining its condemnation in the Social Principles, but were not able to insert specific prohibitions on ordination or marriage of gays and lesbians. That matter would arise again before the next General Conference.

1984 General Conference:
Two Key Voices and "Seven Last Words"

In the early 1980s, Bishop Melvin Wheatley publicly supported the inclusion of gays and lesbians in the church, refusing to sign the 1980 Episcopal Address, which affirmed the statement that homosexuality was "incompatible with Christian teaching." In 1982, he directly challenged the intent to ban homosexuals from ordination when he appointed an openly gay man

56. Ibid., 284.

57. Ibid., 282.

58. "Good News" refers to an evangelical movement within Methodism that began in 1967 (see below). Rex Humbard was a prominent televangelist during this period.

59. *UMC Journal* 1980, 282.

to a church in Denver. An investigative committee within the church found no grounds for charges against the bishop.[60] In October of that same year, the Judicial Council ruled that nothing in the *UMC Book of Discipline* prohibited ordination of self-avowed homosexuals. The decision read in part:

> A probationary member who meets the requirements of the Discipline is eligible for ordination. The Board of Ordained Ministry of the Annual Conference makes inquiry as to the fitness of the candidates for election to full membership, including their educational and personal preparation and the other requirements of the Discipline. These requirements do not refer to sexual orientation. The Annual Conference decides whether to ordain eligible persons and admit them to full membership.[61]

United Methodists who felt betrayed by the Methodist ordination and appointment system came to the 1984 General Conference prepared to make explicit prohibitions against ordaining gays and lesbians, backed by almost a thousand petitions urging that step. The clarity of purpose among delegates on both sides of the issue reflects the work of advocacy groups that had taken up the cause since the UMC first addressed homosexuality. In addition to Affirmation, United Methodists who supported full inclusion of gays and lesbians organized the Reconciling Congregations Program (RCP) in 1983[62] to connect local congregations and individuals. Good News, an evangelical movement within Methodism since 1967, advocated restrictions on ordaining gays and lesbians and on same-sex marriage.

These groups illustrate the increasingly important role that caucuses have played in power struggles within the UMC. Kenneth Rowe writes that caucuses have always been part of such struggles, suggesting that the initial Methodist movement itself was a caucus within the larger eighteenth-century Evangelical Revival.[63] Russell Richey notes that as the church grew in size, caucuses took on the functions of fraternity, revival, and organization that were defining features of conferences in earlier eras, making them "the most obvious and effective expressions of Meth-

---

60. Wheatley's early activism for gay rights was motivated in part by his son John, who was gay, and who died of cancer in 1984 (Green, "Bishop Melvin Wheatley.").

61. UMC Judicial Council Decision No. 513, from the UMC website, Judicial Council Decision archives, http://archives.umc.org/interior_judicial.asp?mid=263&JDID=551&JDMOD=VWD.

62. The group was renamed the Reconciling Ministries Network in 2000.

63. Rowe, "How Do Caucuses," 242.

odist connectionalism (though obviously they divide as well as unite)."[64] Caucuses eventually formed around political leanings, gender, language, and racial/ethnic identity, and since the 1960s, the number has grown to more than twenty such groups related to the UMC. Rowe attributes this proliferation to the political tone of the times, grassroots responses to the increased power of denominational agencies, and unsettled issues from the 1968 merger that formed the denomination. He further notes that caucuses serve as an important force for reshaping the church at times of transition by working outside of the official denominational structure and providing necessary balance to connectional authority. [65]

As the only official voice for the denomination, General Conference is the source of this connectional authority, yet because of its variable nature, it is subject to political pressure from advocacy groups. Caucuses work to influence the election of General Conference delegates, and once those delegates are elected, to sway their votes. As Good News president James Heidinger has noted, that group prepares for each General Conference by working "to get evangelical and traditional delegates elected, petitions channeled, and a series of position papers published which articulate our stand on major issues."[66] Although they exist outside of the denominational structure and thus have no vote or official voice in the proceedings, caucuses that lean both right and left have been a visible presence at General Conference since their founding.

Caucus groups have made the political nature of General Conference conflicts more overt and serve to maintain those conflicts through the intervening four years. Their political maneuverings may determine not only who gets elected as delegates, but also who speaks on the General Conference floor and what they say. The public nature of the proceedings encourages political strategizing by those arguing for or against full inclusion of gays and lesbians, and the publication of the transcripts means that these speeches have impact beyond that immediate context. The speeches often represent carefully crafted statements designed to persuade undecided delegates (and those in the larger church), as much as they express personal passion and commitment. Delegates may or may not recognize the extent to which their presumed heterosexuality privileges their voice and the power that comes with that privilege, yet this is clearly a contest

64. Richey, *Methodist Conference*, 193.
65. Rowe, "How Do Caucuses," 255.
66. Heidinger, "45 Years," par. 40.

for dominance between those who would open more widely the church and its authority structures and those who advocate restricting authority to traditional stake holders.

Karen Oliveto has examined the role of the RCP and the Transforming Congregations Program (TCP), a United Methodist caucus group founded in 1988 to offer gays and lesbians transformational healing from sexual sin. Oliveto argues that the RCP challenges the church on behalf of gays and lesbians, as part of a network of social movements that constitute the larger gay rights movement in the United States.[67] As successful social movements do, the RCP prompts an opposing movement in the more conservative TCP, in the same way that Bourdieu describes the reassertion of orthodoxy when the arbitrary nature of social structures is challenged. Sexual orientation had not been addressed in the first two centuries of American Methodism; however, once the issue of gay rights was raised in the larger U.S. society, a movement and counter-movement arose within the UMC and were codified in caucus groups.

These caucuses became increasingly well organized and influential over time.[68] At the 1984 General Conference, their influence was evident in the consistency of arguments on both sides of the debate and their grounding in scripture and theology. The power of such advocacy groups to affect the election of General Conference delegates was also apparent in delegates' expressed concern about the public nature of their votes or abstentions.[69]

Reports from the Subcommittee on Social Principles and the Committee on Ministry both raised the issue of homosexuality, and at every step it was clear that many delegates sought a specific ban on ordaining gays and lesbians. The statement in the Social Principles remained unchanged, as delegates again rejected an amendment to delete the "incompatibility clause." While the Social Principles affirmed the human and civil rights

67. Oliveto, *Movements*.

68. Additional caucuses have arisen as the struggle over homosexuality has continued. Among groups that advocate full inclusion of gays and lesbians is MIND (Methodists in New Directions), a grassroots organization within the New York Annual Conference founded in 2006. Love Prevails: revolution 3-D evolved out of a support movement for the 2011 trial of Rev. Amy DeLong, who was charged with both being a lesbian and performing a same-sex union. Love Prevails takes a three-pronged, active approach to its witness for change: to encourage LGBTQ Christians and their allies to speak out, or "disclose(t)" themselves; to "divest our prayers, presence, gifts, service and witness from all structures within the church that support the status quo"; and to disrupt local, national, and international gatherings.

69. See *UMC DCA* 1984, 731–32, for comments by Hand, Womelforff, and McCord.

of homosexual persons in its section on the Nurturing Community, the committee added specific support for the employment rights of gays and lesbians under the section on the Social Community, despite fears that this could be used against the church by those seeking ordination. Delegates also accepted the subcommittee's recommendation of nonconcurrence on several petitions that would have banned or permitted ordination of homosexuals, with the understanding that such issues were more properly dealt with under the Disciplinary section on Ministry.

The Committee on Ministry recommended adding to ordination criteria the requirement of "fidelity in marriage and celibacy in singleness," a phrase that delegates dubbed the "seven last words."[70] Two minority reports were offered—one using the more lenient language of "faithfulness and constancy in all relationships" (Minority A),[71] and another adding the seven words plus the sentence: "Since the practice of homosexuality is incompatible with Christian teaching, self-avowed practicing homosexuals are not to be accepted as candidates, ordained as ministers, or appointed to serve in The United Methodist Church" (Minority B).[72] The body struggled to find language that would express trust in the covenant community to ordain qualified candidates, but avoid another Judicial Council reversal. The Majority Report was passed, adding the "seven last words," but only after repeated questions about whether it would prevent the ordination of self-avowed practicing homosexuals. With no clear answer to that question, the delegates asked for an immediate ruling by the Judicial Council.

The Judicial Council returned the next day with a ruling that read:

> Neither ordination nor appointment of self-avowed practicing homosexuals is necessarily precluded by the words "fidelity in marriage and celibacy in singleness" as added to pars. 404, 414, 429, and 431 of the Discipline. The annual conferences have the authority to decide whether candidates for ordination meet the disciplinary requirements.[73]

Delegates promptly called for a reconsideration of their earlier action and entertained a motion to amend the relevant sections of the Discipline by adding an explicit ban on ordaining or appointing self-avowed practicing homosexuals, using the exact language that the body had narrowly

70. Quick, *UMC DCA* 1984, 631.

71. *UMC DCA* 1984, 631–32.

72. Ibid., 632.

73. Ibid., 720.

rejected as Minority Report B the day before. After lengthy debate, presiding bishop Paul Duffy offered a prayer, which was followed by a period of silence while ballots were marked, and spontaneous singing of "Amazing Grace" as the ballots were collected. The amendment passed by a vote of 568 to 404, and a stated ban on the ordination of homosexual persons was added to the 1984 *Book of Discipline*.

In considering the various pieces of legislation related to homosexuality, delegates at the 1984 General Conferences made familiar arguments, and among the most outspoken were two delegates who spoke persuasively for their coalitions and reflected the coordinating efforts of caucuses. David Seamands, clergy delegate from Kentucky, offered the Minority Report B that was eventually approved prohibiting ordination of gays and lesbians. Joseph Sprague, clergy delegate from West Ohio, was on the Church and Society subcommittee that dealt with homosexuality in the Social Principles, and he presented the unsuccessful Minority Report that would have dropped the incompatibility clause, as well as the language protecting civil rights of gays and lesbians.

Sprague was raised Quaker in a conservative congregation in Dayton, Ohio, and he was motivated as a young boy to work for racial justice after witnessing the unfair treatment a black friend experienced. As a young married couple, he and his wife began attending a Methodist church, leading him within a few weeks to consider a call to ordained ministry. He was pastor at various churches, including inner city and university towns; director of religious coalitions in Ohio and Massachusetts; and a delegate to four General Conferences. In 1996, he was elected to the episcopacy, serving for eight years as bishop of the Northern Illinois Conference before retiring in 2004.

An advocate for justice, Sprague has received the American Friends Service Committee Courage of Conviction Award, the Rainbow Push Civil Rights/Peace Award, and the William Sloane Coffin Award for Justice and Peace. Within the UMC he has been at the forefront of progressive movements and was arrested with other gay rights demonstrators at the 2000 General Conference. His book *Affirmations of a Dissenter* drew heresy charges for his challenge to "neoliteralist" interpretations of scripture and his assertions that the virgin birth and resurrection of Jesus might repesent symbolic rather than literal truth. He has also been arrested as part of an interfaith group protesting the Iraq War at the White House.

At the 1984 General Conference, Sprague offered a Minority Report that would have removed the incompatibility clause from the Social Principles, arguing that the church should offer hospitality to all. As the Conference was meeting in Baltimore, where the American Methodist church had been established two hundred years before, Sprague was one of several delegates who referenced that bicentennial. Sprague appealed to founder John Wesley's "quadrilateral" of scripture, tradition, reason, and experience to urge support for this Minority Report. He noted that *scripture* is not a cafeteria line from which people can select passages that serve their purposes, but that "Holy Scripture is a composite feast which reveals the mighty works of God as attested by the community of faith." He remarked that "Jesus was always to be found with the ridiculed and rejected, with the outcasts of the society" and urged the same "graceful hospitality" on the part of the church. He cited a book by Episcopal bishop John Shelby Spong that documents inconsistency within church *tradition* regarding homosexuality, and in the area of *reason*, discussed the inconclusive scientific evidence, which he had examined in his own ten-year study of the issue, leading him to believe that "homosexuality is genetically caused" rather than being "derived behavior." Admitting that he could not speak definitely, he nevertheless asked, "this being the case, do you see that another person's homosexuality is no less Christian than my heterosexuality? The question is how do we behave out of that which is given?"[74] Whereas others were calling for gays and lesbians to restrict their behavior and not act on innate same-sex attraction, Sprague called on the church to observe a similar restriction in not excluding someone on the same basis.

He concluded his appeal by talking about his *experience* with gays and lesbians and their families. He mentioned first a conservative clergy colleague who consulted him when the colleague's son came out as gay and the pastor had to wrestle with seeing his son continue the Christian practices he had been taught, while embracing an identity that the father had always believed was sinful. When Sprague saw the colleague's wife some time later and asked how they were doing, she said, "He's still our boy. He's no different than before he announced how he is, and we love him just the same." Sprague also recounted the diligence and compassion with which a lesbian cared for her partner of twenty-seven years during a lengthy hospital stay, claiming "As a pastor and as a practicing theologian I can say to you that the joy and peace, the fidelity and care, present between those persons in

74. *UMC DCA* 1984, 461.

that hospital room was that which this person does not, and will never find incompatible with Christian teaching." He concluded that those who offered the Minority Report did so believing that it was "full of the truth of God, the fullness of which is still being revealed unto all of us."[75]

Sprague also presented the proposed addition to the Social Principles to protect the civil rights of gays and lesbians, trusting that the General Conference would "want to do only that which is right and just."[76] Several amendments sought to protect the church from those seeking ordination who might use this statement against the church, and Sprague addressed the fears he seemed to think lay behind such actions. He distinguished the theological discussion about the "incompatibility clause," in which delegates were uneasy about the "folks back home," from the current debate about legal rights, in which he sensed concerns about protecting the institution. After reassuring them that he shared both of those concerns to some extent, he spoke of the need for the church to put aside those fears and take a moral lead, asking, "How can the church ask the society to do that which we are not willing to risk doing?"[77]

When questions about how this statement might relate to ordination continued, Sprague replied to the question of whether this was a "creeping step toward ordination of homosexual people"[78] by saying, "Very respectfully sir, I understand nothing in that which is presented before you to have to do with either creeping or running toward ordination."[79] As these questions reveal, guranteeing a ban on the ordination of gays and lesbians was the primary goal of conservatives at the 1984 General Conference, for whom David Seamands served as a spokesmen.

Born in India to missionary parents, Seamands served with his wife as missionaries to that country from 1946 to 1962. He returned to the United States and served as senior pastor of Wilmore United Methodist Church in Kentucky for twenty-two years, after which he became Professor of Pastoral Ministries at Asbury Theological Seminary until his retirement in 1992, serving the last two years as Dean of the Chapel as well. Seamands was considered a pioneer in the field of Christian counseling, and the 1992 Congress of Christian Counseling awarded him the Paraklesis Award, along

75. Ibid., 461–62.
76. Ibid., 549.
77. Ibid., 552.
78. Kim, *UMC DCA* 1984, 552–53.
79. *UMC DCA* 1984, 553.

with James Dobson, Larry Crabb, and Gary Collins. Tapes of his sermons and his healing messages circulated worldwide, and his books, including the best seller *Healing for Damaged Emotions,* sold close to two million copies. He and his wife, Helen, led Marriage Enrichment and Engaged Discovery programs, thus his reputation suffered when sexual misconduct charges were filed against him in 2005, and he admitted to an extra-marital affair that had taken place over a number of years.

Seamands was an active member of Good News, serving on their board and founding the Evangelical Missions Council, which became part of Good News with him as its head. He was a visible spokesperson for evangelical causes in the pages of *Good News* magazine, at their conferences, and as a delegate to six General Conferences (1976 to 1996). At the end of the 1980s, Good News named him one of "Ten Who Shaped the Decade," for his firm stance against homosexual ordination, as well as his expertise on healing damaged emotions,[80] and in 2002 it bestowed on him the Edward W. Robb, Jr. United Methodist Renewal Award, given to one whose life and ministry made significant contributions to renewal within the UMC.[81]

Seamands presented minority reports related to sexuality at four General Conferences, including 1984, when he presented Minority Report B, which was initially rejected but was reconsidered and approved after the Judicial Council ruling was announced. He spoke for those who were determined to secure a ban on the ordination of gays and lesbians. The most consistent note in his and other conservative speeches was the need for moral clarity amid the ongoing unrest about homosexuality. They felt betrayed by the connectional system, and were resolved to do whatever was necessary to close any loophole in the Discipline.

The report added to ordination criteria a prohibition on "self-avowed practicing homosexuals." The statement was necessary, Seamands said, because the covenantal system that the 1980 General Conference had relied on had failed them. The "moral intention" that year had also been to provide a ban on ordaining gays and lesbians, and in lengthy debate, he noted, "we were assured and reassured that we are a connectional system, a covenant family of brothers and sisters who can trust one another" without a specific list. However, "the connectional system was broken, deliberately,

---

80. "Ten Who Shaped the Decade." *Good News* (May/June 1990) 28.
81. *Good News* (March/April 2002) 36.

intentionally, and with nationwide publicity at the highest ecclesiastical level," necessitating explicit, legally binding language.[82]

In voicing many of the same points made by other delegates, Seamands reflected the work of caucuses to effectively train delegates on certain key talking points. As did many conservative delegates, he distinguished between identity and behavior, proclaiming God's unconditional love and grace for all persons and softening what to many, especially moderates, could be an extreme position. He reported that language had been carefully chosen: "'Self-avowed' prevents any witch hunts or key hole investigations or ambushes by Falwell's Raiders. The word 'practicing' precludes any punitive or prohibitory restraints to ordination. It says nothing about sexual orientation."[83] Like Sprague, Seamands acknowledged that same-sex attraction was not chosen, but unlike him, Seamands considered the expression of that attraction in physical acts to be morally unacceptable.

The exclusion of gays and lesbians was presented as a necessity to maintain the highest moral standards for clergy. While some delegates resisted ordination criteria that singled out one specific characteristic or identity, the majority agreed that homosexual practice was an unacceptable norm for UMC clergy. Seamands claimed that God's acceptance of all persons did not mean acceptance of behavior that was contrary to scripture, saying, "There are a thousand-and-one ways for the church to say, 'God loves you and I love you' but lowering moral standards for its ordained clergy is not one of those ways." He went on to say that General Conference not only had the right but the obligation to set high standards, based on the New Testament and on keeping faith with the people who had sent 907 petitions asking for specific language on this issue.[84]

Other delegates felt that the General Conference would overstep its bounds by issuing a specific prohibition, insisting that such discernment rested with annual conference Boards of Ordained Ministry. Speaking against adding the "seven last words," Sprague claimed that these "seven loaded words" were unnecessary because "our board of the ministry is very careful about those who are certified for ministry. When I came in some twenty years ago, if you were warm and could carry a Bible, you were in. That's no longer the case."[85] Whereas conservatives felt they could no longer

82. *UMC DCA* 1984, 632.
83. Ibid.
84. Ibid.
85. Ibid., 639.

trust the covenantal relationship between those boards and the General Conference and were determined to assert their authority over them, those arguing for inclusion sought to retain an open process in which each candidate would be evaluated individually without singling out one criteria for rejection. The prevailing majority, however, believed that homosexual practice was "one of the minimums below which we do not want ordained ministers to fall."[86]

In this bicentennial year, Seamands referred to Methodism's connectional system as its "heart-genius," and once again raised the need for explicit, uniform standards, since a UMC pastor might serve anywhere within the denomination:

> I think if there's any place we need to stay together as sisters and brothers it is in regard to the moral standards for our ordained clergy. If we continue in our present direction, I think it may soon be said of us, "There is no UMC; there are only United Methodist conferences, and each one does what is right in its own eyes." Friends, let us be precise, let's say what we mean and mean what we say. Let our "yes" be "yes" and our "no" be "no." We believe that the purity of our ministry, the unity of our system and the integrity of our church depend upon it.[87]

Seamands ostensibly addressed the same institutional concerns that Sprague spoke to, but his reference to "the purity of our ministry" raises issues of uncleanness associated with homosexuality, especially gay male sex. Sprague spoke to the same associations when he compared the way the church treats gays and lesbians with how it once treated lepers. He pointed out that homosexuality is not like leprosy, but said that both groups have been consistently shunned and judged by religious communities, noting that "in the ancient day it was the priest who decided who was lepers."[88] Sprague pointed out the priestly function of drawing boundaries around what—and who—is clean and unclean, acceptable and not, as the church was doing now with gays and lesbians. Seamands clearly agreed that that was the church's function, but the two disagreed about where that boundary should be drawn.

Some delegates urging support for gays and lesbians saw in this new drawing of boundaries an echo of the church's past exclusions of African

86. Kim, *UMC DCA* 1984, 737.

87. *UMC DCA* 1984, 638.

88. Ibid., 468.

Americans and women. As Bonifacio Mequi put it, claiming that Christian character resides only within heterosexuals "would be as prejudicial and unjust as that kind of prejudice and injustice based on race or creed or color."[89] Race was also a factor in the influx of more conservative delegates from Africa, a result of the UMC's "exciting growth" in the African church, which Richard Looney described as being "more evangelical and more involved in social action."[90] This tilted the vote on homosexuality, as the four African delegates who spoke to this issue clearly viewed homosexuality itself as a sin, unlike many U.S. delegates who drew a distinction between gay identity and practice. To these Africans, any legislation condoning homosexuality would represent a rejection of the Bible[91] and might open the door to infidelity and polygamy.[92] For these delegates, pastors' effectiveness was closely tied to their personal morality; as one said, "How are we going to gain souls for Christ through infidelity?"[93]

Gender was also evident in these discussions as delegates on both sides turned to stories of Jesus healing women. Evelyn Burn used Jesus' defense of the anointing woman in Luke 7:37–50 to urge the same compassionate spirit and the grace to look beyond stereotypes and see individuals.[94] D. L. Maguire drew on the same story, along with the ten lepers Jesus healed (Luke 17:12–19), the Samaritan woman he met at the well (John 4), and the woman caught in adultery (John 8:1–11) to note that Jesus loved, accepted, and showed compassion for these and many more, but he did not ordain them.[95] Bill Roughton likewise used the story of the adulterous woman to point out that compassion for people did not require "endorsement of their lifestyle," asking: "Did Jesus endorse her lifestyle in order to be in ministry to her? Absolutely not! Rather, he offered to her love, caring concern, redemptive grace and he spoke to her those words of redemption, 'Go thou, and sin no more.'"[96] This tendency of male delegates to use gospel stories of

89. Ibid., 738.
90. Ibid., 461.
91. Mayo, *UMC DCA* 1984, 465.
92. Kartwe, *UMC DCA* 1984, 739.
93. Okoko, *UMC DCA* 1984, 641.
94. *UMC DCA* 1984, 733.
95. Ibid., 737.
96. Ibid., 464.

sinful *women* underscores Bourdieu's contention that masculine domination of women is linked to heterosexual domination of gays and lesbians.[97]

In looking at demographics of the various speakers, the most obvious difference was gender: eight women favored inclusion (five clergy and three lay), and only one woman, a lay delegate, spoke for restrictions. While the division between clergy and lay delegates was less clear than in previous years, clergy again dominated the discussion: of those whose position could be clearly discerned from their remarks,[98] eighteen clergy and four lay delegates urged openness or inclusion of gays and lesbians, while twenty-five clergy and nine lay delegates argued for restrictive language.

The gender gap could relate to several points that Bourdieu makes. First, as a dominated group themselves, women may be more likely to advocate for the inclusion of other such persons. Second, the fact that more men favored prohibitions on homosexuality may represent the perceived threat that gay men pose to masculinity. More specifically, men's lack of support may be related to an honor-shame dynamic in the public arena, where one's manliness needs to be validated by other men. As Bourdieu writes, "Manliness, it can be seen, is an eminently *relational* notion, constructed in front of and for other men and against femininity, in a kind of *fear* of the female, firstly in oneself."[99] The public nature of General Conference debates may have encouraged men to "talk tough" about maintaining heterosexual norms, or not speak at all, in order to preserve the respect of other males. This pressure may also have influenced the men who expressed concern about the public nature of the voting process.

Joseph Sprague and David Seamands continued to be prominent voices in the conversation, writing and speaking about this and other issues. Each served as a delegate to several more General Conferences, then Sprague was involved as a presider after his election as a bishop. And as noted above, each faced disciplinary proceedings, but with different implications for their reputations.

Seamands wrote and spoke frequently against homosexuality, basing his case on natural law, as well as scripture. Writing in a 1992 article in *Good News* magazine, he notes that it is incompatible with Christian

97. Bourdieu, *Masculine Domination*, 119–24.

98. In these complex and extended conversations about homosexuality and parliamentary process, it is often difficult to assess a delegate's personal feelings. My count of delegates by status and gender includes only those whose view is obvious from their remarks.

99. Bourdieu, *Masculine Domination*, 53.

teaching for two reasons: first, the positive biblical thread of "a clear, consistent heterosexual track," and second, the scriptural condemnation of "all other forms of sexual intercourse."[100] Seamands refutes arguments that progressives make against biblical passages that deal specifically with same-sex intercourse and places them within a theological context based on the complementarity of the sexes (Genesis 1:27), and a man and his wife cleaving together as one flesh (Genesis 2:24). More importantly, he notes, this is affirmed in the New Testament when Jesus cites Genesis 2:24 in his teachings on marriage and divorce, making it "unmistakably clear that *Jesus interprets the passage to mean there is a sacred order of the sexes which is grounded in creation itself, expresses God's will for humankind—heterosexual, monogamous marriage—and provides the only context for sexual intercourse*" (emphasis in original).[101]

He argues much the same grounds in a 1992 *Good News* article, "Blessing the Unblessable," in response to a same-sex union performed by five United Methodist clergy in Indianapolis. He examines church law, scripture, and church history and finds no basis on which one could bless such a union or the sexual expressions within it.[102] In 1998, he reprised the article, under the same name and with a few updates, in response to the September 1997 same-sex union performed by Rev. Jimmy Creech. He also wrote in both *Good News* and *Christianity Today* about the current state of morality and marriage in the United States, pointing variously to the "amoral media," lax divorce laws, and human pride, or *hubris*, as part of the problem.[103]

The phrase "heterosexual, monogamous marriage" repeats like a drumbeat through Seamands's writing, and having grounded his opposition to same-sex behavior so solidly in that ethic, his own extra-marital affair was a shocking revelation. He admitted that, like so many others, he had fallen into the sin of pride, and had sinned against the victim, the church, his family, and God. Through a facilitated confidential process, Seamands agreed to refrain from ministerial functions and enter a time of penitential prayer and discernment.[104] At age eighty-three, Seamands was less visible in the conservative movement than he had been earlier in his

100. Seamands, "God Made," 14.

101. Ibid., 16.

102. Seamands, "Blessing the Unblessable," 14–17.

103. Seamands and Rutland, "David Seamands," 18–19; Seamands, "Marriage Counterculture."

104. Evers, "Agreement Resolves Complaint."

career, and the affair was little mentioned in the evangelical press, and not at all in *Good News*, likely out of respect for his family and his son Stephen, who was a professor at Asbury and frequent contributor to the magazine. David Seamands died the following year, and his obituary in the magazine made glowing note of his influential career and leadership.

A chain of blog posts at evangelismtoday.blogspot.com from the time the sexual misconduct charges were announced in August 2005 through summer 2013 reveal that people were very ready to forgive David Seamands his failure to live up to his own standard of "monogamous heterosexual marriage." Of more than two dozen entries, only a few, including the original post, express shock and sadness, but the vast majority call for understanding and forgiveness, recalling the biblical stories of King David and the woman caught in adultery; one reads simply: "John 8:1–11," the citation for the latter story. Only four suggest that he was a hypocrite, and another three that God will judge him for his actions. Although undated, the final (anonymous) post refers to Exodus International, the ex-gay ministry that closed its doors in June 2013, apologizing for the hurt they had caused, and notes that Seamands's unforgivable sin was his failure to apologize for his oppostion to the full inclusion of the GLBT community in the UMC. The blogger writes, "One wonders if he was aware of his hypocrisy."[105]

We might expect greater outrage over a pastor who violated the ethical position that he had so consistently promoted, and on which he had argued for the exclusion of others. He had even equated "sex between unmarried singles, pre-marital and extra-marital sex" with same-sex intercourse because they too violate the *objective* biblical ethic of "heterosexual, monogamous marriage" and replace it with a *subjective* standard.[106] Yet he seems to have emerged with his reputation largely intact, and his social and religious capital seems little devalued by the revelation of his own extra-marital affair.

This is due, in part, to his long legacy of work within the evangelical wing of the UMC, capital that could not be wiped out that easily. As *Good News* once claimed, David Seamands had "cast a long shadow."[107] Furthermore, he wrote in his own books and articles of the temptations that surround us and

---

105. Comments on Matt Friedeman, "Another Minister Fails the Test," *Evangelism Today!* blog, August 13, 2005, http://evangelismtoday.blogspot.com/2005/08/another-minister-fails-test.html#c3350962816016301533.

106. Seamands, "God Made," 17.

107. "Ten Who Shaped the Decade." *Good News* (May/June 1990) 28.

the healing power of God's grace for those who have been hurt. Blog posts suggest that those who were touched by his pastoral ministry were quick to extend the same grace to him. Certainly his admission of guilt and his reference to the "victim" of his affair indicate that he understood the breach of trust and abuse of power that his behavior represented,[108] and this admission would make him a sympathetic figure. But Seamands's capital as a white heterosexual man must also be considered, and those who share his condemnation of homosexuality appear far more willing to forgive him a breach of morality than they are to see a monogamous same-sex couple engaged in what to them is an ongoing state of sinful behavior.

Sprague's reputation within the progressive Christian community, on the other hand, has been enhanced by the controversy he sparked, and he is seen as a champion for justice and inclusion. In 1996, the same year Sprague was elected bishop, General Conference passed legislation forbidding the celebration of same-sex unions by United Methodist pastors or in United Methodist churches. Just two years later, charges were filed against a pastor in Sprague's episcopal area for performing a union service for two men. In filing the official complaint, Sprague noted his high regard for the pastor and his own "theological and pastoral disagreement with this component of church law."[109] Even though his ecclesial office required that he enforce a rule with which he disagreed, the standing of that same office allowed him to voice that disagreement within a highly visible forum.

At the 2000 General Conference in Cleveland, Sprague was arrested twice in two days for demonstrating against the Church's exclusive stance towards gays and lesbians—first for taking part in a rally and march outside the conference site, and the next day for a demonstration on the conference floor when delegates voted to retain exclusionary language. Those who support the full inclusion of gays and lesbians in the life of the church view these as courageous acts by someone willing to use his symbolic and religious capital on behalf of those who are excluded from this decision-making arena. Sprague himself sees his arrests as acts of "pastoral solidarity with and for gay and lesbian Christians," writing, "As I had done all of my life, I stood with the outsider. Some members of the Church were outraged. Some were embarrassed. Some were proud of my behavior. I did what I did because I could not fathom a bishop doing less."[110]

108. Smith, "Retired UM Minister," B1.
109. Green, "Complaint Filed."
110. Sprague, *Affirmations*, 102. It is interesting to note that at the 1984 General

Being brought up on heresy charges also increased Sprague's capital among progressive Christians for not allowing conservative readings of certain scripture passages to stand as the only valid interpretation. In his book *Affirmations of a Dissenter*, he writes that both sides acknowledge that the real issue behind contests over homosexuality is biblical authority.[111] In offering a more liberal reading of these other passages, he seeks to unpack ancient religious language that many seekers find "confusing or implausible," acknowledging once again that this will offend some and may even be considered heretical.[112] And indeed, the assertion of orthodoxy in the face of such modern interpretations includes labeling such views as heresy. An essay on Sprague's heresy charges by *Christianity Today* managing editor Chris Armstrong reveals the extent to which conservative Christians feel threatened by such views, comparing them to Jack the Ripper's effect on a community, for endangering the eternal lives of those led astray by such beliefs, and insisting "that the person must be disciplined and his harmful teaching rendered null within the church."[113] Sprague's heresy charges were dismissed after a four-person supervisory response team concluded that, "Bishop Sprague knows Jesus Christ as Lord and Savior, has faith in Christ's saving and transforming power, and is obedient to Christ's teachings."[114]

In his book, Sprague likens the church's treatment of gays and lesbians to its treatment of blacks and, again, lepers. However, he is quick to note that it does not compare "in historic magnitude with the virulence heaped on people of color." The comparison, he notes, "is based on a misunderstanding of the Bible; it negates the clear hospitable witness of Jesus; it fails to accept the preponderance of available scientific data; it perpetuates demeaning prejudices; and, it opens the door to overt and covert violence

---

Conference, Sprague was one of at least sixteen clergy delegates who would later be elected bishop, but only a handful spoke for or against ordaining gays and lesbians. Roy Sano, like Sprague, spoke for inclusion (*UMC DCA* 1984, 637), while Bob Fannin urged the need for strong guidelines in a "mobile, changing world" (*UMC DCA* 1984, 642). Others may well have addressed the issue in other settings or at other General Conferences, notably Susan Morrison, who with Sprague would be arrested at the 2000 General Conference for demonstrating against the church's action on homosexuality. However, their silence could also indicate that the church did not agree with Sprague that outspoken support on such polarizing issues was part of a bishop's role, thus it could indicate that more moderate candidates tend to be elected to the episcopacy.

111. Sprague, *Affirmations*, 20.

112. Ibid., 36–37.

113. Armstrong, "Tangling with Wolves," 51.

114. Gilbert, "Complaints Dismissed."

against gays and lesbians." The question for the church, he writes, regarding sexual orientation, race, and gender, is how to welcome people "as they seek to make the journey of discipleship toward wholeness."[115] For Sprague and others, faithful discipleship could include monogamous same-sex relationship; for Seamands and other conservatives, celibacy was the only faithful option for gay or lesbian disciples.

2012 General Conference:
Geographical and Generational Complications

At the 2012 General Conference, held in Tampa, Florida, it appeared that the UMC was far from resolving its differences about homosexuality, or "human sexuality," to use the church's language at the time. Since 1984, restrictions had tightened against inclusion of gays and lesbians in the church, despite numerous petitions, a statement by fifteen bishops in 1996 expressing the pain the church's position caused them,[116] and regular demonstrations by those advocating inclusion, including those at the 2000 General Conference that resulted in twenty-nine arrests, including two bishops. In addition to the 1996 ban on performing same-sex unions noted above, the 2004 General Conference made certain practices chargeable offences for clergy, including being a "self-avowed practicing homosexual" or performing same-sex unions. This followed a church trial in Bothell, Washington, in which Rev. Karen Dammann, an open lesbian, was found not guilty of "practices declared by The United Methodist Church to be incompatible with Christian teachings," with the jury noting that the Social Principles are advisory in nature and not declarations.[117]

115. Sprague, *Affirmations*, 100–101.

116. The bishops expressed their duty to uphold the Discipline but also "the pain we feel over our personal convictions that are contradicted by the proscriptions in the Discipline against gay and lesbian persons within our church." The statement caused a furor at General Conference, not only for what it said, but because a group of bishops acted outside of and without the knowledge of the rest of the episcopacy. After several closed door meetings at General Conference, the Council of Bishops issued a statement acknowledging the "serious differences" among United Methodists and the bishops on this issue, but affirming their collective and individual commitment to uphold and teach the Discipline.

117. After Dammann, an ordained elder in the Pacific Northwest Annual Conference, revealed to her bishop, Elias Galvan, that she was in a partnered same-sex relationship, Galvan filed a complaint that led to a trial before thirteen clergy of that conference. The jury found no proof that Dammann had engaged in practices declared by the

In 2012, these tensions around sexual orientation were compounded by generational and geographical faultlines. As in previous years, older, more conservative members tended to stand up for traditional values, while younger delegates and others advocated for changes to help stop the loss of young people who found the church's policies out of touch with the times. Tensions between delegates from the United States and those from other parts of the world had heightened, as U.S. membership had declined, and elsewhere, especially Africa, it had grown rapidly. The ratio of delegates showed a dramatic shift, with an expanded delegation from the UMC's Central Conferences overseas, who made up more than one third of the 2012 General Conference (39 percent), having tripled their numbers in eight years, from just 13 percent in 2004. [118]

The influx of African delegates had a significant impact on the discussion and vote on homosexuality. While delegates from these countries represent a variety of perspectives, many of them are theologically conservative, so they were courted by conservative caucuses and informed about certain key pieces of legislation; indeed, as the number of overseas delegates increased, so did the margin on votes related to homosexuality.[119] Less than a century earlier, conservative southern Methodists portrayed African Americans as backward and unfit for leadership, yet more advanced than Africans. Now U.S. conservatives—mostly from the south—claimed that African delegates possessed greater scriptural and moral insight than some of their U.S. counterparts, at least on this issue.

Advocates of inclusion, on the other hand, found themselves in the awkward position of supporting the cultural diversity that comes with being a global church, while strategizing against African delegates who

---

UMC to be incompatible with Christian teaching. In addition to the lack of evidence that Dammann was sexually active and could not be compelled to incriminate herself, the jury wrote that while there were "passages that contain the phrasing 'incompatible with Christian teaching,' we did not find that any of them constitute a declaration," and therefore did not rise to the level of church law ("Jury Issues Statement on Decision in Dammann Case," UMNS news release, March 22, 2004, http://archives.umc.org/interior.asp?ptid=2&mid=3762).

118. With a set number of delegates, General Conference reflects population shifts in the proportion of delegations from various regions.

119. In a 2004 article entitled "Light from the Dark Continent," Mark Tooley, director of the United Methodist committee of the Institute on Religion and Democracy, credited the successful votes at that year's General Conference to increased membership in Africa. The addition that year of one million members from the Methodist Church of Cote D'Ivoire, he claimed, would make "any 'pro-gay' shift by future General Conferences increasingly impossible" (Tooley, "Light," 63).

rejected the ordination of gays and lesbians. In 2012, liberal Methodists trod a delicate line, recognizing that in matters of sexual justice, some African cultures lagged behind North America,[120] and wrestling with how best to seek justice for gay and lesbian Africans without appearing racist or paternalistic.

Aware of these and other stresses facing the body, General Conference planners, through articles in the *Daily Christian Advocate* (DCA), encouraged delegates to follow John Wesley's guidance and engage in "holy conferencing" throughout their time together, and a period was set aside for "holy conversation" in small groups around the topic of human sexuality. While no record of the small group sessions exist, the DCA transcript of the following evening's plenary includes a speech by Mark Miller, who was a lay delegate from New Jersey, a music leader for past General Conferences, and an openly gay man. Miller spoke of the harm that came to LGBT persons who felt they were bullied in those sessions.[121]

When dealing with legislation on human sexuality, the plenary body voted down two proposals that would have admitted the church's division on homosexuality—one from the Global Young People's Convocation that called on the Church to "refrain from judgment regarding homosexual persons and practices until the Spirit leads us to new insight,"[122] and one offered by pastors of two of the UMC's largest congregations[123] that affirmed the current position, recognized a significant minority who disagreed, and urged "respectful coexistence" rather than schism.[124]

---

120. Some African church leaders support criminalization of and severe punishment for homosexuality, including a law passed in Uganda in February 2014 that includes life imprisonment for certain acts. These clergy seek to resist the imposition of more liberal sexual ethics as unbiblical and as part of the continuing effect of western colonialism (Nzwili, "African clerics," 15–16).

121. In a video interview on the Love Your Neighbor website (May 3, 2012), Miller talks about the slow process of change in the church and compares it to the history of racism and sexism. He speaks of the need to understand each other's perspectives as deeper revelations come to light, adding, "You could be pessimistic and say that it's all about power, but I would be more generous than that." http://gc12.org/blog/mark-miller-gay-delegates-are-here/.

122. *UMC DCA* 2012, 270–71.

123. Presented by Adam Hamilton of UMC Church of the Resurrection in Kansas City, KS, a church of eighteen thousand members and co-authored by Mike Slaughter of Ginghamsburg UMC in Dayton, OH, which hosts about five thousand worshippers each week.

124. *UMC DCA* 2012, 2677.

Tensions between the United States and Central Conferences surfaced in the debate, particularly with conservative African delegates. A delegate from Katanga alluded to bestiality,[125] drawing an apology from his translator, a reaction from the house, and a reminder from the presiding bishop of the rules of holy conferencing. The loss of young members in the United States was also debated, with some claiming that they found the current language on homosexuality offensive and out-of-touch, and others insisting that young people were seeking clear biblical morals. Other delegates spoke of the gay and lesbian persons, including youth, who were being hurt by the policy.

Here and elsewhere delegates drew on scripture and on John Wesley, specifically Wesley's admonition to "do no harm," which Mark Miller had used in his remarks. Opponents of the amendment called for fidelity to scripture and to the church's "historic witness."[126] As we have seen in previous debates, the language of change cut both ways, with some arguing that change was necessary to be relevant to younger generations[127] and others insisting that accommodation on this issue would represent accommodation to secular culture and an accommodation of sin.[128] One delegate quoted John Wesley, saying:

> I'm not afraid that the people called Methodist should ever cease to exist in Europe or America, but I am afraid less they only should exist as a dead sect having a form of religion without the power, and this undoubtedly will be the case unless they hold fast both [*sic*] the doctrine, spirit, and discipline which they first set out.[129]

The demographics of the speakers were similar to that in previous discussions: all of the speakers in favor of retaining the current language were male, several from the southern United States, and of the three non-white speakers, two were from Africa. A more diverse group spoke in favor of inclusive language, including white and black men, a black woman, and three white women, one of them a young adult and one a self-identified lesbian. Speeches were fairly evenly divided among lay and clergy delegates.

As significant as the speeches themselves is what the written record reveals about what was happening "off-stage," or on the periphery of the

125. Tshoz, *UMC DCA* 2012, 2711.

126. Wende, *UMC DCA* 2012, 2678.

127. See *UMC DCA* 2012 for speeches by Swenson and Ihlo, 2710.

128. See *UMC DCA* 2012 for speeches by Dunnam, 2677, and Connolly, 2712.

129. *UMC DCA* 2012, 2712.

plenary sessions. Several progressive caucuses[130] had organized a Common Witness Coalition called "Love Your Neighbor," and their efforts were evident in demonstrations on the plenary floor, including the day that these amendments failed. Following the vote, protesters occupied the plenary floor singing, and when they ignored the presiding bishop's requests to leave, the bishop dismissed the body early, canceling the rest of that session. Protesters only dispersed when bishops agreed to let an openly gay pastor offer a prayer,[131] after which they proceeded to the next agenda item, leaving any other legislation on human sexuality unaddressed.

The Coalition's work was also evident in the "Stand with Mark" campaign that emerged around Miller's speech and went viral on Twitter. Miller invited other gay delegates to stand with him as he spoke, making gay and lesbian persons within the church and the General Conference a visible reality, something rarely seen in previous years. Amory Peck, one of three persons to take part in the Laity Address to General Conference, came out as a lesbian in a news conference following the address. Saying she was probably the first out, gay person to make the address, she remarked, "I was sad that I could not say that openly. But the Laity Address is about bringing people together. Of course gays and lesbians are active in the church, but there is fearfulness in being open about it. I wish we could lift the silence because the silence is crushing."[132]

The Church and Homosexuality

In the forty years between 1972 and 2012, the gay rights movement became more active and visible in the U.S. public square. In the 1980s, it coalesced around the AIDS crisis, which some religious conservatives depicted as God's judgment on homosexuals. The 1990s and later saw greater acceptance through the portrayal of gay characters in the media and gay and

130. Those groups were Affirmation, Black Methodists for Church Renewal, Methodist Federation for Social Action (descendent of the earlier MFSS), National Federation of Asian American United Methodists, Native American International Caucus, and Reconciling Ministries Network.

131. The next session began with a statement calling for unity and healing by Bishop Rosemarie Wenner, after which Frank Wulf offered a prayer for healing ("After Prayer, Gay Rights Protest Ends," *United Methodist Reporter*, May 3, 2012. http://www .unitedmethodistreporter.com).

132. *Love Your Neighbor Newsletter*, April 26, 2012, 11. http://www.general conference2012.org/neighbornews.html.

lesbian celebrities who came out. Over these years, UMC policies regarding homosexuality became increasingly restrictive, while the tone of General Conference discussions moved from expressed fear to affirmation of gay *persons*, but rejection of same-sex intimacy as sinful. Since 1984, homosexuality has been the subject of tense and extensive debate at every General Conference, and despite repeated attempts to at least acknowledge the church's division on the subject, the "incompatibility clause," the "seven last words," and the ban on ordination of "self-avowed practicing homosexuals" remained intact, as of the 2012 General Conference. As that gathering revealed, the division has been exacerbated by other tensions that threaten church unity.

The General Conference represents the full diversity of the denomination, thus its lay and clergy delegates have kept up with the church's global growth. While the church may celebrate the richness of diverse cultures this brings to the body, especially in worship, music, and other programs, it raises problems as well, some of which will be addressed in chapter 5. This diversity is also evident in the various positions expressed towards homosexuality, which can be described as total rejection, partial rejection, qualified acceptance, and full acceptance.[133] General Conference delegates have expressed all of these positions at times, although the fully rejecting view has fallen largely silent within General Conference conversations. The UMC's official policy has remained in the middle, which conservatives and moderates would see as qualified acceptance, and gay persons and those advocating their full inclusion would view as partial rejection.

The greatest tension lies between traditionalists who support orthodox beliefs and values, and progressives who assert the need for changing norms to meet changing social conditions and to reflect God's continuing revelation. For traditionalists, scripture is clear on this matter, since all biblical passages addressing same-sex behavior are negative.[134] Those who support ordination of gays and lesbians and same-sex marriage note that the concept of homosexuality as a sexual orientation was unknown until modern times, thus prohibitive scriptures convey understandings of same-sex intimacy as an unnatural behavior for presumably heterosexual

133. See Comstock, *Unrepentant, Self-Affirming,* 13–14, and Nelson, "Homosexuality and the Church," 65–67, for variations of this schema.

134. Scripture passages that have been understood to address same-sex sexual activity include the story of Sodom and Gomorrah (Genesis 19:1–29), laws related to impurity in Leviticus (18:22 and 20:13), and references in early Christian epistles describing sexual sins (Romans 1:18–32, 1 Corinthains 6:9–10, 1 Timothy 1:8–11).

persons. Biblical scholars have articulated alternative interpretations of these passages, arguing that they should be read in light of changing social conditions.[135] In their 2012 amendment to recognize the church's division, Adam Hamilton and Mike Slaughter wrote that a significant minority in the UMC read the relevant scriptural passages as they read passages about "polygamy, concubinage, slavery, and the role of women in the church,"[136] which are widely viewed as products of a different social context. For many modern readers these are not matters on which to stake the unity of the church.

For conservatives, though, the sinful nature of same-sex intimacy represents a moral absolute. However, religious and pastoral arguments have shifted over the years in light of new knowledge, and the stereotype of gay men as sexual predators and as sexually promiscuous eventually dropped away, as monogamous same-sex couples and responsible single gays and lesbians came to the fore. As the behavioral sciences have demonstrated that sexual orientation does not appear to be chosen,[137] arguments have shifted to the need for gays and lesbians to resist acting on their inborn, same-sex desire, and comparisons to alcoholism emerged. In the face of competing interpretations of scriptural passages that address same-sex sexual behavior, conservatives such as David Seamands focused instead on passages that affirm gender complementarity as the created norm (the

135. In addition to biblical scholars, many scholars who look at religion and sexual orientation either defend traditional readings or offer alternative interpretations of the passages that address same-sex sexual behavior. Among them are: McNeill, *The Church and the Homosexual*, 37–66; Scanzoni and Mollenkott, *Is the Homosexual*, 54–72; Nelson, *Embodiment*, 181–88; Boswell, *Christianity, Social Tolerance*, 91–117; and Jung and Smith, *Heterosexism*, 65–84. In Siker, ed., *Homosexuality in the Church*, Richard B. Hays (3–17) and Victor Paul Furnish (18–35) offer competing readings of these texts.

136. *UMC DCA* 2012, 2677.

137. While there are numerous theories about the origins of homosexuality, there is no conclusive evidence from the biological or behavioral sciences, suggesting that there might be a complex of causative factors. The American Psychiatric Association removed homosexuality from its list of pathologies in 1974, yet there remains a diversity of opinions about the degree to which it is rooted in biology or socialization, the extent to which conscious choice is involved, and the degree to which sexual orientation can be changed. Most arguments rely on the work of Alfred Kinsey and others in the 1940s, which articulated a range of sexual orientations, from totally heterosexual to totally homosexual, with most people somewhere between those poles. The lack of concrete scientific evidence about sexual orientation allows for a range of interpretations to support the range of moral and theological assessments.

"Adam and Eve, not Adam and Steve" argument).[138] This is consistent with a surprising trend among evangelical Christians to rely less on biblical passages as the moral authority on this matter and appeal at times to science, medicine, and natural order.[139] Even with these shifting arguments, conservative United Methodists have remained steadfast in their opposition to ordaining gays and lesbians who are sexually active, suggesting that the stated arguments mask deeper resistance at an unconscious level.

Many United Methodists are comfortable with the church's current position and see it as middle ground that acknowledges both biblical norms and modern understandings of sexual orientation. Sometimes referred to as "love the sinner, hate the sin," this posture claims that all persons are sinners in need of grace, and that homosexuality itself is not an immoral choice but a sinful tendency to be resisted. While those holding this position are quick to distinguish it from total rejection of gays and lesbians, their definition of any same-sex sexual expression as sinful limits the welcoming message they intend to convey, since many gays and lesbians interpret their position as: "I love you, but unless you resist the sexual desire God gave you, I believe you are condemned to hell."

In 2005, the UMC Judicial Council Decision 1032 reinforced this position's requirement that gays and lesbians relinquish their "sinful" behavior by supporting the exclusion of an actively gay man from church membership. The ruling reversed a decision by Bishop Charlene Kammerer of the Virginia Annual Conference, who had ruled that the pastor of a local church did not have the right to refuse membership to an openly gay man. The Judicial Council upheld the pastor's right to determine when a person is ready to affirm membership vows. While conservative Methodists hailed the decision as support for high moral standards, others considered it a stark contradiction to the church's contemporaneous advertising campaign of "Open Hearts, Open Minds, Open Doors."

The UMC is not alone in its struggles with homosexuality. In recent years, the Episcopal Church, the Evangelical Lutheran Church of America (ELCA), and the Presbyterian Church (USA) (PCUSA), have voted to ordain gays and lesbians, and in response have seen conservative congregations break away to form new denominational bodies. Several years of

138. Such passages include the creation of humans as male and female in Genesis 1:27, the creation of Eve as Adam's companion in Genesis 2:21–24, and Jesus' citation of those passages in Matthew 19:4–6.

139. Thomas and Olson, "Evangelical Elites."

tension followed the 2003 election of Gene Robinson as the first openly gay bishop in the Episcopal Church. During those years, a number of congregations allied with conservative dioceses in the worldwide Anglican Communion, mostly in Africa and South America, before coalescing in June 2009 as the Anglican Church of North America. In August 2010, theological conservatives within the ELCA and the Canadian Lutheran Church came together as the North American Lutheran Church in response to the ELCA's 2009 vote to allow gays and lesbians to be ordained and married. After the PC(USA) lifted its ban on ordaining gays and lesbians in 2010, the Evangelical Covenant Order of Presbyterians formed in January 2012.

Speaking about what was at stake for those who left, Mark Tooley of the conservative Institute on Religion and Democracy said, "When orthodox and conservative Christians made homosexuality their flash-point issue, and they lost those struggles, in many ways they had no choice but to create these new structures."[140] Tooley's remark gives some indication of the division that could occur within the UMC should ordination of gays and lesbians be approved.

The UMC differs from the other mainline churches that have split in several important ways. Each of the other denominations encompasses the United States alone, whereas the global nature of the UMC has contributed to its difficulties. Its situation most closely resembles the U.S.-based Episcopal Church's affiliation with the global Anglican Communion. The alliance of U.S. Episcopal congregations with conservative dioceses outside the United States could provide the model for a divided UMC, if it comes to that. Also like the Episcopal Church, a trust clause in the deed of every United Methodist congregation requires that its property remain with the denomination if it secedes.[141] In January 2012, a court in Virginia found against seven break-away congregations that brought suit against the Episcopal Church in an effort to retain their property. Rulings in Connecticut, Wisconsin, and Texas likewise granted ownership to the Episcopal Church over congregations that had left.[142] Thus, while onlookers might wonder why United Methodists are still together, those within know that leaving comes at a high price.

The UMC is also distinguished from other Protestant denominations by its connectional polity, which has contributed to the maintenance of its

140. Quoted in Burke, "Splinter Groups," 14.

141. *UMC Discipline* 2012, par. 2503.

142. As of this writing, appeals were pending in the Texas case.

restrictive policies in two ways. First, given the theological diversity within the church, delegates have sought to avoid a situation in which gay pastors might be sent to congregations that are resistant to their leadership, as the church in earlier years used the same rationale to resist the ordination of women. Second, centrists have been willing to approve a more conservative position in order to keep peace within the church, making the current policy a palatable option. Denominations with congregational polity, on the other hand, can allow each congregation more leeway in deciding its own course in such matters.

The connectional nature, as well as the distinctive structure of Methodism, has also yielded conflict over the authority of General Conference versus that of annual conference Boards of Ordained Ministry. The tightening of legislative language about homosexuality and the corresponding codification of a monogamous heterosexual norm represent the General Conference's assertion of its authority in defining ministerial credentials, often in response to Judicial Council decisions that have upheld annual conference or episcopal support of gay clergy, such as the Karen Dammann case. The struggle over homosexuality itself revolves on issues of authority—both the belief that the moral deficiency of "self-avowed practicing homosexuals" precludes their authority as clergy, and the authority of scripture and church teaching in addressing the issue.

The majority of General Conference delegates have upheld traditional readings of scripture and the maintenance of traditional norms related to marriage and family structures, which they believe are threatened by more permissive ethics and contextual interpretations of scripture. This position makes a conscious appeal to the past in the midst of modernizing forces, as Bishop G. Lindsey Davis does in claiming that the UMC has "chosen to maintain the orthodox Christian stance, which has dominated Christian understanding for two thousand years."[143] In response to understandings that homosexuality is an orientation rather than a conscious choice, some have portrayed the rejection of homosexual behavior as self-sacrifice, which is required of all Christians, but especially those aspiring to the higher calling of ordained ministry.[144]

Traditionalists stake claims of orthodoxy in response to prophetic movements that challenge such presuppositions as human constructions that are subject to change. Bourdieu would describe the UMC requirement

143. Foreword to Dunnam and Malony, *Staying the Course*, 10.
144. Kirkley, *UMC DCA* 1984, 633.

of celibacy as "bad faith," in which those in power promise spiritual rewards for the repression of worldly interests,[145] those interests being sexual activity for those outside of heterosexual marriage. Udis-Kessler also uses the term "bad faith" to describe a moral alchemy that occurs when an in-group (heterosexuals) claims that what is virtuous for them (monogamous marriage) becomes a "threat to society" when practiced by the out-group of gays and lesbians.[146] Udis-Kessler echoes Bourdieu with her claim that Christianity's battle over homosexuality is a struggle about domination and the power to assign meaning and define reality.

The dominant group in General Conference, namely white, male clergy who present as heterosexual, use their power to erect barriers that restrict other groups' access to power, as previous struggles over race and gender illustrate. As Bourdieu claims, prophetic movements that challenge the institutional structure find themselves forced to operate outside the institution and without institutional protection, which is captured in the UMC bans on ordination of gays and lesbians and elimination of funding for "pro-gay" groups. The effectiveness of such restrictions to preserve the interests of the UMC seat of power is evident in the dearth of openly gay speakers in the General Conferences covered in this chapter. Only in recent years have gays and lesbians self-identified within General Conference sessions, and as Amory Peck said, even in 2012, there was still fear in doing so.[147]

The prophetic movement advocating full inclusion of gays and lesbians challenges understandings of sin, the validity of sexist and sexual dualisms, theological constructs, and biblical interpretations, which have all served historically to guarantee the interests of those in power. These understandings establish boundaries that determine not only who is in power, but group membership itself. Delegates who expressed fear that UMC members would leave the denomination if it approved pro-gay policies reflect the function of boundaries to prevent those inside from leaving, as well as those outside from entering. Religious groups have always drawn

145. Bourdieu, "Genesis and Structure," 21.

146. Udis-Kessler, *Queer Inclusion*, 112.

147. The ability of gays and lesbians to conceal their sexual orientation makes it impossible to discern the sexual identity of speakers; in addition, the bias against them would discourage many from speaking up. Literature from PFLAG (Parents and Friends of Lesbians and Gays) at the 2000 General Conference claimed that there had been only two openly gay speakers in twenty-nine years of General Conference debates on the subject (Udis-Kessler, *Queer Inclusion*, 133).

boundaries establishing both insiders and outsiders, but Bourdieu, echoing Weber, describes how the nature of such boundaries changed, as primitive religion became rationalized. In the process, understandings shifted: magic became morality, and the fault, or blemish, became sin. The power to define sin lies with religious specialists who naturally seek to preserve their own interests;[148] whereas Bourdieu is referring to priests, the same power can apply to both UMC clergy and General Conference delegates.

UMC delegate Roy Sano reflected this understanding of boundaries when he compared delegates who would restrict ordination to the Pharisees in Jesus' time. Using the language of the "two keys" as the power to both bind and to loose (Matthew 16:19), he said:

> I believe their proposal is more likely to mislead us in these days, when a flood of letters call us back to scribal religion and Pharisaic piety. I would submit that under such circumstances as we find ourselves today, Jesus was more intent on bridling or binding the scribes and Pharisees. By contrast, he turned loose those who apparently crossed over or transgressed the boundaries which were drawn apparently in the created order. In his day, Jesus released in no uncertain terms salvation through the Samaritans who epitomized transgressors of the boundaries. The followers, like Paul, did not ask the converts to change their identity. Hence, they did not ask for circumcision, a major battle in the early church. I would submit these are the biblical analogies to guide us today.[149]

The question of boundaries is especially noticeable in regard to sexual relations that represent disorder, or a breakdown in social structures, thus the threat that homosexuality poses to gender norms and to marriage and traditional family structures. Bourdieu, among others, attributes heterosexism to the same hierarchical dualism that creates sexism. According to this dualism, same-sex relationships, specifically between men, cast one man in the female role of being dominated (penetrated) by another. The dominated man is thus seen as one who suffers the humiliation of being "feminized," relinquishing the symbolic capital that comes with maleness.[150] The earliest Methodist discussions, like Bourdieu's work on sexual orientation, focused on gay men; however, the same dualism would portray women in lesbian couples as not being appropriately under male authority. While the ratio-

148. Bourdieu, "Genesis and Structure," 8–9.

149. *UMC DCA* 1984, 637.

150. Bourdieu, *Masculine Domination*, 22.

nale behind anti-gay ideology is complex, there is clearly a threat to male gender identity and a corresponding loss of power. Bourdieu notes the religious significance of such reordered relationships when he writes of the "taboo of the sacrilegious feminization of the masculine."[151] After the 1978 and 1982 cases of gay men being charged, which were mentioned above, the most publicized cases of openly gay UMC clergy have been women.[152] The increase in women corresponds to their increase among ordained clergy, but the decline of gay men could indicate that they are less willing to test the boundary of feminization that would diminish their perceived authority. Men are not the only ones who experience feelings of threat from such disorder, but also anyone who is comfortable with traditional gender roles and family and social structures.

This breakdown of social boundaries and the structures they inscribe is intensified by the repugnance that many feel toward male same-sex intercourse, raising issues of pollution and purity. These feelings are evident in the speeches of delegates who refer to homosexuality as "perversion" or "debauchery," and in Seamands's language about "the purity of our ministry, the unity of our system and the integrity of our church."[153] In her seminal work on purity, Mary Douglas writes that our concept of uncleanness is related to both hygiene and respect for convention, or order;[154] thus, holiness is related both to maintaining social categories and ritual protection of bodily orifices.[155] In defying the heterosexual norm, gays and lesbians transgress boundaries of social order, while gay men further transgress hygienic boundaries in anal intercourse. Douglas notes that anal, or excremental, eroticism is associated with the "magic" of primitive, non-rational

---

151. Ibid., 119.

152. In addition to Karen Dammann, Rose Mary Denman, herself a conservative, came out in 1987 and was found in violation of the 1984 legislation she had supported. The Judicial Council in 1994 allowed Jeanne Knepper to continue in the ordination process, despite charges that she was a "self-avowed practicing homosexual." Beth Stroud lost her clergy credentials in a church trial in 2004 after coming out to her congregation near Philadelphia, and Amy DeLong was tried in 2011 for performing a same-sex union in Wisconsin and for being a noncelibate gay clergyperson when she and her partner registered under Wisconsin's Domestic Partnership Law. DeLong was acquitted on the latter charge and suspended for twenty days for performing the same-sex union, the shortest penalty that any UMC jury has handed down in such cases.

153. UMC DCA 1984, 638.

154. Douglas, Purity and Danger, 7.

155. Ibid., 126.

cultures,[156] reinforcing the idea that gay men more closely resemble sexualized women than rationalized men, and thus are equally unfit for religious leadership. These vestiges of ancient ideas of purity are combined with the notion that sexual pleasure is sinful, resulting in a modern sexual ethic that allows only one acceptable sexual arrangement, namely procreative sex within the context of monogamous heterosexual marriage,[157] as David Seamands and others insisted.

The sense of defilement or disorder associated with homosexuality is heightened in the current debate by the social unrest of the times. In her study of the 2000 General Conference, Udis-Kessler describes the need that delegates felt to protect the institutional church from an invasion of the secular world. For many, she writes, the prohibitions in the Discipline were regarded as though "they were dams holding back the floodwaters of heresy and apostasy. Conservatives seemed to fear that if they allowed the dams to be weakened, even by merely agreeing to disagree on homosexuality, the church would be awash in worldliness and would no longer recognizably be the church."[158] Boundaries were drawn around what was designated as holy and absolute, at the same time barring whatever was secular, profane, and changeable, and offering clear moral standards for United Methodist leadership.

Similarly, Daniel Maguire locates heterosexism and homophobia in fear of diversity and fear of change. The gay rights movement came on the heels of the 1960s, adding layers of change and diversity to the social transformations that occurred in that pivotal decade. What is at stake in such changes, Maguire notes, is both personal and political.[159] He writes:

> Fear of two persons who love each other and want to bond permanently, legally, and if they choose, religiously, would not on its face, seem to presage social disaster. Why does it engender such panic?
>
> It does seem to be a rule of life that when an issue becomes suddenly inflamed in society, it rarely has anything to do with the issue. It has everything to do with power. Powerholders, like animals who sense earthquakes before others, first feel the distant tremors that threaten their foundations and their privileges.

156. Ibid., 118.

157. Jordan, *Ethics of Sex*, 107.

158. Udis-Kessler, *Queer Inclusion*, 146.

159. Maguire, "Heterosexism, Not Homosexuality," 2–3.

> All of this helps to explain the shocking enigma of misplaced moral indignation in the political arena and among religious people.[160]

Maguire ponders why such indignation is not aimed at worldwide poverty and starvation, global warming, and military build-ups. "But no," he writes. "In countries such as the United States, a demonic, fear-driven pelvic orthodoxy, with scandalous over-absorption in issues like same-sex marriage, contraception, and abortion, consumes politics, churches' legislatures, and judiciaries."[161] Greenberg and Brystyn cite a similar response in late antiquity, where "profound social change,"[162] along with factors that John Boswell identified in his landmark work *Christianity, Social Tolerance, and Homosexuality*,[163] became the seeds of current anti-homosexual feelings in western culture and religion.

This idea was not lost on General Conference delegate Thomas Starnes, who quoted an article by Reinhold Niebuhr from the 1950s that named triviality, or attention to "petty moralisms," as the church's greatest sin. Starnes quoted Niebuhr that the church, when confronted with slavery, had focused on "drinking, cussing, card playing, and other fleshly concerns." Starnes concluded:

> I cannot imagine that in our heart of hearts we honestly think that whether or not we ordain gays or lesbians is the central moral issue facing us in this [American Methodism's] Bicentennial year.

160. Ibid., 4.

161. Ibid.

162. Greenberg and Brystyn, "Christian Intolerance," 542.

163. In his *Christianity, Social Tolerance, and Homosexuality: Gay People in Western Europe from the Beginning of the Christian Era to the Fourteenth Century* (1980) Boswell claims that modern intolerance of homosexuality is rooted in the late Middle Ages, when the quest for order and uniformity was codified in the merger of theology and canon law. Rather than an orthodox perspective that has been consistent throughout church history, the attitude in ancient societies was generally tolerant of same-sex behavior; however, Hellenistic philosophy contributed dualisms to Western Christian thought that help set up such distinctions. Boswell's work is seen as groundbreaking scholarship in the field of gay and lesbian studies, but has been challenged by those on the left and the right. As a Catholic and an openly gay man, Boswell was criticized by gay radicals for letting the church off too easy, and by conservative Christians for not portraying the church's consistent witness against same-sex behavior. An extensive list of reviews, summarizing each one's critique of Boswell's work is on Fordham University's People with a History: An Online Guide to Lesbian, Gay, Bisexual, and Trans* History site, the John Boswell Page. http://www.fordham.edu/halsall/pwh/index-bos.asp.

> If, in a time of unprecedented hunger, the threat of nuclear anni-
> hilation, the chains of racism and sexism, we think that this issue
> deserves the time and energy we are giving it, then God help us as
> a church.[164]

Underlying this concern with "trivial" issues, of course, is a deeper theological division within the church, described variously as conservatives versus liberals, tradition versus progress, or orthodoxy versus heresy, part of the larger arc of transformation prompted by modernism. The eruption of this underlying division into overt conflict at times of change occurs when prophetic forces call into question existing social boundaries and structures, along with underlying but unrecognized power dynamics, masked by religious arguments. Delegate Roy Sano's reference to "boundaries which were drawn apparently in the created order"[165] suggests that at least some General Conference delegates shared the viewpoint that such distinctions are social products, not divine fiat.

William Abraham speaks stringently against such contentions and argues for the importance of maintaining the UMC's stance on homosexuality when he writes:

> Now I am aware that our convictions and the way we hold them
> are shot through with all sorts of distortion, sin, cultural bag-
> gage, personal prejudice, and the like. Yet on the matter before
> us, conservatives are both tenacious and urgent. This is not ac-
> cidental. They are tenacious because the position they hold is not
> just a matter of human judgment or opinion. It is construed as the
> teaching of our Lord in divine revelation. They are urgent because
> they believe that the rejection of divine revelation involves the
> unraveling of the fabric of faith and the radical undermining of
> the canonical commitments of The United Methodist Church. For
> better or worse, they foresee chaos and division if the position of
> *The Book of Discipline* were revised.
>
> It is a very serious mistake to reduce this tenacity to lust for
> power; politics; conventional, bourgeois morality, homophobia,
> white male patriarchy; and the like. At one level, what is at stake is
> the measure of cognitive dissonance any community can endure.
> ... Much more important is that what is at stake are the foundations

164. *UMC DCA* 1984, 735.

165. Ibid., 637.

of the Church in the Word of God and the place of The United Methodist Church within the church catholic and apostolic.[166]

Abraham bases his claim on the power of divine revelation as a "threshold concept" through which one enters an entirely new world. He acknowledges that both liberals and conservatives can convincingly cite scripture, as well as the other prongs of the Wesleyan quadrilateral, but notes that the real difference lies in an "epistemology of theology" in which revelation becomes the seat of knowledge. Even as he acknowledges the human element in interpreting revelation, Abraham claims the status of divine revelation for the conservative viewpoint. However, liberal Methodists also understand inclusion of all persons, including gays and lesbians, to be God's desire for the church. Abraham speaks to the deep significance this issue represents for conservatives, yet liberals cling just as firmly to a contradictory ideal, as expressed by the fifteen bishops in 1996, and by the retired bishops and black scholars in their statements in 2011.

Likewise United Methodists use the language of pain to describe the effect that the UMC's position has on gays and lesbians, while more conservative members describe the pain they experience in being labeled as victimizers for beliefs they understand as fidelity to the word of God. At the 1984 General Conference, delegates on all sides of the UMC debate noted their pain in voting as they did, and the pain their vote may have caused others. In 2012, Mark Miller spoke of the harm done to gay and lesbian United Methodists in that year's small group sessions. The language of pain and injury used across the board reflects the conviction with which United Methodists hold contrasting experiences of God's revelation, as well as the theological and scriptural grounding they find for divergent positions. At the same time, the public nature of the General Conference speeches and the strategies of caucus groups raise the possibility that such language, while rooted in sincere belief, may also represent carefully crafted statements that are intended to sway undecided delegates to one position or another.

In surveying U.S. delegates to the 1996 General Conference, James Wood found that although both sides were deeply committed, conservatives were far more likely to leave the denomination if more liberal policies were approved (25 percent of delegates versus 2 percent who were "liberal leavers").[167] Wood's numbers, of course, do not account for those who had already left the church over its restrictive policies, and those numbers in-

166. Abraham, "The Church's Teaching," 29.
167. Wood, *Where the Spirit Leads*, 27.

crease as the policies persist and are strengthened.[168] Wood's demographic profile identified the same gender gap that is evident in the speeches covered in this chapter. Wood found that 82 percent of the "conservative leavers" were men, while 85 percent of the "liberal leavers" were women;[169] similarly, 71 percent of all female delegates did not believe homosexuality is a sin, compared to 43 percent of male delegates.[170]

As General Conference speeches examined here reveal, United Methodists on all sides of the issue are frustrated with the amount of time and energy expended on concerns related to homosexuality, yet after four decades of debate, no parties show signs of relenting in the course that they perceive as God's vision for the church. Delegates have compared this conflict to the church's struggles with racism and sexism, and while there are similarities, the three issues have distinct differences, which will be explored in the next chapter.

The issue of homosexuality in the church is complex, highly charged, and defined by misrecognized fears related to rapid social change and the perceived threat to familiar social institutions and the sense of security they represent. Underlying this conflict are the church's historic discomfort with issues of sexuality, and dualistic constructions that codify that unease into categories of sexual insiders (monogamous heterosexuals and celibates) and outsiders (everybody else). These have been magnified in recent years by cultural differences between different generations and African countries where the church has grown.

In offering possible solutions, some have envisioned a removal of sanctions against ordaining gays and lesbians to allow for regional decisions, and to force study and productive conversation around the issue. Removing sanctions would also signal an openness that could bring gays and lesbians out of the closet and into full engagement with local congregations, resulting in personal encounters that could reduce stereotypes and lead to greater acceptance—a hope that experienced a setback with Judicial Council Decision 1032 supporting a pastor's right to determine whether openly gay persons are fit for church membership. It is also highly unlikely

---

168. I first became aware of the church's positions on this matter in 1984, when a gay couple left our church to join the Unitarian Universalist Church because of the UMC's policy decisions that year.

169. Wood, *Where the Spirit Leads*, 29.

170. Ibid., 87.

that conservatives would agree to the removal of the restrictive language thay have fought so hard to add and retain over the years.

Even more people envision a restructuring of the denomination that allows for geographic regions to set their own policy on the matter, but that may not satisfy conservative concerns about connectionalism. Arriving at the current position has been an arduous process, and given the entrenched nature of the resistance to ordaining gays and lesbians, any significant change to the policy may well lead to division, a possibility that will be explored in chapter 5.

5

Looking Back, Looking Forward
What the Future Can Learn from the Past

"For Methodism to thrive it requires energy, change, mobility, and flux."

—DAVID HEMPTON

IN THE 1910S AND 1920S, male delegates to the Methodist Episcopal Church, South (MECS) General Conference were considering the place of African American Methodists in a unified church, while the (Methodist Episcopal Church) MEC General Conference discussed women's ordination. Meanwhile, southern white women reached out in mission to black women and lobbied for racial equality and women's rights. Their actions illustrate that these issues are often interrelated and that they coincide in such periods of change.

In 1920, two white members of the MECS Woman's Missionary Council (WMC) met with the leadership of the National Association of Colored Women (NACW), believing that hearts and attitudes would only be changed through personal contact. Southern white women continued to work with and for black women through the WMC and the Commission on Interracial Cooperation (CIC). Focusing on the social spheres where they had some degree of power, white women worked to provide childcare, improve skills and working conditions of domestic workers, and increase educational opportunities for black women, so they could "aspire to larger usefulness."[1] In the 1930s, MECS women opposed the formation

1. Knotts, "Race Relations," 210.

of the Central Jurisdiction in the merger with the MEC and The Methodist Protestant Church (MPC), believing that the segregated structure contradicted the relational ethic of Jesus' teaching. In hopes of defeating the plan, women succeeded in electing fifty-four female delegates to the 1938 MECS General Conference when the merger was considered, but white male voices promoting racial separation prevailed.

The extent of white women's influence on these issues reflects their dual status as a privileged race and a subordinated sex. They reached out to black women, who are doubly disadvantaged, and used their own advantage as white persons to seek racial equality. Yet gender inequality limited their influence in the General Conference and in the larger society, thus they found themselves working outside of recognized power structures. Their focus on improving conditions of black women's domestic work reinforced a social arrangement that restricted African Americans to subservient roles and posed no threat to white women seeking employment outside the home. At the same time, white women had power within the private sphere of the home to set wages and working conditions for their domestic workers. Recognizing the limits based on their sex, white southern women lobbied for women's ordination, even as their own writings perpetuated androcentric religious imagery, urging "human brotherhood" under "Divine fatherhood."[2]

In her articles documenting southern white women's efforts to address racism and sexism in the church, Alice Knotts describes the degree of change the south faced at this time, which led white men to reassert their power.[3] Even as they recognized the "comfort of traditional patterns," some white southern women rejected the idea that racial separation was part of God's plan.[4] Through their intentional efforts to "change race relations in the South," these white women began to "bring to conscious awareness things they knew deeply underneath the surface,"[5] or as Bourdieu would say, to recognize the misrecognized.

The interactions of these southern women, both white and black, illustrate that issues of race and sex are not neatly separated; the tensions over sexual orientation that arose several decades later added another layer

---

2. *Twenty-Seventh Annual Report of the Woman's Missionary Council*, 1937, 157, quoted in Knotts, "The Debates," 41.

3. Knotts, "Race Relations," 199–200.

4. Knotts, "The Debates," 40–41.

5. Knotts, "Methodist Women," 240.

of complexity. Different forms of domination may overlap, and certain groups may be dominated in one area while dominant in another. Whereas the previous chapters analyzed how each form of domination played out in controversies over Methodist leadership, this chapter will consider the three dimensions together, looking for intersections, common threads, significant distinctions, and interrelationships.

The course of these three groups of people as they moved toward full, unqualified leadership has not been uniform or consistent, often overlapping and even competing with each other. At times, different oppressed groups supported each other, as did the southern white women introduced above. Just as often, however, one group advanced its interests at the expense of another marginalized group, whether consciously or not. The most noticeable interactions have been between race and gender, which have a longer history than questions of sexual orientation. In the nineteenth century, many Methodists, notably those involved in the Holiness movement, argued for abolition as well as women's rights, recognizing both as forms of subjugation. Some abolitionists, however, were content to see slavery ended but did not go on to advance racial equality.

Likewise, early feminism took on a racist tone when white women criticized the Fifteenth Amendment that granted voting rights to black men but denied them to women, both white and black. Sexism was present in black Methodism as well as in the larger Methodist bodies, as women in the African Methodist Episcopal Church (AMEC) were denied ordination until 1960, and Jarena Lee was discouraged from preaching by Richard Allen, the denomination's founder and first bishop. The African Methodist Episcopal Church, Zion (AMEZC), on the other hand, removed the word "male" from its ordination requirements in 1868, and ordained a female deacon in 1896 and a woman elder two years later. Such complexities continue to the present and will be explored in this chapter.

Context of Social Change

As noted above, a striking similarity among the three contests for leadership is their occurrence during and just after periods of significant social change, supporting Bourdieu's claim that disruption to social order creates a sense of disorder or threat, which may prompt a reassertion of orthodoxy. Even so, these contests for power result in a continual process of transformation that follows a larger arc of social change, as resistance is eventually overcome. As Bourdieu notes, the form of any religion's beliefs and practices at a given point in time differs from its original content;[6] in other words, no original, unaltered form of any religion exists, since their various forms will always be contingent upon the societies in which they occur.

Bourdieu uses the scientific term hysteresis, to describe the lag between significant or sudden change and subsequent adjustments in habitus and the resulting structural shifts. Even after social change has occurred, it may take many years, or even the passing of a generation before patterns of thought and social relationships catch up. Those who were shaped by an older habitus are not equipped to deal with new field conditions.[7] The dialectic nature of habitus requires disruption from prophetic change movements such as those explored here. The turn of the twentieth century and the period around the 1960s were marked by rapid, often dramatic social change that tested the boundaries of social institutions, authority structures, and toleration of difference. The resistance examined here occurred just after those periods of change, as people shaped by an older habitus struggled to adapt to new social realities. In examining General Conference speeches from those eras, I was prepared to search for clues to this resistance, but was surprised at the overt nature and the frequency of arguments based explicitly on resistance to social change, which delegates offered as often, or more so, than biblical or theological rationales.

Many Christians were especially unsettled by the ideological challenge of modernism, as religion was regarded as one of several specialized fields that might convey "truth." In response, both eras in question saw assertions of religious orthodoxy, through the emergence of Christian fundamentalism in the 1920s and the rise of the "Religious Right" in the 1980s. In linking the anxiety of Christian fundamentalism to the challenges of modernism, Karen McCarthy Brown writes that Enlightenment thinking created the expectation that we could control our own fate and possess "an unchanging truth."[8] Religious fundamentalists, she writes, "reject Enlightenment rationalism while continuing to imitate its drive for clarity and control."[9] Citing religion's "orientational role," Brown writes that the central goal of the early religious fundamentalists in the 1920s was "to make of their religion an Archimedean point in the midst of a changing world."[10] They desired social

---

6. Bourdieu, "Genesis and Structure," 18.

7. Bourdieu, *Outline*, 83.

8. Brown, "Fundamentalism," 193.

9. Ibid., 186.

10. Ibid., 179–80.

control that clearly delineated social boundaries—"between the righteous and the sinful, between life and death, and not coincidentally, between men and women."[11] Harvey Cox notes that fundamentalists fight not only an outside threat, but the "fifth column" of progressives within their faith group,[12] thus the vehemence of the internal struggle among Methodists in these debates.

In the Methodist transcripts examined here, concerns about modernism are most explicitly expressed by MECS delegates in 1938 who argued that a stronger, unified church could better resist such secular influences as communism, atheism, and immorality. Throughout these transcripts, however, those promoting change made the most direct references to modernity, equating it with progress, specifically in granting women greater rights. Those concerned about such changes spoke to the overarching uncertainty of the era and the rapid pace of change, asserted the church's continuing relevance, denounced secular influences, and promoted the need for stability that the church provided. Arguing for reunification, delegate H. P. Anker, missionary to Congo, gave voice to fears that may have been behind other arguments:

> Is modernism the thing we are afraid of? If so, why don't we say so? I am not a modernist but we can't put a fence around a church and keep modernism out. I don't believe we need worry about that. Being separate won't keep us out of that issue.[13]

More common were remarks about how these larger contours of change were experienced on the personal level as changes to familiar patterns of family, school, and church—the institutions that serve as primary sites of socialization. Changes in the early twentieth century prompted defense of traditional racial and gender relationships in an effort to preserve social stability and security, as would later movements for civil and human rights based on race, gender, and sexual orientation. Addressing sexism in the church, Beverly Harrison recognizes the validity of such feelings, writing, "Societies . . . have a way of wanting to survive—to hang in there and not fall apart. They tolerate what they tolerate because it *feels* like it is functional to survival. Change makes all of us feel insecure."[14] Indeed, a

11. Ibid., 177.
12. Cox, *Future of Faith*, 152.
13. *MECS DCA* 1938, 9.
14. Harrison, "Sexism," 196.

sense of insecurity is detectable in resistant Methodists during both periods of change, even if the root of that insecurity goes unnamed.

During the later wave of change around the 1960s, Harrison, James Nelson, and others proposed new ethical and theological models to address changing norms related to sexuality, marriage, and family. Writing in 1978, Nelson claimed that the traditional functions of marriage were changing due to increased mobility, new understandings of sex roles, urbanization, industrialization, and technological changes that offered reliable birth control and longer life spans. Nelson cited a study indicating the plurality of family arrangements in the United States, where only 37 percent fit the normative "nuclear family" structure of two parents and their children in one household; [15] by the 2010 census only 20 percent of households fit that norm.[16] Nelson concluded that marriage was "increasingly becoming a choice rather than an imperative."[17]

Throughout the two eras examined here, social change movements contributed to a sense of unrest that delegates felt most keenly on the personal level, although that unrest mirrored tensions in the church and within the larger U.S. society. In the 1910s, MECS delegates expressed a sense of personal disorientation by lamenting the loss of clearly defined racial relationships, even ties of affection, between slaves and their masters, an example of the hysteresis effect that Bourdieu describes. In the Civil Rights movement of the 1950s and 1960s, individual Methodists experienced racial tension as schools, neighborhoods, and businesses were desegregated. Feminism also played out at the personal level, with the principal argument made against ordaining women in the 1920s being preservation of their roles as wives and mothers. These concerns persisted into the 1950s as Methodist Church (MC) delegates considered restricting full clergy rights to single women and widows. The sexual changes in the 1960s, and particularly the gay rights movement that arose in the 1970s, prompted The United Methodist Church (UMC) and other churches to define monogamous heterosexual marriage as the only appropriate site for sex. Just as personal relationships were the locus of much stress, some people saw them as the place where attitudes could be altered, as did the southern women discussed at the beginning of this chapter.

15. Nelson, *Embodiment*, 130–31.

16. "Households and Families" 2010 U.S. Census Brief. http://www.census .gov/prod/cen2010/briefs/c2010br-14.pdf.

17. Nelson, *Embodiment*, 131.

Throughout these changes, many Christians felt that the church's influence was waning. The UMC bishops expressed that concern in their 1972 Episcopal Address when they warned of the church's irrelevance in the face of scientific progress, and urged the church to make clear its moral standards, in order to remain relevant in a changing world. Mark Jordan identifies such feelings regarding the sexual changes in the 1960s when he notes that the "Sexual Revolution" was not an ethical dilemma for the church as much as its loss of authority to regulate and even define sexual acts and identities, a role taken over by secular bureaucracies.[18] Feelings of change that people experienced in their personal lives were compounded by a sense that the institutional church was losing moral influence in the larger society.

Although a sense of instability related to change is understandable, Beverly Harrison echoes Bourdieu when she writes that society comes apart not because of change, but because people "keep insisting that something is 'natural' or 'inevitable' or 'desirable' well past the point when what is done is any longer humanly tolerable, much less wise."[19] Methodism's conflicts over leadership by African Americans, women, and gays and lesbians illustrate this resistance, as many expressed pain and fear associated with losing social structures and relationships that defined life as they knew it. Changes to leadership positions carried both practical and symbolic significance, as people clung to familiar structures against a tide of change. Conflict ensued as others affirmed the need to keep up with changing times, and as these voices multiplied, change did occur, in the cases of race and gender, proving Bourdieu's point that despite the durability of social structures, they continually evolve.

Similar Patterns

In addition to the context of social change, the three issues considered here share other similarities. One similarity is that, while some delegates saw social changes as beneficial to the church as well as society, others portrayed change as a loss of something vital. In arguing for a segregated MC, MECS delegates lamented the loss of southern ways, including racial segregation, which their denomination embodied. On the brink of merging with the MEC and MPC, delegates claimed that the unification plan did not "offer

18. Jordan, *Ethics of Sex*, 133.

19. Harrison, "Sexism," 196.

the protection to Southern Methodism" that previous plans had[20] and urged preservation of the "peculiar genius of our Southern institutions."[21] Abolition had brought radical changes to southern economic and social life, but Jim Crow laws had maintained racial segregation in most institutions and social spaces. In the 1910s, the white membership of the MECS resisted the loss of a religious space that was similarly segregated. They also expressed fear that their smaller denomination, along with its distinctive values, programs, and priorities, would be swallowed up by the larger MEC.

MEC delegates debating women's ordination in the 1920s were similarly concerned about the loss of traditional family structures and gender roles. The repeated calls for women to retain the high calling of motherhood served to protect the idealized Victorian middle-class family, tended by a pious wife and mother who was content to remain in that sphere. As currents in the larger society threatened that ideal, delegates urged the church to maintain traditional patterns, with men in charge of both church and home.

UMC delegates who sought to restrict ordination of gays and lesbians most often cited a loss of clear moral values and urged the church to speak definitively on this issue, which challenged traditional notions of sexuality, as well as family structures. For many of them, accommodation of homosexual practice represented the church's capitulation to the immorality of the times. Seeking stability in the church against an uncertain world, one delegate said, "It is very necessary that in a mobile, changing world, such as we now experience, that standards be stated and observed."[22] Delegates made repeated references to moral standards and the requirement that clergy commit themselves to the "highest ideals of the Christian life."[23]

In addition to fearing their own loss of something valuable, opponents of change in all three cases also proposed benefits for the dominated group. In a segregated church, MECS delegates argued, less developed African Americans would benefit from having leadership over their own race, which would grant them the experience that might someday qualify them for leadership over whites. MECS delegates understood it as their Christian duty—their "sacred obligation"—to care for their "brothers in black," continuing the paternalistic relationship that existed between the MECS

20. Bell, *MECS DCA* 1938, 7.

21. Smith, *MECS DCA* 1918, 100–101.

22. Fannin, *UMC DCA* 1984, 642.

23. Quick, *UMC DCA* 1984, 631.

and the Colored Methodist Episcopal Church (CMEC). MEC delegates who argued against ordaining women claimed to be protecting them from the public sphere and safeguarding them for the higher calling of home and motherhood. Being restricted to local ordination, they would also be spared the "limitations that an itinerant ministry must place upon anyone who enters it with honesty of purpose."[24] Having moved away from the harsh condemnation of gay men as sexual predators that prevailed at the 1972 UMC General Conference, delegates in the 1980s advocated a stance described as "love the sinner, hate the sin," which was rooted in Christian love for gays and lesbians, and a desire that they repent of their sinful behavior so they could experience the fullness of God's grace.

In each of these cases, the assumed benefit to the dominated group is part of the theological argument used to justify their exclusion from leadership, and meets the need for the dominant group to legitimate their own "good fortune" at the expense of others. As an element of the dominant group's habitus, misrecognition of their own gain favors the perpetuation of an unequal social order, and even its justification by religious beliefs and structures. Such arguments allow delegates who seek to exclude certain groups from leadership to see that exclusion as a requirement that the groups seeking leadership repress their own "worldly interests" in order to uphold God's order—a stance that is reinforced by the simultaneous implication that the challengers are selfish, worldly, and ungodly. Not only would the dominant group derive "spiritual satisfaction," but through the maintenance of divinely mandated social orders, the *dominated* group would benefit spiritually as well.

While Bourdieu points to the use of religious beliefs to reinforce and justify unequal social arrangements, Methodist delegates just as often cited practical reasons for excluding other groups from leadership. In all three cases, most explicitly regarding women's ordination, delegates cited the connectional nature of Methodism as part of the problem. Until all congregations in the denomination were ready to welcome the new group into leadership, it would be unfair to them and to those who made appointments to allow for that possibility. Both the MEC and MECS were content to segregate black Methodists from whites—the only thing at issue was the nature of that segregation. Ordination of women posed practical difficulties for families by women working outside the home, and particular problems for clergy couples. Amid the uncertainty about whether homosexuality is a

24. Taylor, *MEC DCA* 1924, 234.

conscious choice, delegates focused on sexual *practice* and the requirement of celibacy or heterosexual marriage. Even as they revealed differing beliefs about the sinful nature of a person's sexual orientation, delegates relied on the practical, tangible criterion of sexual behavior.

With all three issues, it was advocates of expanding leadership, more than resisters, who used religious rationale, often pointing to scriptures that support inclusion. Champions of women's ordination cited Joel 2 and Galatians 3, which erase gender division, and in 1938, on the brink of unification, most delegates lauded the spiritual and evangelical possibilities of a unified MC that outweighed racial difficulties. Advocating for ordination of gays and lesbians, one delegate rejected religious rationales for exclusion, saying: "In the history of our church too often Scripture and tradition have been used to oppress people," then went on to name specifically "the oppression of Blacks and the keeping of women from ordination."[25] Instead, delegates argued, Christian values mandate inclusion of all, and particularly those on the margins of society.

Underlying the resistance expressed in both theological and practical terms is the insistence that boundaries be maintained. The issue of boundaries is fundamental to each of the specific issues, but also to discussions of inclusion themselves. Southern delegates in the 1910s affirmed clear racial boundaries, to avoid any chance or appearance of "social equality." Likewise, acceptable social space for women had been clearly circumscribed, and MEC delegates in the 1920s resisted any challenges to those boundaries by the feminist movement. As discussed in chapter 4, the various boundary issues in regard to homosexuality include the breach of acceptable moral boundaries, the perversion of gender order when a male takes a passive role, and the violation of body boundaries in the male same-sex act itself, which only heightens restrictions some Christians impose on any sexual behavior.

Contests over bodily boundaries can be projected externally as threats against one's own group, thus some experience homosexuality as a danger to heterosexual marriage. In theorizing a "culture war" between liberals and conservatives in this country, James Hunter writes that few issues generate more anxiety than homosexuality.

> The reason is plain: few other issues challenge the traditional
> assumptions of what nature will allow, the boundaries of the
> moral order, and finally the ideals of middle-class family life more

25. McIntosh, *UMC DCA* 1984, 737.

radically. Homosexuality symbolizes either an absolute and fundamental perversion of nature, of the social order, and of American family life, or it is simply another way in which nature can evolve and be expressed, another way of ordering society, and an alternative way of conducting family life.[26]

Methodists made essentially the same arguments about changing roles for women and African Americans in the 1910s and 1920s. Both groups had detractors who defended traditional roles; however, whereas some delegates affirmed women's changing roles as a natural progression, MECS delegates agreed that racial equality remained a distant prospect, while a few argued that merging with the MEC represented a step in that direction.

Conflicts over authority are contests about boundaries. Religious and social change may redefine who is "in" a group and who is not, as well as who qualifies for leadership. Symbolic systems define the boundaries of a particular group, and religious rituals consecrate those boundaries as well as setting apart certain persons for priestly functions that allow them to both set and transgress boundaries. Methodist ordination is closely guarded not only for its symbolic and ritual power, but for its legislative role as well, and it is only effective if recognized and accepted by all group members. Methodist delegates who expressed resistance to ordaining women and gays and lesbians represented one or more of the following: 1) those who refused to consecrate certain groups for moral or theological reasons; 2) those whose own interest would be weakened by expanding ordination criteria; and 3) those seeking stability in the midst of a larger sense of social disorder caused by shifting boundaries.[27] Even though problematic, boundaries are a necessary part of self-definition for any group—at issue in these discussions is whether the boundaries circumscribing acceptable leadership could be moved and, if so, how far.

The loosening of boundaries results in a sense of threat to both individual and group identity, and each of the issues discussed here raised a complex of anxieties. Black Methodist clergy represented a threat to white clergy and congregations, in part because of the stereotypes of sexualized black men as threats to white women, and sexualized black women as threats to white marriage. Women seeking ordination posed a threat to

26. Hunter, *Culture Wars*, 189.

27. No delegates expressed the second of these viewpoints and most would claim the first as their true motivation. While many were indeed acting out of religious impulses, my analysis understands this to be, at least in part, the use of religion to legitimate hidden, misrecognized interest.

either replace male clergy or feminize their profession. Gay men threatened manliness and family order. James Nelson sees the church's current tensions over homosexuality as a catch-all for other fears that "functions symbolically as a carrier of meanings and issues far beyond itself. It is a funnel into which are poured a host of disparate anxieties about authority, about increasing cultural diversity, about perceived threats to personal security."[28]

Religious conservatives' concern for social order is often manifest in efforts to control issues of the body and sexuality through such issues as abortion, same-sex marriage, and sex outside of marriage. Conservative members of the UMC reflected such a desire for control over the bodies of those who are racially or sexually "other." Nelson, Harrison, Mark Jordan, and other scholars confront such notions by exploring our inescapable embodiment as a source of pleasure and blessing rather than curse, and as the very site of spiritual connection to each other and our communion with God.

These assertions are made in the face of centuries of alienation between human embodiment and spirituality. All three groups in question have historically been constructed as contrary to the rational, transcendent male by their association with embodied, sexual, and sinful nature. African Americans were depicted as hypersexual, even animalistic, and their portrayal by MECS delegates as morally deficient echoes such claims. The idealization of the Victorian woman lay like a veneer over centuries of associating women with Eve and her responsibility for humanity's fall into sin, an act captured in original sin's link with concupiscence, or sexual desire that detracts from our spiritual nature. As noted, the sinful nature of same-sex sexual behavior was directly asserted as evidence that gays and lesbians are unfit for religious leadership.

The bodily nature of all three issues discussed here not only reveals Christianity's ongoing discomfort with sexuality, but it also illustrates the embodied nature of habitus, through which the entire history of power relations that shaped the church continue to shape future generations. Changing relationships based on race, gender, or sexuality run counter to the habitus that each person holds in his or her own body. Resistance rests at a deep, somatized level beyond our conscious awareness.

In Western culture, these power relations and the boundaries that preserve them are codified in a system of dualisms that underlie social and

28. Nelson, *Body Theology*, 17.

religious meaning. Specifically, the distinctions just noted that separate the three groups from white straight men are captured in a sexist dualism that privileges men over women, a spiritual dualism that privileges spirit and mind over body, and a dualism of white/light, over black/dark that imposes its order on races. This dualistic mode of thinking frames the oppositional "us versus them" posture that is evident in these discussions and in the maintenance of boundaries that delineate insiders and outsiders. Especially in discussions of homosexuality, some Methodists insist on delineation between good and evil and defend the need for clearly defined relationships and morals in a complex and changing world. Others recognize that life rarely falls into such sharp binaries, nor people into rigid categories, but that race and sexuality are more complex. For these Methodists, the church must dismantle oppressive policies and practices and reflect new understandings of human society and relationships. The Methodist debates themselves do not fall neatly into two camps, but many are uncertain as to what course the church should follow, and may find themselves supporting one perspective to an extent, without giving their wholehearted assent.

Whatever the motivation, these issues represent struggles for control not only of Methodist leadership but also of the defining worldview that the church offers its members and reflects to the outside world. This function leads us back to Bourdieu's central argument that contests for power are prompted by the capital that various groups possess and want to keep, or do not possess and wish to accrue, by maintaining or changing the prevailing *habitus*. He writes that what is at stake in contests for religious power is to control the worldview of the church membership, or their religious *habitus*, which will dispose them "to act and think in conformity with the principles of a (quasi-) systematic view of the world and human existence."[29] In reading these Methodist transcripts, such struggles for power remain hidden for the most part, but come into plain view more often than one might expect.

Religion is a symbolic system steeped in power relations that are codified in rigid boundaries defining individual and group identity; preserving or dismantling those relations is at issue in these conversations. Although often framed in rational terms, the conflict both within and among Christians is a visceral one that largely eludes conscious, rational expression. Karen Brown notes that the fundamental question is who we are as human beings: "Are we cerebral masters of our environment, or are we embodied

29. Bourdieu, "Legitimation," 126.

creatures enmeshed within it?"[30] What these three issues ultimately share is the ability to raise both strong resistance and equally strong support for changing authority structures, leading to open conflict that may or may not articulate all the underlying factors from which those feelings sprang. Using Brown, Bourdieu, and others, scholarship can help describe and understand the fundamental nature of these conflicts in the hope of exposing their constructed nature and defusing their power over us, but Bourdieu's discussion about how deeply such tensions lie suggests that we may never be able to fully embrace and understand them.

Distinct Dynamics

Despite the similar dynamics and underlying meaning systems of these three issues, there are striking differences as well, most obviously the character of the dominated group and the nature of resistance aimed at them. Racial tensions in the United States rest in part on the fact that African Americans were the only immigrant group that was forcibly removed from their homeland, separated from all that was familiar, and subjected to the brutalities of slavery and continuing oppression after abolition. As discussed in chapter 2, neither the dominant nor dominated group could fail to recognize such an overt and often violent form of domination, in which whites, and particularly slave owners, enjoyed clear social and economic benefits, although the collective habitus over time brought a sense of normalization and the recognition of slavery and segregation as "the way things are." Despite overt challenges and changes in laws and institutional structures, white dominance persists in the United States, and whiteness is perceived by many as normative, thus, whites are less racialized than other ethnic groups are.

White southerners in the early decades of the twentieth century were a generation or two away from institutional slavery, which still shaped their meaning systems and their social and economic structures, and thus their habitus. Strict segregation and continued violence in the form of lynchings served to enforce white dominance and quash black resistance. No other group considered here was as thoroughly demeaned, with the entire black race portrayed as being intellectually, spiritually, and socially inferior, or as one white delegate described them, "two thousand years behind us in the

---

30. Brown, "Fundamentalism," 186.

achievements of civilization."[31] Racial division marked not only American society, but also the American Christian church, including Methodism. This division allowed MECS delegates to deny African Americans leadership in the larger, predominately white denomination, deeming them better suited to leadership in all-black churches.

By contrast, women were not degraded but lauded, when they fulfilled their expected roles as wives and mothers and remained within their circumscribed realm of the home. Methodist women such as Frances Willard, Anna Howard Shaw, and Madeline Southard proved women's capacity for leadership outside the home as well, through their involvement in the national women's movement, their own mission organizations, and the temperance movement. As a result, few delegates challenged their fitness for leadership, but instead claimed for decades that the church was not ready to accept them as ordained clergy.

Male domination of women goes unrecognized by both sexes, to some degree. While the benefits to men are obvious, even some women feel a sense of comfort and security with men in control, since they have been socialized into a subordinate role. Bourdieu points to visible evidence of women's complicity, and even preference, for male dominance in the fact that many women still today are attracted to men who are older and taller than they are, to the extent that *they* feel diminished if they are with shorter, or "diminished" men.[32] The first discussions of Methodist women's leadership occurred during the earliest wave of feminism, when such contours of male domination were just beginning to be exposed.

Statistically, women are not a minority group, and within most churches, including Methodism, they have historically accounted for a sizable majority of the membership, yet many have seemed content to be excluded from ordained leadership. The cause of women's ordination posed no threat of a divided church, in part, perhaps, because of women's acquiescence to their subordinated role, but also because of the impractical nature of a church divided along gender lines. Some women, such as Anna Howard Shaw, left the MEC for denominations that allowed their ordination, and over the time period surveyed here, increasing numbers of women challenged their ecclesial domination and sought full clergy rights. Yet as late as 1956, women still argued against that step, while theologian

31. Prettyman, *MECS DCA 1918*, 98.
32. Bourdieu, *Masculine Domination*, 35.

and feminist Georgia Harkness and others recognized that men held the power to effect change.

Perhaps the most obvious difference between homosexuality and the other two issues is the outward ease with which it can be concealed. While racial mixing has resulted in persons who identify as black, but whose skin is light enough to "pass" as white, and transgender persons may live counter to their biological sex, most people cannot, or do not, disguise their race or sex. A person's race and sex are therefore an inescapable and recognizable element of their social location and interaction with others. Historically though, many, if not most, gays and lesbians in western culture have lived closeted lives, under the strength of the heterosexual norm—a form of symbolic violence in which gays and lesbians accept the stigma that culture assigns to their sexual orientation. As discussed in chapter 4, this issue has a shorter history of open debate than the other two, in large part because gays and lesbians remained an invisible minority for much of Christian history.

Concealment produces internal dissonance to the extent that it threatens mental and emotional health, and prompts some to consider or even commit suicide. Because gays and lesbians are products of a heterosexist habitus, they have been socialized to "act straight." Just as gays in the U.S military during its period of "don't ask, don't tell" learned how to "pass" as straight, the UMC's similar posture has led many to practice a similar concealment and silence, in order to serve as ordained clergy. This arrangement has a trade-off to the internal tension it creates, since concealment allows for the accumulation of social and religious capital, especially among white men who are privileged by gender and race. Because concealment allows access to power, some reject the comparison of gay rights to other liberation movements, most notably the Civil Rights movement, where African Americans had no such opportunity to conceal their race in order to gain power.

The UMC discussions mirror debates in the larger society about the degree to which homosexuality is a conscious choice, and many conservatives now accede to the idea that one does not choose a sexual orientation or attraction. Framing their argument as a condemnation of one's lifestyle rather than the person, they insist that ordination can only be granted to gays and lesbians who choose not to act on their same-sex attraction. The moral status of gays and lesbians in the UMC treads a middle line between the degradation of African Americans and the voiced admiration for women—they are granted "sacred worth," yet they are required to deny their sexual desire in order to be ordained, forcing a split between sexual identity and behavior.

Many feel that this issue may divide the church, as it is split along racial lines. Rather than a fissure between gay Christians and heterosexuals, this division would be along lines of acceptance. The predominately gay Metropolitan Community Church is the most visible example of a denomination that was born out of the exclusion that gay Christians have experienced. Within Methodism, lines of acceptance are already drawn at the local level, as individuals, congregations, and other communities have declared their acceptance and affirmation of gay and lesbian Christians by affiliating with the Reconciling Ministries Network. The Transforming Congregations program also functions at the local level to offer healing from sexual sin, which they extend to homosexuality.

The tone of the rhetoric against homosexuality reflects a resolve and insistence that the church's condemnation of same-sex practice must be clear and total. Delegates have consistently voted down any attempts to remove restrictive language, as well as amendments that would admit the church's division on the issue. In addressing race and gender, delegates allowed for the possibility of change in the future. MECS delegates talked of helping African Americans to become more developed, allowing for the possibility that they would at some future point be qualified for leadership. Even in the 1920s, most delegates acknowledged women's fitness for ministry, while claiming that "the time was not ripe" for their leadership. No such allowance has been made regarding same-sex behavior. The strength of the opposition indicates that what is at stake for many United Methodists is not just the unity of the church, but its fidelity to Christian ideals and standards in a time of competing moralities. In the UMC debates examined here, delegates insisted that the pluralistic times be met with a clear and unapologetic Christian moral vision.

As Bourdieu and others have pointed out, power relations are embedded in language, which, like religion, is a symbolic system that is both structured and structuring. The language used to describe each group seeking leadership served to convey and shape their positions relative to the dominant group, and to identify the posture of those engaged in debate. The discussions of race used the common parlance of the time, referring to African Americans as "Negroes" or as "colored persons." More telling are singular references to "the Negro" or "the brother in black," abstractions that reduced African Americans to a common identity, ignoring individual differences.

Similarly, the 1972 UMC discussions used objectifying language of "the homosexual." By the 1980s, however, such references were largely dropped, signaling the changed approach of rejecting behavior rather than persons. Those who supported ordination of gays and lesbians avoided abstraction by using "homosexual" only as an adjective, using instead the less derogatory noun forms of "gays," or "gay men" and "lesbians." While dropping singular references, opponents of gay rights continued to use the plural form, casting "practicing homosexuals" as outside the circle of faithful Christians who could be considered for ordained leadership.

Interestingly, no such abstraction or objectification is evident in references to women, as very few delegates made singular references to "the woman." This may reflect the social distance that the mostly white, heterosexual delegates had from African Americans and from openly gay men and lesbians, as compared to their distance from women. Given the intimacy of family structures, all of the delegates would have known and loved individual women as their mothers, wives, sisters, etc.; therefore, it was more difficult to objectify them or to portray them as morally unfit for leadership. Because of racial segregation, few white delegates in the early twentieth century would have been personally acquainted with African Americans as social equals. Likewise the heterosexist norm greatly reduced the possibility that delegates, especially in the 1970s or 1980s, would encounter openly gay persons. Delegates' social distance from these two groups made it easier to pass judgment and codify that distance in church structures. Studies suggest that personal acquaintance with members of dominated groups and the opportunity to experience them as religious leaders contribute to their acceptance,[33] thus the continued distancing of African Americans and of gays and lesbians is self-reinforcing.

Social distance allowed for blackness and homosexuality to be construed as forms of deviance, whereas no such characterization of women was expressed. Race was clearly not under a person's control, and so African Americans' deviance from the racial "norm" of whiteness took the form of an illness or defect. Some delegates described homosexuality in similar terms, and opponents of their ordination insisted that homosexual

33. This is noted by Ruth Wallace in her study of laywomen serving Catholic parishes, (*They Call Her Pastor*, 165) and by Thomas and Olson's look at evangelicals' changing views on homosexuality ("Evangelical Elites," 266).

behavior took the more serious form of sin, a deviance from social values and norms that threatened the wellbeing of the collective. Such sinners could only be restored to wholeness through confession and repentance of their sinful actions, which would also allow their restoration to the group.

Overlapping Patterns of Domination

The issues examined here not only share differences and similarities, but they overlap in several ways. The most obvious overlap is chronological, although delegates tended to avoid dealing with more than one issue at a time. The MECS first allowed women as delegates in the 1920s, overlapping with their conversations about race. At the time of the 1939 merger to form the MC, however, the southern church did not yet grant women any clergy rights. When the MEC discussed women's ordination in the 1920s, some delegates pointed to reunification as a reason to delay granting them that right, fearing resistance from the southern church. Although women in the MC gained full clergy rights in 1956, they did not enter ordained ministry in large numbers until the feminist movement of the 1970s, overlapping with the gay rights movement. Rooted in the same dualisms that privilege rationalized men, gay rights may have compounded the sense that white, heterosexual men were being pushed aside.

In her article "Misogyny and Homophobia: The Unexplored Connections," Beverly Harrison directly addresses the common sexual and economic sources of these two issues. She roots both in a patriarchal ideology that is rational and disembodied, and that springs from a Christian theology that degrades the body. She uses the potent terminology of "misogyny" and "homophobia," claiming that they are forms of hatred and anger that emerge from an ideology of control and that also have economic and political roots. It is no accident, she writes, that by seeking full humanity, the two groups have become scapegoats who are blamed for "destroying traditional values," when what is really eroding morals is "a political-economic system which makes every human consideration except the maximization of profit irrelevant."[34] Gays and lesbians, women, and African Americans are discredited when they seek social justice that would involve a redistribution of economic resources, as well as social and political influence. What is

---

34. Harrison, "Misogyny," 10.

needed, Harrison writes, is an adequate sexual ethic to replace outdated values that have "sacralized unjust power relations."[35]

Cornel West also links these issues to economic inequality within U.S. capitalism,[36] as well as to white cultural conservatism that seeks to control social order by degrading the bodies of those construed as "other."[37] This "othering" takes the form of distinction from rational men, as noted above, where the groups may be cast as sexualized beings who are more like animals or exotic savages. When two or more of these identities are combined, the effect is heightened, leading to their further marginalization.

We also find these groups marginalizing each other. Multi-racial churches may be less willing to accept women's leadership,[38] while some have noted the discrimination against gays and lesbians in some black churches. Theories on the causes of black sexism and black heterosexism range from the human tendency to scapegoat the most vulnerable and degrade those who are different,[39] to black men's lack of self-love, itself a product of society's deep racism.[40]

Kelly Brown Douglas attributes black heterosexism to several influences that coalesce as a "perfect storm" of factors. First is resistance within the black community to equating gay rights with Civil Rights, and especially with slavery. Although some Civil Rights leaders have worked for gay and lesbian rights, including James Lawson in the UMC, others feel that the comparison amounts to "pimping" the Civil Rights movement for the sake of gays and lesbians, whose oppression is not comparable to what African Americans have endured. Douglas also writes that, in response to attacks on their own sexuality and on black families, blacks have adopted a "hyper-proper sexuality" and the norm of a male-centered family, which are based on white heterosexist patriarchy.[41] Finally, she notes, black condemnation of same-sex behavior may spring from respect for biblical authority and a hermeneutic of struggle that emphasizes right conduct, along with a Platonized rejection of the body that crept into black Christianity during

---

35. Ibid., 11.
36. West, "Christian Love," 407.
37. West, *Race Matters*.
38. Yancey and Kim, "Racial Diversity," 108.
39. West, "Christian Love," 402, 405.
40. Hopkins, "Toward a Positive," 579.
41. Douglas, "Heterosexism," 190.

eighteenth-century revivals.[42] Both racism and heterosexism, she writes, involve one group denying the humanity of another.[43]

A notable example of one marginalized group charging another with discrimination is the body of womanist writings that some black women have produced in response to the white focus of mainstream feminism. The term "womanist" was coined by Alice Walker to describe "a black feminist or feminist of color," with a second part of Walker's definition being "a woman who loves other women, sexually and/or nonsexually."[44] Womanists start with the distinctive history of black women who were raped and reduced to the status of breeders during slavery, noting not only their abuse by white men, but by white women and black men who vented their own experiences of being dominated by in turn dominating black women.[45] The dual themes of racism and sexism have run throughout black women's history and served as a linchpin between the social movements for black rights and for women's rights.[46]

Notably, black women were the perfect foil for white Victorian women, who were viewed as the apex of virtue. The two groups were depicted as opposites, with white women seen as delicate, pale, and asexual, and black women as strong, dark, and sexually active. Douglas claims that black women were even blamed for black men's sexual depravity that was thought to endanger white women, since black women lacked sufficient virtue to instill it in their sons.[47] Black women continue to be demeaned or ignored by men of both races and by white women, and when the rights of one dominated group compete with another, black women are generally left out. As the title of one book claims, *All the Women Are White, All the Blacks Are Men, but Some of Us Are Brave.*[48] Womanists bring to light the distinctive history of black women's domination in society and in the church. While at least one black female delegate is identified in General Conference minutes,[49] their story as a doubly discriminated group is largely absent from the Methodist records examined here.

42. Ibid., 194–95.
43. Ibid., 198.
44. Walker, "Preface," xi–xii.
45. Williams, "The Color of Feminism," 52.
46. Giddings, *When and Where*, 6.
47. Douglas, "Daring to Speak," 239.
48. Hull, et al., *All the Women are White*, 1982.
49. Moorer, *MEC DCA* 1920, 565.

Even more invisible are black lesbians, who fault even womanists for neglecting their situation as a triply marginalized group. While womanism offers black women a context for defining their experience and forging new theologies, the lesbian voice is often silenced even within womanism, despite Walker's inclusion of women who love "other women, sexually and/or nonsexually." Black lesbians are at the bottom of every dualism involved in constructing traditional ethics of race, gender, and sexuality, and the racist strain in feminism and the sexist and heterosexist strains in black communities serve to exclude black lesbians at every turn. Using Zora Neale Hurston's line that black women are the "mule of the world," Douglas notes that even they may join black men in "seizing heterosexual privilege."[50]

The various forms of discrimination examined here form an intricate web of struggles for power and inclusion. Once admitted as General Conference delegates, African Americans and women did not always support the cause of other marginalized groups, as when the sole black delegate to speak to women's admission as lay delegates in 1888 opposed the move. While members of one group may seek their own advantage at the expense of another, the common foe is an ideology of white heterosexual male privilege, and a Christian theology that legitimates their dominance. While I could not always identify the race or even the gender of some delegates, what was obvious in transcripts throughout the years I surveyed was the continued dominance of white, male, presumably heterosexual clergy.

Bourdieu is helpful in looking at the various groups in relation to their field positions and accumulation of capital. The dualisms that serve to degrade, or at least to dis-empower, certain groups define positions within the various fields they inhabit. Because of the homologous nature of fields, the religious field, like the larger society, affords more symbolic capital to white heterosexual men. In subfields where these men are absent, other characteristics produce symbolic capital, for example maleness in black churches, whiteness in women's movements, and heterosexuality in both. Even those who fight against their own domination in one field may unwittingly dominate others in a different field. Bourdieu's understanding of *collusio* as a type of collective habitus explains how one group may discriminate against another group through no conscious intention, but simply as the accumulated practice of that group acting in its own best interest.

Bourdieu himself comes up short by posing a dichotomous model of dominant/dominated to consider these overlapping and multiple forms

50. Douglas, "Daring to Speak," 242–43.

of discrimination. Even as he critiques such binary opposition, Bourdieu perpetuates it, just as one marginalized group tends to focus on its own experience of subjugation and thus perpetuate discrimination of another "out-group." Methodist delegates occasionally compared the church's historic exclusion of one group to whatever issue was under debate, while others argued the uniqueness of a particular form of exclusion. Despite modern liberation movements, resistance remains strong to leadership that does not conform to the white heterosexual male norm. This resistance is shaped by a habitus that not only affirms that leadership norm, but also discredits other groups as being less rational and morally debased.

Implications for The United Methodist Church

With its representative General Conference, American Methodism resembles a democracy more than the hierarchical Roman Catholic Church that Bourdieu describes. His theories, however, are equally applicable, as differentiated groups and agents compete for their own interests. Although Methodism is sometimes described as a hierarchical denomination because of its chain of bishops and district superintendents, those leaders' power lies in appointing clergy, whereas the power to change policy and structures resides with the quadrennial General Conference.

The General Conference process is messy, inefficient, and often painful, and the diversity of viewpoints is evident in the political nature of the legislative process and the proliferation of caucus groups. The four-year span between meetings, the disparate voices within the church, and the tendency to defer to resistant members mean that the church often lags behind the society in accepting and accommodating change.

At the same time, UMC General Conferences, like other denominational assemblies, can facilitate the negotiation of difference by providing space for diverse opinions to be expressed, an orderly process for seeking resolution, and common ground as the context for debate.[51] This historical look at some of the most painful chapters in American Methodism suggests that conflicts may not be resolved for decades, and even after institutional change occurs, division and anger may linger at the personal level.

The 2012 General Conference, however, offered signs that change could happen sooner rather than later. In addition to its continuing

51. Wood and Bloch, "The Role," 124.

stalemate on the issue of sexual orientation, General Conference failed to pass two different plans that would have restructured the denomination for more effective and efficient ministry, given the decline in U.S. membership, increased growth in Africa, and the mounting costs of being a global denomination. A last-minute alternative, called Plan UMC, was passed after much discussion, but on the final day of the gathering, the Judicial Council found it to be unconstitutional. Guaranteed appointments for clergy, which women had secured in 1956, were eliminated as part of the Consent Calendar on recommendation from committee, with no plenary discussion, although that move would later be overturned by a Judicial Council ruling as well. Delegates were not out of Tampa before they were calling this the "do-nothing General Conference," and advocates of change, especially, felt as if they had moved backward rather than forward.

While there may have been little progress in terms of legislation, the 2012 General Conference saw an overt critique of white male heterosexual dominance that prophetic movements over the past century had been challenging in piecemeal fashion. The church's commissions that deal with race and gender, which were both headed by black women, monitored General Conference proceedings to see whose voices and interests were most prevalent. Monitoring teams made daily reports in plenary sessions and in the *Daily Christian Advocate* (DCA) newspaper about issues of power and privilege they observed.

Monitors reported that fewer than 5 percent of delegates were under the age of thirty, and even fewer were people of color. Over the week of plenary sessions, white men from the United States dominated the discussion and were called on most frequently by bishops, even if women's hands were raised. Only one African woman delegate spoke the entire session. Monitors questioned how much bishops were steering discussion by the persons they called on to speak, specifically during the conversation on sexual orientation on May 3. The team also noted issues of white privilege, and the tendency of many delegates to label others with pejorative language, such as "those people," "colored people," or people from the "Bible belt."[52]

The monitors exposed many of the issues addressed in this book, which have remained at an unconscious level for many, especially the dominant. Recognizing the misrecognized in such a public way seemed to empower

52. From Daily Editions of the *UMC DCA* 2012, http://www.umc.org/site/c. lwL4KnN1LtH/b.8064117/k.AF6A/General_Conference_2012_Daily_Christian_Advocate_DCA.htm.

those in the minority to make their own challenges to the dominant voices. During discussion of Plan UMC, delegates who were from subordinated groups began to ask about the crafters of the plan. They asked who they were, where they were from, and if they could see them, even making specific reference to skin color. As one delegate said:

> I would really like to see who was writing this petition because I need to know . . . that they had thought about me as a young person or me as a person of color when they were writing that petition . . . because that is what we have been talking about for the past few minutes, is representation of the racial and ethnic caucuses and representation of women and representation of young people.[53]

The conversation left the presiding bishop, in his own words, "perplexed," and after consulting with other bishops, he turned aside all such questions and returned to parliamentary procedure[54]—a rational, Western type of discourse that privileges the already dominant voices. Throughout the sessions, Central Conference delegates expressed confusion about substitute motions and amendments to amendments, revealing lack of familiarity with Robert's Rules. The return to that format only heightened the difference between the dominant voices at General Conference and newer voices trying to make themselves heard.

The stark difference in a declining U.S. church and the growth overseas has made it clear to many that the current structure is unsustainable. General Conference itself is a perfect example of the difficulties faced by the church: a growing number of delegates from outside the United States presents an ever-increasing budget for travel, translation, and hospitality,[55] with the biggest share of the cost borne by a shrinking U.S. membership that faces an even sharper decline with the die-off of the Baby Boomers. A global denomination poses substantive challenges as well as practical, as delegates vote on matters with which they are unfamiliar, and last-minute legislation may not get translated, as was the case with Plan UMC, which was not available to Central Conference delegates who could not read English.

53. Lopez, *UMC DCA* 2012, 2519.

54. Watson, *UMC DCA* 2012, 2520.

55. The 2016 General Conference Commission voted to reduce the target number of delegates from 1000 to 850, a move that will save the denomination around $600,000 (Hahn, "2016 General Conference.").

The 2008 General Conference had addressed these problems with its own restructuring plan that would have designated the United States as a Regional Conference, similar to Central Conferences in other parts of the world. There was little overt acknowledgment of how these changes would affect the tensions over homosexuality, but U.S. conservatives argued successfully against the change, hoping, no doubt, to retain the votes of conservative overseas delegates in denominational policy. The question still before the church is whether it can negotiate a new regional structure that will address the larger issues facing it and accommodate internal differences over homosexuality, or whether conservatives will block any such attempts in order to keep voices and votes within one structure, and insisting that a ban on ordaining gays and lesbians be denomination-wide.

As conservatives may fear, it is likely that an independent U.S conference would approve ordination of gays and lesbians, given the greater acceptance of homosexuality within U.S. culture[56] and among General Conference delegates themselves. James Wood's survey of 1996 General Conference delegates from the United States revealed that more than half (54 percent) disagreed that homosexuality is sinful.[57] As this study has shown, previous conflicts about race and gender led eventually to inclusion of the groups under consideration.[58] Unlike that resistance, however, those who oppose ordaining gays and lesbians are absolute, allowing for no possibility of change down the road. Thus even a regional restructure could lead to schism, if conservative U.S. congregations follow the Episcopal pattern of affiliating with more conservative conferences in Africa, even at the risk of losing their property.

Between the 2012 and 2016 General Conference, tensions and talk of division ramped up and centered on same-sex marriage, given the passage of marriage equality in increasingly more states. Charges were filed against two clergy, Frank Schaefer and Tom Ogletree, who performed weddings for their gay sons. In November 2013, Schaefer was stripped of his clergy

56. Among other studies, Thomas and Olson's look at evangelical Christians' changing responses to homosexuality notes that by shifting their moral arguments away from the Bible and towards less orthodox sources such as science, medicine, and the natural order, they have opened the possibility of following the larger culture to more liberal views on the issue ("Evangelical Elites," 268–69).

57. Wood, *Where the Spirit Leads*, 85. Wood also surveyed General Conference delegates in 2004, and raw data provided by his widow reveals that a slight majority of delegates that year (52.5 percent) continued to hold that view.

58. It is notable, however, that the three African American Methodist denominations (AMEC, AMEZC, and CMEC) remain as separate denominations.

status,[59] and in March 2014, a "just resolution" was reached in Ogletree's case. Other pastors and congregations performed or hosted unions, or declared they would if asked, while some withheld apportionment dollars, vowing they would not remit these assessed funds to the denomination until church policy was revised.

In the interim between General Conferences, bishops stepped to the fore in addressing these tensions. New York Area Bishop Martin McLee, who helped resolve Ogletree's case, called for a halt to trials for pastors who perform same-sex marriages, while Bishop Grant Hagiya of the Greater Northwest Annual Conference handed down twenty-four-hour suspensions to two pastors who performed same-sex unions. Great Plains Area Bishop Scott Jones, on the other hand, preached that one hundred violations in that conference would result in an equal number of suspensions and trials. Retired Bishop Melvin Talbert performed a same-sex marriage in Alabama, against the wishes of Birmingham Area Bishop Debra Wallace-Padgett and the executive committee of the Council of Bishops. This and the statement by retired bishops calling for removal of all restrictive language regarding homosexuality[60] reveals dissent within the Council of Bishops that mirrors the division within the church.

Talbert is one of eight active and retired bishops who contributed essays to a 2014 book entitled *Finding Our Way: Love and Law in The United Methodist Church*. While Talbert calls for disobedience, and Bishop Gregory Palmer and African Bishop John Yambasu write of the need to uphold the prohibitions in the Discipline, most of the bishops strike a moderate note aimed at preserving unity, rather than achieving uniformity of belief and practice. Those voices claim that in order to find reconciliation, both sides must have the humility to accept the possibility that they could be wrong. Retired bishop Reuben Job, one of the book's editors, proposed a three-step process for the two years leading up to the 2016 General Conference: 1) stop all propaganda that judges and distances others; 2) declare a moratorium on both celebrations of and trials related to same-sex unions; and 3) enter a time of concentrated prayer and discernment that seeks reconciliation and preserves unity.[61]

The book illustrates how bishops use their symbolic capital to call for and model the search for common ground and acceptance of difference

---

59. An appeals board reinstated Schaefer's credentials in June 2014.

60. See chapter 1.

61. Job, "Trust God," 108–10.

that the church needs, giving direction to the church in the interim between General Conferences. At the same time, the book highlights how little power United Methodist bishops have to resolve conflict and effect change. While many United Methodists would resonate with this effort, those on either extreme will not be satisfied, and will continue to push for or resist change, disrupting efforts to preserve unity. The bishops can urge reconciliation, hoping that hearts and minds are opened and that delegates to the 2016 General Conference will find a way to resolve the stalemate and hold the denomination together. In the end, however, only that body can change policy and speak for the denomination, and the depth of division and influence of caucus groups makes quick resolution unlikely.

The book was released in May 2014, and before the month was over, eighty pastors and theologians posted a statement on the Good News website calling for an amicable split, a statement resulting from their own period of discernment. These religious leaders cited not just the differences around sexual orientation, but also crises of organizational discipline, authority of scripture, and discipleship, especially in the violation of covenant by those who willingly disobeyed the *Book of Discipline* and bishops who failed to hold them accountable. The Good News statement points out the reality that irreconcilable division exists throughout the church—among laity, clergy, and the Council of Bishops. They write: "Talk of a 'middle-way' or of 'agreeing to disagree' is comforting and sounds Christ-like. However, such language only denies the reality we need to admit. Neither side will find 'agreeing to disagree' acceptable."[62]

Talks of restructuring continued as well, with various plans making their way to the 2016 General Conference. While none of the contributors of *Finding Our Way* call for schism, Bishop Kenneth H. Carter, Jr. suggests in his chapter what a divided church might look like. He envisions a three-way split among progressive, evangelical, and mainstream churches. Noting the potential effect of such a division throughout the denomination, Carter calls it a "violent process" that would neither glorify God nor advance the church's stated mission to make disciples of Jesus Christ for the transformation of the world. Another possibility is creating structures that would allow for reunion after a period of separation.[63] An April 2014 cover

---

62. No authors are cited for the statement, which is entitled, "Regarding United Methodism's Future." http://goodnewsmag.org/2014/05/regarding-united-methodisms -future/

63. Carter, "Disarm," 68–69.

story in *The Christian Century* discussed restructuring options that would allow jurisdictional autonomy, or two parallel national denominations with different policies on homosexuality. Such a split would be most difficult for congregations that have managed to stay unified by building bridges among its members, the approach many of the bishops advocate.[64]

A fracture over homosexuality, rather forced by restructuring or not, along with the schisms in other denominations, may be part of a larger re-formation within Christianity—a re-formation that makes explicit the times of change that this book addresses and the resulting division within the church. Referred to as the Fourth Great Awakening[65] or the Great Emergence,[66] this transformation is likened to the Reformation of the sixteenth century or the Great Schism of 1054, but is happening gradually and globally. Harvey Cox describes it as the start of a new "Age of the Spirit," characterized by spiritual quest rather than doctrine, global reach, and a turn from patriarchy and hierarchy to leadership rooted in community.[67] Catching this wave of change within Christianity may be necessary for the UMC to survive, and can be seen as a sign of new life, rather than death or defeat.

David Hempton in fact argues that change is inherent to Methodism, which experienced dramatic growth in the nineteenth century because of its combination of zeal and organization.[68] He notes that Methodism cannot survive on institutional consolidation alone, but requires "energy, change, mobility, and flux."[69] The church has maintained momentum because its stagnation in the U.S. has been offset by its vitality and growth overseas. This may also have contributed to tensions between regions where the church is more settled and those on the charismatic edge—tensions that were heightened by theological differences.

The global nature of the church can bring a Wesleyan renewal that provides both structural and theological grounding. Hendrik Pieterse points out that a recovery of connectionalism understood theologically, rather than as the bureaucratic structure of the church, can bring new life to the UMC. United Methodists who are preoccupied with tensions between the U.S. church versus those of the rest of the world have fallen prey to

64. Frykholm, "A Time to Split," 25.
65. Bass, *Christianity after Religion*.
66. Tickle, *Great Emergence*.
67. Cox, *Future of Faith*, 223.
68. Hempton, *Methodism*, 153.
69. Ibid., 200.

center-periphery, or "us-them," thinking, which affects much of Western Christendom.[70] Instead Pieterse recommends theological reflection using Methodist historian Russell Richey's understanding of connectionalism with three characteristics that could lead to a more authentic Methodist identity as a church that: 1) is a single whole with internal relationships that are radically mutual; 2) sees boundaries as gift not as threat; and 3) engages theology as practice.[71] Pieterse and Richey both emphasize the role of the Holy Spirit in opening the church to change and new direction,[72] thus the spiritual renewal that Cox and others describe are consistent with Wesleyan theology.

This Christian change movement is most evident in the UMC in its growth overseas, especially in Africa, but the loss of young people in the U.S. church suggests that it has not capitalized on other aspects of the movement. The UMC does not keep membership numbers by age group, but the average age of its members is fifty-seven, compared to the average age of the U.S. population at thirty-five. In addition, only 6 percent of UMC clergy are under the age of thirty-five,[73] another sign that the church's survival depends on gaining and retaining young people. As a young delegate pointed out at the 2012 General Conference, 91 percent of young people outside the Christian church find it anti-homosexual and 87 percent find it judgmental.[74] The church's position on sexual orientation and its resolution of the issue are key to attracting young people, and therefore to its survival.

The inevitable backlash to the change movement within Christianity takes the form of a reassertion of orthodoxy—a defense of the status quo. Indeed, if we are in the midst of a religious transformation on the scale of the Reformation, the resistance of those who value tradition is normal and to be expected. Changes in leadership are accompanied by changes in worship style, spiritual experience, and the very definition of who is a Christian.

70. Pieterse, "Worldwide," 4–7.

71. Ibid., 14–19.

72. Ibid., 22–23.

73. According a 2013 report "Clergy Age Trends in The United Methodist Church," issued by the Lewis Center for Church Leadership at Wesley Theological Seminary, 5.91 percent of ordained elders in the UMC are under age thirty-five, which continues a slight growing trend from a low of 4.61 percent in 2005. The percentage of young ordained deacons is higher, standing at 9.15 percent in 2013, although the total number in this recently formed category of ministry is still comparatively small.

74. Swenson, 2012 UMC DCA, 2710. Barna Group statistics (Kinnamon and Lyons, UnChristian, 34).

Cox claims an end to the Age of Belief, in which church membership has relied on assenting to correct doctrine, and the beginning of an Age of the Spirit rooted in spiritual experience and discipleship.[75] Boundaries that were once firm are now shifting and porous, prompting the response that those boundaries are fixed by God and immovable, the same pattern we see as any religious habitus undergoes challenge and is exposed as an arbitrary human construction.

Of the changes that Methodists have faced in the past century, the current situation may be the most significant, with financial and membership pressures within, and influences from a larger Christian change movement afoot. The church may be closer to schism than at any time since 1844, yet remaining intact without a restructuring plan could be more costly. Institutional conflicts over race and gender took decades to resolve, and in both cases only happened after a generation or two died off. If the UMC waits for the impending die-off of the Baby Boom generation, it could find its greatest membership located outside the United States, and without the theological reflection that Pieterse recommends, many may find this a unwelcome change.

Implication for U.S. Society

Despite its decline in U.S. membership, the UMC remains one of the largest Protestant denominations in the country, second only to the Southern Baptist Convention. Unlike the SBC, which is predominantly conservative, the UMC continues to embrace conservative, liberal, and moderate forces. While diversity in the UMC is the root of its ongoing tensions, it also mirrors the composition of the country; therefore, an analysis of these tensions can have application beyond the denomination.

While some rush to describe opposite poles in a "culture war" on these and other issues, such a depiction runs the risk of ignoring or underestimating those in the middle. For example, James Wood's surveys of General Conference delegates and their view on homosexuality offered the options of conservative, very conservative, liberal, and very liberal, thereby forcing true moderates into one of two opposing camps. Even so, only 3 percent considered themselves very conservative and only 4 percent very liberal,[76] suggesting a large "moderate middle."

75. Cox, *Future of Faith*, 8.
76. Wood, *Where the Spirit Leads*, 88.

In surveying leaders in six Protestant denominations, Daniel Olson and William McKinney[77] looked for evidence of this liberal/conservative divide and found a much more nuanced situation. In plotting their responses, they found that 73 percent of United Methodists did not fall into either opposing camp, and they classified the largest group (33 percent) as centrist—the rest being independents (24 percent) or bipartisans (16 percent). A 2008 survey by Public Religion Research asked mainline Protestant clergy about their political ideology and found the UMC to be the most evenly split. Whereas most denominations tilt either right or left of center, United Methodists were balanced at the polar ends, with 38 percent liberal, 39 percent conservative, and a sizable group of moderates (23 percent).[78] Methodists have often been seen as a reflection of the American mainstream and a centrist denomination that represents the American middle class.

The large Methodist denominations that are studied here may reflect the larger U.S. society (or their region, in the case of the MECS), as much as any privatized religious group can mirror a larger culture. This historical examination demonstrates how polarizing issues around race and gender became mainstream within this mainstream denomination. Although racism and sexism still exist in the United States and in American Methodism, public rhetoric and policy in the church and the country reject both as unacceptable forms of discrimination. The church's conflicts over ordination of gays and lesbians and same-sex unions mirror the larger public debate about gay marriage—a debate that is framed as a defense of traditional family values and norms. Thus the struggles of American Methodists over sexual orientation may be instructive for the nation as a whole, as it wrestles with the same tensions, while this historic look at race and gender can demonstrate how an acceptable position was finally attained.

It is interesting to note that, unlike the larger society, American Methodism has largely avoided divisive battles over abortion. The UMC Social Principles affirm the availability of a safe legal procedure under certain conditions, rejecting abortion on demand or for birth control or gender selection, a compromise position that captures the sentiment of the moderate Methodist center. This research would suggest that consensus on abortion

77. Olson and McKinney, "United Methodist Leaders."

78. *Clergy Voices: Findings from the 2008 Mainline Protestant Clergy Voices Survey*, 12. http://publicreligion.org/site/wp-content/uploads/2011/06/2008-Mainline-Protestant-Clergy-Voices-Survey-Report.pdf.

was arrived at more easily than other issues because, like divorce, abortion does not involve issues of leadership or threaten the interest of white male heterosexual clergy. Also, while the UMC may advocate a particular position, the legality of abortion rests with government, whereas ordination and the blessing of same-sex unions lie within the church's power. However, legalized abortion, dating to 1973, was seen as part of the sexual permissiveness and changing moral norms at that time. Abortion was discussed as part of the UMC's Social Principles in 1972, and, like divorce, contributed to the overall sense of social instability around family structures that the discussion of gay rights only intensified.

The Only Constant Is Change

This book set out to explore the questions: Who holds power in the UMC, not just to lead churches, but to decide who those leaders will be? How do changes in authority structures occur, and why is it such a long and painful process? Finally, how are the stories of marginalized groups within the church interrelated?

While this exploration has focused on the resistance to change, human history reflects that change is the norm rather than the exception. One need only look at changing social structures and habits, technology, and other scientific modifications in the past century, or even in recent decades, to see how quickly humans change their individual lives, their social relationships, and the physical world around them. Much of this change is intentional, including advances in medicine, communication, transportation, industry, and other areas, but these changes may bring unintentional consequences such as global climate change and drug-resistant bacteria, whose impact is not completely known.

The changes in authority structures explored here were intentional as well, as groups and individuals with marginal interest or influence have sought an equal share of social capital. The democratic nature of the Methodist General Conference allows for a participatory decision-making process, but one that is drawn out and difficult, because of the way ingrained power relationships resist change. Once those power shifts do occur, members of a newly empowered group may use their capital to argue either for the leadership of other groups, or against others' advancement, so as to not jeopardize their own newly-gained status.

Despite the inevitable resistance, power relations *do* change, as the current leadership of African Americans and women in the UMC proves. A century ago, both the MEC and MECS General Conferences were overwhelmingly comprised of white male clergy, with a small percentage of lay delegates; the MEC had an even smaller number of laywomen delegates, and the MECS had none. Fifty-five years ago, the MC had just begun to grant women full clergy rights, and forty-five years ago the newly formed UMC was in the process of dismantling the Central Jurisdiction to allow black pastors to serve throughout the denomination.

While the clergy ranks of the UMC are still predominantly white and male, the church has been intentional about electing a Council of Bishops that would represent diversity at the highest level of leadership. Currently only 43 percent of active bishops in the United States are white men. Of the forty-seven active bishops, eleven are female (23 percent) and ten (21 percent) are African American, all male. Additionally, the church has two Hispanic bishops, both female, and six Asian or Asian-American bishops, all male.[79] The pace of change may seem slow to those who are working for greater inclusion, yet the church's diverse leadership today occurred because the white men who comprised General Conferences one hundred years ago were persuaded to allow other voices into that arena. That persuasion came from forces within the church, as well as from external social change movements. Had those delegates acted solely in their own interest, change would not have occurred, and the church would still be led by white men.

For some members of the General Conference and the church, change happens all too quickly, and they seek a point of stability amid ongoing change. Those who argue for the maintenance of traditional social structures hearken to a particular point in history that provided a sense of comfort and/or their own accumulation of social or religious capital. The Victorian era saw the coalescence of an ideal American family, in which the father worked outside the home and the mother remained contentedly at home. Those resisting the ordination of women and of gays and lesbians spoke of such structures as God's natural order for humans, as revealed in the Bible, yet few such families exist in the Hebrew or Christian scriptures.[80] Opponents of gay marriage who claim a biblical mandate for

79. Statistics from UMC InfoServ, email message to author, November 30, 2012.

80. See Virginia Ramey Mollenkott's list of "diverse forms of family" that are mentioned or implied in scripture in her book *Sensuous Spirituality*, 194–97.

that family structure use scripture to justify or legitimate their own social preference, while failing to recognize the constructed nature of that or any social arrangement, since their resistance lies at a deep, unconcscious level.

Such misrecognition is aided by the circular nature of change, in which it is difficult to pinpoint the origin of a particular wave of transformation, or separate out the mutual reinforcement of agents and structures. Therefore, this research is unable to offer a clear explanation of when and how a particular wave of social change begins, or the origin of the resistance that it provokes. By "thinking with Bourdieu" and others, I have examined the complexity of these issues and have tried to unravel a few of the many strains from which they emerge. My hope is that this discussion offers insights into the nature of resistance that may go beyond conscious rationales, while I acknowledge that exposing such currents does not lead to their easy resolution. These conflicts raise ultimate questions of meaning that shape our worldview, and resolving them requires a "symbolic revolution," as Bourdieu suggests. However, recognizing the arbitrary nature of social relations through which people have been excluded from Methodist leadership allows for the possibility that such relations may be changed. While racism and sexism continue at some level, the dissolving of institutional barriers demonstrates that change, while difficult, is possible. Tracing the ongoing story of these issues can offer a roadmap through current tensions and those that may arise in the future.

Bibliography

Methodist Resources

Methodist Episcopal Church. *Journal of the General Conference.* New York: Carlton and Porter, 1868.

Methodist Episcopal Church. *Journal of the General Conference.* New York: Carlton and Porter, 1880.

Methodist Episcopal Church. *Journal of the General Conference.* New York: Carlton and Porter, 1888.

Methodist Episcopal Church. *Journal of the General Conference.* New York: Eaton and Mains, 1920.

Methodist Episcopal Church. *Journal of the General Conference.* New York: Eaton and Mains, 1824.

Methodist Episcopal Church, South. *Journal of the General Conference.* [Nashville, TN?], 1914.

Methodist Episcopal Church, South. *Journal of the General Conference.* [Nashville, TN?], 1918.

Methodist Church. *Journal of the General Conference.* Nashville, TN: Methodist Publishing House, 1956.

United Methodist Church. *Journal of the General Conference,* 1972.

United Methodist Church. *Journal of the General Conference,* 1976.

United Methodist Church. *Journal of the General Conference,* 1980.

United Methodist Church. *Journal of the General Conference,* 1984.

Methodist Episcopal Church, South. *Daily Christian Advocate,* 1914.

Methodist Episcopal Church, South. *Daily Christian Advocate,* 1918.

Methodist Episcopal Church, South. *Daily Christian Advocate,* 1938.

Methodist Episcopal Church. *Daily Christian Advocate,* 1880.

Methodist Episcopal Church. *Daily Christian Advocate,* 1888.

Methodist Episcopal Church. *Daily Christian Advocate,* 1920.

Methodist Episcopal Church. *Daily Christian Advocate,* 1924.

Methodist Church. *Daily Christian Advocate,* 1956.

United Methodist Church. *Daily Christian Advocate,* 1972.

United Methodist Church. *Daily Christian Advocate,* 1980.

United Methodist Church. *Daily Christian Advocate,* 1984.

United Methodist Church. *Daily Christian Advocate,* 2012.

Evangelical United Brethren Church. *The Discipline of the Evangelical United Brethren Church.* Dayton, OH: Board of Publication of the Evangelical United Brethren Church, 1967.

Methodist Church. *Doctrines and Discipline of the Methodist Church, 1964.* Nashville, TN: The Methodist Publishing House, 1964.

United Methodist Church. *The Book of Discipline of The United Methodist Church.* Nashville, TN: United Methodist Publishing House, 1968.

United Methodist Church. *The Book of Discipline of The United Methodist Church.* Nashville, TN: United Methodist Publishing House, 1972.

United Methodist Church. *The Book of Discipline of The United Methodist Church.* Nashville, TN: United Methodist Publishing House, 1976.

United Methodist Church. *The Book of Discipline of The United Methodist Church.* Nashville, TN: United Methodist Publishing House, 1980.

United Methodist Church. *The Book of Discipline of The United Methodist Church.* Nashville, TN: United Methodist Publishing House, 1984.

United Methodist Church. *The Book of Discipline of The United Methodist Church.* Nashville, TN: United Methodist Publishing House, 2012.

Manuscripts from Methodist Archives: Methodist Episcopal Church, *Journal of the General Conference,* 1880; and Methodist Episcopal Church, Committee Reports and Resolutions, 1880.

Other Resources

Abraham, William J. "The Church's Teaching on Sexuality: A Defense of The United Methodist Church's Discipline on Homosexuality." In *Staying the Course: Supporting the Church's Position on Homosexuality,* edited by M. D. Dunnam and H. N. Maloney, 15–31. Nashville: Abingdon, 2003.

———. "Staying the Course: On Unity, Division and Renewal in The United Methodist Church." In *Ancient and Postmodern Christianity: Paleo-Orthodoxy in the 21st Century, Essays in Honor of Thomas C. Oden,* edited by K. Tanner and C. A. Hall, 170–82. Downers Grove, IL: InterVarsity, 2002.

Adkins, Lisa, and Beverley Skeggs, eds. *Feminism after Bourdieu.* Oxford: Blackwell, 2004.

Albanese, Catherine L. *America, Religions and Religion.* 4th ed. Belmont, CA: Thomson Wadsworth, 2007.

Allen, Richard. *The Life Experiences and Gospel Labors of the Rt. Rev. Richard Allen.* Philadelphia: F. Ford and M. A. Riply, 1880.

Anderson, Margaret L. "Whitewashing Race: A Critical Perspective on Whiteness." In *White Out: The Continuing Significance of Racism,* edited by A. W. Doane and E. Bonilla-Silva, 21–34. New York: Routledge, 2003.

Armour, Ellen T. *Deconstruction, Feminist Theology, and the Problem of Difference.* Chicago: University of Chicago Press, 1999.

Armstrong, Chris. "Tangling with Wolves: Why We Still Need Heresy Trials." *Christianity Today* (August 2003) 50–51.

Atack, Jeremy, and Peter Passell. *A New Economic View of American History from Colonial Times to 1940.* 2nd ed. New York: Norton, 1994.

Bass, Diana Butler. *Christianity after Religion: The End of Church and the Birth of a New Spiritual Awakening.* New York: HarperOne, 2012.

Bell, Daniel M. "Will Homosexuality Split the Church?" In *Questions for the Twenty-First Century Church,* edited by R. E. Richey, W. B. Lawrence, and D. M. Campbell, 271–79. Nashville: Abingdon, 1999.

Berger, Peter L. *The Heretical Imperative: Contemporary Possibilities of Religious Affirmation.* Garden City, NY: Anchor, 1979.

———. *The Sacred Canopy: Elements of a Sociological Theory of Religion.* New York: Anchor, 1967.

Berger, Peter L., and Thomas Luckmann. *The Social Construction of Reality: A Treatise in the Sociology of Knowledge.* Garden City, NY: Doubleday, 1966.

Berlinerblau, Jacques. "Toward a Sociology of Heresy, Orthodoxy, and Doxa." *History of Religions* 40 (2001) 327–51.

Beuttler, Fred W. "Making Theology Matter: Power, Polity, and the Theological Debate over Homosexual Ordination in the Presbyterian Church (U.S.A.)." *Review of Religious Research* 41 (1999) 239–61.

Blackmon, Douglas A. *Slavery by Another Name: The Re-Enslavement of Black Americans from the Civil War to World War II.* New York: Doubleday, 2008.

Blount, Jackie M. "The Feminization of Teaching from 1850–1900." *Journal of the Midwest History of Education Society* 23 (1996) 41–48.

Bonilla-Silva, Eduardo. *Racism without Racists: Color-Blind Racism and the Persistence of Racial Inequality in the United States.* Lanham, MD: Rowman & Littlefield, 2003.

———. *White Supremacy and Racism in the Post-Civil Rights Era.* Boulder, CO: Lynne Rienner, 2001.

Bonilla-Silva, Eduardo, et al. "When Whites Flock Together: The Social Psychology of White Habitus." *Critical Sociology* 32 (2006) 229–53.

Boswell, John. *Christianity, Social Tolerance, and Homosexuality: Gay People in Western Europe from the Beginning of the Christian Era to the Fourteenth Century.* Chicago: University of Chicago Press, 1980.

Bourdieu, Pierre. "The Field of Cultural Production, or: The Economic World Reversed." *Poetics* 12 (1983) 311–56.

———. "Genesis and Structure of the Religious Field." *Comparative Social Research* 13 (1991) 1–44.

———. *In Other Words: Essays toward a Reflexive Sociology.* Stanford, CA: Stanford University Press, 1990.

———. "Intellectual Field and Creative Project." In *Knowledge and Control: New Directions for the Sociology of Education*, edited by M. F. D. Young, 161–88. London: Collier Macmillan, 1971.

———. *Language and Symbolic Power.* Cambridge, MA: Harvard University Press, 1991.

———. "Legitimation and Structured Interests in Weber's Sociology of Religion." In *Max Weber, Rationality and Modernity*, edited by S. Lash and S. Whimster, 119–35. London: Allen & Urwin, 1987.

———. *The Logic of Practice.* Stanford, CA: Stanford University Press, 1990.

———. *Masculine Domination.* Translated by Richard Nice. Stanford, CA: Stanford University Press, 2001.

———. *Outline of a Theory of Practice.* Translated by Richard Nice. Cambridge: Cambridge University Press, 1977.

———. *Practical Reason: On the Theory of Action.* Stanford, CA: Stanford University Press, 1998.

———. *Sketch for a Self-Analysis.* Translated by Richard Nice. Chicago: University of Chicago Press, 2007.

Bourdieu, Pierre, and Loic J. D. Wacquant. *An Invitation to Reflexive Sociology.* Chicago: University of Chicago Press, 1992.

————. "On the Cunning of Imperialist Reason." *Theory, Culture, and Society* 16 (1999) 41–58.

Brewer, Paul R. "The Shifting Foundations of Public Opinion about Gay Rights." *Journal of Politics* 65 (2003) 1208–20.

Brown, Karen McCarthy. "Fundamentalism and the Control of Women." In *Fundamentalism and Gender*, edited by J. S. Hawley, 175–201. New York: Oxford University Press, 1994.

Browning, Peter. "Homosexuality, Ordination, and Polity." *Quarterly Review* 14 (1994) 161–79.

Buisson-Fenet, Hélène. "De la dissonance à l'esprit critique. Sur quelques façons d'être clerc et homosexuel." *Social Compass* 46 (1999) 75–84.

Burke, Daniel. "Splinter Groups Turn into Churches." Religion News Service (RNS) news release in *The Christian Century* (March 21, 2012) 14–15.

Burr, Chandler. "Homosexuality and Biology." In *Homosexuality in the Church: Both Sides of the Debate*, edited by J. S. Siker, 116–34. Louisville: Westminster John Knox, 1994.

Butler, Judith. *Gender Trouble: Feminism and the Subversion of Identity*. New York: Routledge, 1990.

————. "Performativity's Social Magic." In *Bourdieu: A Critical Reader*, edited by R. Shusterman, 113–28. Oxford: Blackwell, 1999.

Cadge, Wendy. "Vital Conflicts: The Mainline Denominations Debate Homosexuality." In *The Quiet Hand of God: Faith-Based Activism and the Public Role of Mainline Protestantism*, edited by R. Wuthnow and J. H. Evans, 265–86. Berkeley: University of California Press, 2002.

Cadge, Wendy, et al. "How Denominational Resources Influence Debate about Homosexuality in Mainline Protestant Congregations." *Sociology of Religion* 69 (2008) 187–207.

Caldwell, Gilbert Haven. "The Last Prejudice." In *The Loyal Opposition: Struggling with the Church on Homosexuality*, edited by T. Sample and A. E. DeLong, 99–109. Nashville: Abingdon, 2000.

Calhoun, Craig, et al., eds. *Bourdieu: Critical Perspectives*. Chicago: University of Chicago Press, 1993.

Campbell, Dennis M. "Does Methodism Have a Future in American Culture?" In *Questions for the Twenty-First Century Church*, edited by R. E. Richey, W. B. Lawrence, and D. M. Campbell, 9–23. Nashville: Abingdon, 1999.

Campbell, Scott. "Who Will Decide? The Looming Battle Over Doctrine in The United Methodist Church." In *United Methodism at Risk: A Wake-Up Call*, edited by L. Howell, 119–24. Kingston, NY: Information Project for United Methodists, 2003.

Cannon, Katie G. *Black Womanist Ethics*. Atlanta: Scholars, 1988.

Carter, Kenneth H., Jr. "Disarm." In *Finding Our Way: Love and Law in The United Methodist Church*, edited by R. P. Job and N. M. Alexander, 53–69. Nashville: Abingdon, 2014.

Cary, John Jesse, ed. *The Sexuality Debate in North American Churches 1988–1995: Controversies, Unresolved Issues, Future Prospects*. Lewiston, NY: Edwin Mellon, 1995.

Chambers, Patricia Price, and H. Paul Chalfant. "A Changing Role or the Same Old Handmaidens: Women's Role in Today's Church." *Review of Religious Research* 19 (1978) 192–97.

Chaves, Mark. *Ordaining Women: Culture and Conflict in Religious Organizations.* Cambridge, MA: Harvard University Press, 1997.

———. "The Symbolic Significance of Women's Ordination." *Journal of Religion* 77 (1997) 87–114.

Chaves, Mark, and James Cavendish. "Recent Changes in Women's Ordination Conflicts: The Effects of a Movement on Intraorganizational Controversy." *Journal for the Scientific Study of Religion* 36 (1997) 574–84.

Chodos, Howie, and Bruce Curtis. "Pierre Bourdieu's *Masculine Domination*: A Critique." *The Canadian Review of Sociology and Anthropology* 39 (2002) 397–412.

Clark, J. Michael, et al. "Institutional Religion and Gay/Lesbian Oppression." In *Homosexuality and Family Relations*, edited by F. W. Bozett and M. B. Sussman, 265–84. New York: Harrington Park, 1990.

Coleman, Monica A. "Must I Be Womanist?" *Journal of Feminist Studies in Religion* 22 (2006) 85–96.

Collier, Karen Y. "A Union that Divides: Development of a Church Within a Church." In *Heritage and Hope: The African American Presence in United Methodism*, edited by G. S. Shockley, 99–115. Nashville: Abingdon, 1991.

Collins, Patricia Hill. *Fighting Words: Black Women and the Search for Justice.* Minneapolis: University of Minnesota Press, 1998.

Comstock, Gary David. *Unrepentant, Self-Affirming, Practicing: Lesbian/Bisexual/Gay People within Organized Religion.* New York: Continuum, 1996.

Cone, James H. *A Black Theology of Liberation.* Philadelphia: J. B. Lippincott, 1970.

———. *God of the Oppressed.* Maryknoll, NY: Orbis, 1997.

———. *Risks of Faith: The Emergence of a Black Theology of Liberation, 1968–1998.* Boston: Beacon, 1999.

Connolly, Paul. "Racism and Postmodernism: Towards a Theory of Practice." In *Sociology after Postmodernism*, edited by D. Owen, 65–80. London: Sage, 1997.

Cook, Roger. "Andy Warhol, Capitalism, Culture, and Camp." *Space and Culture* 6 (2003) 66–76.

Cox, Harvey. *The Future of Faith.* New York: HarperOne, 2009.

Countryman, L. William. *Dirt, Greed, and Sex: Sexual Ethics in the New Testament and Their Implications for Today.* Philadelphia: Fortress, 1988.

Culver, Dwight W. *Negro Segregation in The Methodist Church.* New Haven: Yale University Press, 1953.

Dallas, Joe. "Another Option: Christianity and Ego-Dystonic Homosexuality." In *Homosexuality in the Church: Both Sides of the Debate*, edited by J. S. Siker, 137–44. Louisville: Westminster John Knox, 1994.

Daly, Mary. *Beyond God the Father: Toward a Philosophy of Women's Liberation.* Boston: Beacon, 1985.

———. *The Church and the Second Sex.* New York: Harper & Row, 1968.

Davis, Angela. "Reflections on the Black Woman's Role in the Community of Slaves." *The Black Scholar* 3 (1971) 2–15.

Davis, Morris L. *The Methodist Unification: Christianity and the Politics of Race in the Jim Crow Era.* New York: New York University Press, 2008.

Dayton, Lucille S., and Donald W. Dayton. "Your Daughters Shall Prophesy: Feminism in the Holiness Movement." *Methodist History* 14 (1976) 67–92.

Deal, William E., and Timothy K. Beal. *Theory for Religious Studies.* New York: Routledge, 2004.

Bibliography

Deer, Cécile. "Doxa." In *Pierre Bourdieu: Key Concepts*, edited by M. Grenfell, 119–30. Stocksfield, UK: Acumen, 2008.

Desmarchelier, Carmel. "Teachers' Understanding of Homosexuality and Body Image: Habitus Issues." *Journal of Men's Studies* 8 (2000) 237–53.

Dianteill, Erwan. "Pierre Bourdieu and the Sociology of Religion: A Central and Peripheral Concern." *Theory and Society* 32 (2003) 529–49.

Dillon, Michele. "Pierre Bourdieu, Religion, and Cultural Production." *Cultural Studies—Critical Methodologies* 1 (2001) 411–29.

Doane, Ashley Woody, and Eduardo Bonilla-Silva, eds. *White Out: The Continuing Significance of Racism*. New York: Routledge, 2003.

Douglas, Kelly Brown. "Daring to Speak: Womanist Theology and Black Sexuality." In *Embracing the Spirit: Womanist Perspectives on Hope, Salvation, and Transformation*, edited by E. M. Townes, 234–46. Maryknoll, NY: Orbis, 1997.

———. "Heterosexism in the Black American Church Community: A Complicated Reality." In *Heterosexism in Contemporary World Religion: Problem and Prospect*, edited by M. M. Ellison and J. Plaskow, 177–200. Cleveland: Pilgrim, 2007.

Douglas, Mary. *Purity and Danger: An Analysis of Concepts of Pollution and Taboo*. London: Routledge & Kegan Paul, 1966.

Du Bois, W. E. B. "Of the Faith of the Fathers." [From *The Souls of Black Folk* (1903).] In *Du Bois on Religion*, edited by P. Zuckerman, 47–56. Walnut Creek, CA: AltaMira, 2000.

———. "Religion in the South." [From *The Negro in the South* (1907).] In *Du Bois on Religion*, edited by P. Zuckerman, 69–89. Walnut Creek, CA: AltaMira, 2000.

———. "Will the Church Remove the Color Line?" [From *The Christian Century* (1931).] In *Du Bois on Religion*, edited by P. Zuckerman, 173–79. Walnut Creek, CA: AltaMira, 2000.

Duff, Nancy J. "How to Discuss Moral Issues Surrounding Homosexuality When You Know You Are Right." In *Homosexuality and Christian Community*, edited by C. Seow, 44–57. Louisville: John Knox, 1996.

Dunlap, E. Dale. "Homosexuality and the Social Principles." In *The Loyal Opposition: Struggling with the Church on Homosexuality*, edited by T. Sample and A. E. DeLong, 71–87. Nashville: Abingdon, 2000.

Dunnam, Maxie D., and H. Newton Malony, eds. *Staying the Course: Supporting the Church's Position on Homosexuality*. Nashville: Abingdon, 2003.

Ellison, Marvin M. "Beyond Same-Sex Marriage: Continuing the Reformation of Protestant Christianity." In *Heterosexism in Contemporary World Religion: Problem and Prospect*, edited by M. M. Ellison and J. Plaskow, 13–36. Cleveland: Pilgrim, 2007.

Ellison, Marvin M., and Judith Plaskow, eds. *Heterosexism in Contemporary World Religion: Problem and Prospect*. Cleveland: Pilgrim, 2007.

Epstein, Steven. "Queer Encounter: Sociology and the Study of Sexuality." In *Queer Theory/Sociology*, edited by S. Seidman, 145–67. Cambridge, MA: Blackwell, 1996.

Evers, Kevin. "Agreement Resolves Complaint against Longtime Kentucky Pastor." UMNS news release, August 1, 2005. http://www.umc.org/site/c.gjJTJbMUIuE/b.937171/k.AF1E/Agreement_resolves_complaint_against_longtime_Kentucky_pastor.htm.

Fisher, R. D., et al. "Religiousness, Religious Orientation, and Attitudes Towards Gays and Lesbians." *Journal of Applied Social Psychology* 24 (1994) 614–30.

Fowler, Bridget, ed. *Reading Bourdieu on Society and Culture*. Oxford: Blackwell, 2000.

———. "Reading Pierre Bourdieu's *Masculine Domination*: Notes Towards an Intersectional Analysis of Gender, Culture and Class." *Cultural Studies* 17 (2003) 468–94.

Fowler, Bridget, and Fiona Wilson. "Women Architects and Their Discontents." *Sociology* 38 (2004) 101–19.

Frank, Thomas Edward. *Polity, Practice, and the Mission of The United Methodist Church.* Nashville: Abingdon, 1997.

Frykholm, Amy. "A time to split?" In *The Christian Century* (April 16, 2014) 22–25.

Fulkerson, Mary McClintock. "Gender—Being It or Doing It? The Church, Homosexuality, and the Politics of Identity." *Union Seminary Quarterly Review* 47 (1993) 29–46.

Furnish, Victor Paul. "The Bible and Homosexuality: Reading the Texts in Context." In *Homosexuality in the Church: Both Sides of the Debate*, edited by J. S. Siker, 18–35. Louisville: Westminster John Knox, 1994.

———. "The United Methodist Experience." In *The Sexuality Debate in North American Churches, 1988–1995: Controversies, Unresolved Issues, Future Prospects*, edited by J. J. Cary, 169–85. Lewiston, NY: Edwin Mellen, 1995.

Giddings, Paula. "The Last Taboo." In *Race-ing Justice, En-Gendering Power: Essays on Anita Hill, Clarence Thomas, and the Construction of Social Reality*, edited by T. Morrison, 441–63. New York: Pantheon, 1992.

———. *When and Where I Enter: The Impact of Black Women on Race and Sex in America.* New York: William Morrow, 1984.

Gifford, Carolyn De Swarte. "'My Own Methodist Hive': Frances Willard's Faith as Disclosed in Her Journal, 1855–1870." In *Spirituality and Social Responsibility: Vocational Vision of Women in The United Methodist Tradition*, edited by R. S. Keller, 81–98. Nashville: Abingdon, 1993.

Gilbert, Kathy L. "Complaints Dismissed against Bishop Joseph United Methodist News Service (UMNS) news release, February 18, 2003. http://archives.umc.org/umns/news_archive2003.asp?ptid=2&story=%7B5DF87400-53AC-4DA9-BA21-1FCFD370AD22%7D&mid=2406.

Gilbert, Kathy L. and Heather Hahn. "Same-gender debate rekindles schism talk." UMNS news release, May 29, 2014. http://www.umc.org/news-and-media/same-gender-debate-rekindles-schism-talk.

Grant, Jacquelyn. "Black Women and the Church." In *All the Women Are White, All the Blacks Are Men, but Some of Us Are Brave*, edited by G. T. Hull et al., 141–52. New York: Feminist Press at The City University of New York, 1982.

Green, Linda. "Bishop Melvin Wheatley dies at 93." UMNS news release, March 3, 2009. http://archives.gcah.org/xmlui/handle/10516/377.

———. "Complaint Filed against Chicago Pastor for Same-Sex Service." UMNS news release, October 21, 1998. http://www.umaffirm.org/cornews/dell3.html.

Greenberg, David F., and Marcia H. Brystryn. "Christian Intolerance of Homosexuality." *American Journal of Sociology* 88 (1982) 515–49.

Grenfell, Michael, ed. *Pierre Bourdieu: Key Concepts.* Stocksfield, UK: Acumen, 2008.

Griffin, Horace L. *Their Own Receive Them Not: African American Lesbians and Gays in Black Churches.* Cleveland: Pilgrim, 2006.

Hahn, Heather. "2016 General Conference to See Drop in Delegates." UMNS blog post, October 20, 2013. http://umcconnections.org/2013/10/20/2016-general-conference-see-drop-delegates.

Hardy, Cheryl. "Hysteresis." In *Pierre Bourdieu: Key Concepts*, edited by M. Grenfell, 131–48. Stocksfield, UK: Acumen, 2008.

Harkness, Georgia. *Women in Church and Society: A Historical and Theological Inquiry.* Nashville: Abingdon, 1972.

Harrison, Beverly Wildung. *Making the Connections: Essays in Feminist Social Ethics*, edited by C. S. Robb. Boston: Beacon, 1985.

———. "Misogyny and Homophobia: The Unexplored Connections." *Integrity Forum* (1981) 7–13.

———. "Sexism and the Contemporary Church: When Evasion Becomes Complicity." In *Sexist Religion and Women in the Church: No More Silence!*, edited by A. L. Hageman, 195–216. New York: Association, 1974.

Hartman, Keith. *Congregations in Conflict: The Battle over Homosexuality.* New Brunswick, NJ: Rutgers University Press, 1996.

Hatch, Nathan O., and John H. Wigger, eds. *Methodism and the Shaping of American Culture.* Nashville: Kingswood, 2001.

Hays, Richard B. "Awaiting the Redemption of Our Bodies: The Witness of Scripture Concerning Homosexuality." In *Homosexuality in the Church: Both Sides of the Debate*, edited by J. S. Siker, 3–17. Louisville: Westminster John Knox, 1994.

Heidinger, James V., II. "45 Years of Vison for Renewal and Reform." September 19, 2013. http://goodnewsmag.org/2013/09/45-years-of-vision-for-renewal-and-reform/.

Hempton, David. *Methodism: Empire of the Spirit.* New Haven: Yale University Press, 2005.

Hildebrand, Reginald F. "Methodist Episcopal Policy on the Ordination of Black Ministers, 1784–1864." *Methodist History* 20 (1982) 124–42.

———. *The Times Were Strange and Stirring: Methodist Preachers and the Crisis of Emancipation.* Durham: Duke University Press, 1995.

Hill, Renee L. "Power, Blessings, and Human Sexuality: Making the Justice Connections." In *Beyond Colonial Anglicanism: The Anglican Communion in the Twenty-First Century*, edited by I. T. Douglas and K. Pui-lan, 191–203. New York: Church Publishing, 2001.

———. "Who Are We for Each Other? Sexism, Sexuality and Womanist Theology." In *Black Theology: A Documentary History, Vol. 2: 1980–1992*, edited by J. H. Cone and G. S. Wilmore, 345–51. Maryknoll, NY: Orbis, 1993.

hooks, bell. *Ain't I a Woman: Black Women and Feminism.* Boston: South End, 1981.

Hopkins, Dwight N. "Lies above Suspicion: Being Human in Black Folk Tales." In *Deeper Shades of Purple: Womanism in Religion and Society*, edited by S. Floyd-Thomas, 282–90. New York: New York University Press, 2006.

———. "Toward a Positive Black Male Heterosexuality." *Anglican Theological Review* 90 (2008) 575–81.

Hull, G.T., et al. *All the Women Are White, All the Blacks Are Men, but Some of Us Are Brave.* New York: Feminist Press at The City University of New York, 1982.

Hunt, Mary. "Eradicating the Sin of Heterosexism." In *Heterosexism in Contemporary World Religion: Problem and Prospect*, edited by M. M. Ellison and J. Plaskow, 155–76. Cleveland: Pilgrim, 2007.

Hunter, James Davison. *Culture Wars: The Struggle to Define America.* New York: BasicBooks, 1991.

Hunter, James Davison, and Alan Wolfe. *Is There a Culture War? A Dialogue on Values and American Public Life.* Washington, DC: Pew Research Center and Brookings Institution, 2006.

Hutchison, William R. *Religious Pluralism in America: The Contentious History of a Founding Ideal.* New Haven: Yale University Press, 2003.

Irons, Kendra Weddle. "From Kansas to the World: M. Madeline Southard, Activist and Pastor." *Methodist History* 43 (2004) 33–44.

———. "M. Madeline Southard (1877–1967) on 'Ecclesial Suffrage.'" *Methodist History* 45 (2006) 16–30.

Jacobson, Matthew Frye. *Barbarian Virtues: The United States Encounters Foreign Peoples at Home and Abroad, 1876–1917.* New York: Hill and Wang, 2000.

Jakobsen, Janet R., and Ann Pellegrini. *Love the Sin: Sexual Regulation and the Limits of Religious Tolerance.* New York: New York University Press, 2003.

Jenkins, Richard. *Pierre Bourdieu.* London: Routledge, 1992.

Job, Reuben P. "Trust God." In *Finding Our Way: Love and Law in The United Methodist Church,* edited by R. P. Job and N. M. Alexander, 101–15. Nashville: Abingdon, 2014.

———, and Neil M. Alexander. *Finding Our Way: Love and Law in The United Methodist Church.* Nashville: Abingdon, 2014.

Jones, Stanton L., and Don E. Workman. "Homosexuality: The Behavioral Sciences and the Church." In *Homosexuality in the Church: Both Sides of the Debate,* edited by J. S. Siker, 93–115. Louisville: Westminster John Knox, 1994.

Jordan, Mark D. "'Both as a Christian and as a Historian': On Boswell's Ministry." In *The Boswell Thesis: Essays on* Christianity, Social Tolerance, and Homosexuality, edited by M. Kuefler, 88–107. Chicago: University of Chicago Press, 2006.

———. *The Ethics of Sex.* Malden, MA: Blackwell, 2002.

———. *The Invention of Sodomy in Christian Theology.* Chicago: University of Chicago Press, 1997.

Jung, Patricia Beattie. "Sexual Diversity and Ordained Ministry." *Union Seminary Quarterly Review* 57 (2003) 67–87.

Jung, Patricia Beattie, and Ralph F. Smith. *Heterosexism: An Ethical Challenge.* Albany: State University of New York Press, 1993.

Keller, Rosemary Skinner. "Georgia Harkness—Theologian of the People: Evangelical Liberal and Social Prophet." In *Spirituality and Social Responsibility: Vocational Vision of Women in the United Methodist Tradition,* edited by R. S. Keller, 205–30. Nashville: Abingdon, 1993.

———. "Women and the Nature of Ministry in the United Methodist Tradition." *Methodist History* 22 (1984) 99–114.

Kinnaman, David, and Gabe Lyons. *UnChristian: What a New Generation Really Thinks About Christianity . . . And Why It Matters.* Grand Rapids: Baker, 2007.

Kirby, James E. *The Episcopacy in American Methodism.* Nashville: Kingswood, 2000.

Kirby, James E., et al. *The Methodists.* Westport, CT: Greenwood, 1996.

Knotts, Alice. "The Debates Over Race and Women's Ordination in the 1939 Methodist Merger." *Methodist History* 29 (1990) 37–43.

———. "Methodist Women and Interracial Fairness in the 1930s." *Methodist History* 27 (1989) 230–40.

———. "Race Relations in the 1920s: A Challenge to Southern Methodist Women." *Methodist History* 26 (1988) 199–212.

Kolden, Marc. "Homosexual Ordination: The Real Issue?" *Dialog* 33 (1994) 63.

Krais, Beate. "Gender and Symbolic Violence: Female Oppression in the Light of Pierre Bourdieu's Theory of Social Practice." In *Bourdieu: Critical Perspectives,* edited by C. Calhoun et al., 156–77. Chicago: University of Chicago Press, 1993.

———. "Gender, Sociological Theory and Bourdieu's Sociology of Practice." *Theory, Culture and Society* 23 (2006) 119–34.

Kuefler, Mathew, ed. *The Boswell Thesis: Essays on* Christianity, Social Tolerance, and Homosexuality. Chicago: University of Chicago Press, 2006.

Lakey, Othal Hawthorne. *The History of the CME Church*. Rev. ed. Memphis: CME, 1996.

Lehman, Edward C., Jr. *Gender and Work: The Case of the Clergy*. Albany: State University of New York Press, 1993.

———. *Women Clergy: Breaking through Gender Barriers*. New Brunswick, NJ: Transaction, 1985.

Lewis, Amanda E. "Some Are More Equal than Others: Lessons on Whiteness from School." In *White Out: The Continuing Significance of Racism*, edited by A. W. Doane and E. Bonilla-Silva, 159–72. New York: Routledge, 2003.

Lincoln, C. Eric, and Lawrence H. Mamiya. *The Black Church in the African-American Experience*. Durham: Duke University Press, 1990.

Lindsay, D. Michael. "Elite Power: Social Networks within American Evangelicalism." *Sociology of Religion* 67 (2006) 207–27.

Loftus, Jeni. "America's Liberalization in Attitudes Toward Homosexuality, 1973 to 1998." *American Sociological Review* 66 (2001) 762–82.

Love, Janice. *United Methodism in a World Context: Navigating the Local and the Global*. Occasional Paper 100. Nashville: United Methodist General Board of Higher Education and Ministry, 2006.

Lovell, Terry. "Bourdieu, Class, and Gender: 'The Return of the Living Dead'?" In *Feminism after Bourdieu*, edited by L. Adkins and B. Skeggs, 37–56. Oxford: Blackwell, 2004.

———. "Resisting with Authority: Historical Specificity, Agency and the Performative Self." *Theory, Culture and Society* 20 (2003) 1–17.

———. "Thinking Feminism With and Against Bourdieu." *Feminist Theory* 1 (2000) 11–32.

Lynch, John E. "Ordination of Women: Protestant Experience in Ecumenical Perspective." *Journal of Ecumenical Studies* 12 (1975) 173–97.

Maduro, Otto. *Religion and Social Conflict*. Translated by Robert R. Barr. Maryknoll, NY: Orbis, 1982.

Magalis, Elaine. "Shall She Be Allowed to Preach." In *Conduct Becoming to a Woman: Bolted Doors and Burgeoning Missions*, 137–54. New York: Women's Division, United Methodist Board of Global Ministries, 1973.

Maguire, Daniel C. "Heterosexism, Not Homosexuality, Is the Problem." In *Heterosexism in Contemporary World Religion: Problem and Prospect*, edited by M. M. Ellison and J. Plaskow, 1–11. Cleveland: Pilgrim, 2007.

Mariner, Kirk. "The Negro's Place: Virginia Methodists Debate Unification 1924–25." *Methodist History* 18 (1980) 155–70.

Martin, Dale B. "Heterosexism and the Interpretation of Romans 1:18–32." In *The Boswell Thesis: Essays on* Christianity, Social Tolerance, and Homosexuality, edited by M. Kuefler, 130–51. Chicago: University of Chicago Press, 2006.

Martin, Joan. *More than Chains and Toil: A Christian Work Ethic of Enslaved Women*. Louisville: Westminster John Knox, 2000.

Mathews, Tom. "Battle Over Gay Rights." *Newsweek*, June 6, 1977, 16.

Mathews, Donald G. "'Christianizing the South'—Sketching a Synthesis." In *New Directions in American Religious History*, edited by D. G. Hart and H. S. Stout, 84–115. New York: Oxford University Press, 1997.

McCaughan, Edward J. "Race, Ethnicity, Nation, and Class within Theories of Structure and Agency." *Social Justice* 20 (1993) 82–103.

McCombs, Phil, and John Feinstein. "Anita Bryant Visit Here Sparks Demonstration; 'Gay Rights Now' Chanted by 2,000 Marchers." *Washington Post*, January 23, 1978, Metro, C1.

McFarland, Sam. G. "Religious Orientations and the Targets of Discrimination." *Journal for the Scientific Study of Religion* 28 (1989) 324–36.

McGhee, Derek. "Looking and Acting the Part: Gays in the Armed Forces—A Case of Passing Masculinity." *Feminist Legal Studies* 6 (1998) 205–44.

McGuire, Meredith B. "New-Old Directions in the Social Scientific Study of Religion: Ethnography, Phenomenology, and the Human Body." In *Personal Knowledge and Beyond: Reshaping the Ethnography of Religion*, edited by J. V. Spickard et al., 195–211. New York: New York University Press, 2002.

McLeod, Julie. "Feminists Re-Reading Bourdieu: Old Debates and New Questions about Gender Habitus and Gender Change." *Theory and Research in Education* 3 (2005) 11–30.

McNay, Lois. "Gender, Habitus, and the Field: Pierre Bourdieu and the Limits of Reflexivity Theory." *Theory, Culture and Society* 16 (1999) 95–117.

McNeill, John J. *The Church and the Homosexual.* Kansas City: Sheed Andrews and McMeel, 1976.

Meisenhelder, Tom. "Toward a Field Theory of Class, Gender, and Race." *Race, Gender and Class* 7 (2000) 76–95.

Melton, J. Gordon. "Schism in American Methodism." *AME Zion Quarterly Review* 96 (1984) 2–18.

Messer, Donald E., and William J. Abraham, eds. *Unity, Liberty, and Charity: Building Bridges Under Icy Waters.* Nashville: Abingdon, 1996.

Mollenkott, Virginia Ramey. "Overcoming Heterosexism—To Benefit Everyone." In *Homosexuality in the Church: Both Sides of the Debate*, edited by J. S. Siker, 145–49. Louisville: Westminster John Knox, 1994.

———. *Sensuous Spirituality: Out from Fundamentalism.* New York: Crossroad. 1992.

Moon, Dawne. *God, Sex, and Politics: Homosexuality and Everyday Theologies.* Chicago: University of Chicago Press, 2004.

Murguia, Edward, and Tyrone Forman. "Rethinking Whiteness Historiography: The Case of Italians in Chicago, 1890–1945." In *White Out: The Continuing Significance of Racism*, edited by A. W. Doane and E. Bonilla-Silva, 49–62. New York: Routledge, 2003.

Murray, Peter C. *Methodists and the Crucible of Race, 1930–1975.* Columbia: University of Missouri Press, 2004.

———. "The Origins of Racial Inclusiveness in the Methodist Church." *The Journal of Religious Thought* 45 (1989) 57–69.

———. "The Racial Crisis in the Methodist Church." *Methodist History* 2 (1987) 3–14.

Myers, Kristen. *Racetalk: Racism Hiding in Plain Sight.* Lanham, MD: Rowman and Littlefield, 2005.

———. "White Fright: Reproducing White Supremacy through Casual Discourse." In *White Out: The Continuing Significance of Racism*, edited by A. W. Doane and E. Bonilla-Silva, 129–44. New York: Routledge, 2003.

Nason-Clark, Nancy. "Ordaining Women as Priests: Religious vs. Sexist Explanations for Clerical Attitudes." *Sociological Analysis* 48 (1987) 259–73.

Bibliography

Nelson, James B. *Between Two Gardens: Reflections on Sexuality and Religious Experience.* New York: Pilgrim, 1983.

———. *Body Theology.* Louisville: Westminster John Knox, 1992.

———. *Embodiment: An Approach to Sexuality and Christian Theology.* Minneapolis: Augsburg, 1978.

———. "Homosexuality and the Church." *Christianity and Crisis* 37 (1977) 63–69.

Noll, William T. "A Welcome in the Ministry: The 1920 and 1924 General Conferences Debate Clergy Rights for Women." *Methodist History* 30 (1992) 91–99.

Norwood, Frederick A. *The Story of American Methodism.* Nashville: Abingdon, 1974.

Nzwili, Fredrick. "African clerics: Gay rights equal colonialism," RNS news release in *The Christian Century* (April 2, 2014) 15–16.

O'Donnell, Saranne P. "The Question of Eligibility of Women to the General Conference of the Methodist Episcopal Church—1888." In *Woman's Rightful Place: Women in United Methodist History*, edited by D. K. Gorrell, 11–26. Dayton, OH: United Theological Seminary, 1980.

Oliveto, Karen Phyllis. "Movements of Reform and Movements of Resistance: Homosexuality and the United Methodist Church: A Case Study." PhD diss., Drew University, 2002.

Olson, Daniel V. A., and William McKinney. "United Methodist Leaders: Diversity and Moral Authority." In *The People(s) Called Methodist: Forms and Reforms of their Life*, edited by W. B. Lawrence, D. M. Campbell, and R. E. Richey, 109–26. Nashville: Abingdon, 1998.

Olson, Laura R., and Wendy Cadge. "Talking about Homosexuality: The Views of Mainline Protestant Clergy." *Journal for the Scientific Study of Religion* 41 (2002) 153–67.

Orsi, Robert, ed. *Gods of the City: Religion and the American Urban Landscape.* Bloomington: Indiana University Press, 1999.

Parrish, Carrie. *Journey of Women toward Ordination in the United Methodist Tradition: An Examination of the Efforts of Women to Become Ordained in the Methodist Tradition Since the Mid-Nineteenth Century.* Commission on the Status and Role of Women, North Carolina Conference, United Methodist Church, 1983.

Patton, Cindy. "Queer Space/God's Space: Counting Down to the Apocalypse." *Rethinking Marxism* 9 (1996–97) 1–23.

Petersen, Larry R., and Gregory V. Donnenwerth. "Religion and Declining Support for Traditional Beliefs about Gender Roles and Homosexual Rights." *Sociology of Religion* 59 (1998) 353–71.

Phillips, L. Edward. "Homosexual Unions and the Social Principles: Blessing the Incompatible?" In *The Loyal Opposition: Struggling with the Church on Homosexuality*, edited by T. Sample and A. E. DeLong, 88–95. Nashville: Abingdon, 2000.

Pieterse, Hendrik R. "A Worldwide United Methodist Church? Soundings toward a Connectional Theological Imagination." *Methodist Review* 5 (2013) 1–23.

Pitts, Jesse R. "Personality and the Social System." In *Theories of Society: Foundations of Modern Sociological Theory*, edited by T. Parsons et al., 2:685–716. New York: Free Press of Glencoe, 1961.

Plaskow, Judith. "Dismantling the Gender Binary within Judaism: The Challenge of Transgender to Compulsory Heterosexuality." In *Heterosexism in Contemporary World Religion: Problem and Prospect*, edited by M. M. Ellison and J. Plaskow, 13–36. Cleveland: Pilgrim, 2007.

Rabaka, Reiland. "The Souls of White Folk: W. E. B. Du Bois's Critique of White Supremacy and Contributions to Critical White Studies." *Journal of African American Studies* 11 (2007) 1–15.

Ratzinger, Joseph. "Letter to the Bishops of the Catholic Church on the Pastoral Care of Homosexual Persons." In *Homosexuality in the Church: Both Sides of the Debate*, edited by J. S. Siker, 39–48. Louisville: Westminster John Knox, 1994.

Rey, Terry. *Bourdieu on Religion: Imposing Faith and Legitimacy*. London: Equinox, 2007.

———. "Marketing the Goods of Salvation: Bourdieu on Religion." *Religion* 34 (2004) 331–43.

Richey, Russell E. *Early American Methodism*. Bloomington: Indiana University Press, 1991.

———. "Is Division A New Threat to the Denomination?" In *Questions for the Twenty-First Century Church*, edited by R. E. Richey et al., 105–16. Nashville: Abingdon, 1999.

———. *The Methodist Conference in America: A History*. Nashville: Kingswood, 1996.

Richey, Russell E., et al., eds. *Perspectives on American Methodism: Interpretive Essays*. Nashville: Kingswood, 1993.

Rogers, Jack. "Sex, Philosophy, and Politics: How and What the Church Must Decide in the Debate over Ordination of Homosexuals." In *Homosexuality in the Church: Both Sides of the Debate*, edited by J. S. Siker, 161–77. Louisville: Westminster John Knox, 1994.

Rowe, Kenneth E. "How Do Caucuses Contribute to Connection?" In *Questions for the Twenty-First Century Church*, edited by R. E. Richey et al., 242–57. Nashville: Abingdon, 1999.

———. "The Ordination of Women: Round One; Anna Oliver and the General Conference of 1880." In *Perspectives on American Methodism: Interpretive Essays*, edited by R. E. Richey et al., 298–308. Nashville: Kingswood, 1993.

Rudy, Kathy. "The Social Construction of Sexual Identity and the Ordination of Practicing Homosexuals." *Journal of Religious Ethics* 25 (1997) 127–46.

Ruether, Rosemary Radford. *Sexism and God-Talk: Toward a Feminist Theology*. Boston: Beacon, 1983.

Ruether, Rosemary Radford, and Eleanor McLaughlin, eds. *Women of Spirit: Female Leadership in the Jewish and Christian Traditions*. New York: Simon and Schuster, 1979.

Rutledge, Kathleen K. "Pondering a Divorce." *Christianity Today* 48 (2004) 49–52.

Sample, Tex, and Amy E. DeLong, eds. *The Loyal Opposition: Struggling with the Church on Homosexuality*. Nashville: Abingdon, 2000.

Sano, Roy. "Homosexuality and the Church: Evangelical Commitment and Prophetic Responsibility." In *The Loyal Opposition: Struggling with the Church on Homosexuality*, edited by T. Sample and A. E. DeLong, 43–52. Nashville: Abingdon, 2000.

Scanzoni, Letha, and Virginia Ramey Mollenkott. *Is the Homosexual My Neighbor? Another Christian View*. San Francisco: Harper and Row, 1978.

Scharen, Christian Batalden. "Subject to Discipline: Authority, Sexuality, and the Production of Candidates for Ordained Ministry." *Journal of the American Academy of Religion* 66 (1998) 313–44.

Schlager, Bernard. "Reading CSTH as a Call to Action: Boswell and Gay-Affirming Movements in American Christianity." In *The Boswell Thesis: Essays on* Christianity,

Social Tolerance, and Homosexuality, edited by M. Kuefler, 74–87. Chicago: University of Chicago Press, 2006.

Schmidt, Jean Miller. *Grace Sufficient: A History of Women in American Methodism.* Nashville: Abingdon, 1999.

Schubert, J. Daniel. "Suffering." In *Pierre Bourdieu: Key Concepts*, edited by M. Grenfell, 183–98. Stocksfield, UK: Acumen, 2008.

Scott, James. *Domination and the Arts of Resistance: Hidden Transcripts.* New Haven: Yale University Press., 1990.

Seamands, David A. "Blessing the Unblessable." *Good News* (November/December 1992) 14–17.

———. "Blessing the Unblessable." *Good News* (May/June 1998) 19–22.

———. "God Made Them Male and Female: Scripture's Consistent Heterosexual Track." *Good News* (January/February 1992) 14–17.

———. "A Marriage Counterculture." *Christianity Today* (December 14, 1992) 27–28.

———. "Perfectionism Fraught with Fruits of Self-Destructionism." *Christianity Today* (April 10, 1981) 24–26.

Seamands, David, and Mark Rutland. "David Seamands and Mark Rutland on the Church's Integrity Crisis." *Good News* (July/August 1988) 18–21.

Shopshire, James M. "Black Methodist Protestants, 1877–1939: Protest and Change among African Americans within Predecessor Organizations of the United Methodist Church." In *The Recovery of Black Presence: An Interdisciplinary Exploration*, edited by R. C. Bailey and J. Grant, 177–91, 242–45. Nashville: Abingdon, 1995.

Sigmund, Paul E. *Liberation Theology at the Crossroads: Democracy or Revolution?* Oxford: Oxford University Press, 1990.

Siker, Jeffrey S., ed. *Homosexuality in the Church: Both Sides of the Debate.* Louisville: Westminster John Knox, 1994.

Skeggs, Beverley. "Context and Background: Pierre Bourdieu's Analysis of Class, Gender, and Sexuality." In *Feminism after Bourdieu*, edited by L. Adkins and B. Skeggs, 19–33. Oxford: Blackwell, 2004.

Sledge, Robert Watson. *Hands on the Ark: The Struggle for Change in the Methodist Episcopal Church, South, 1914–1939.* Lake Junaluska, NC: Commission on Archives and History, The United Methodist Church, 1975.

Smaje, Chris. "Not Just a Social Construct: Theorising Race and Ethnicity." *Sociology* 31 (1997) 307–27.

Smith, Peter. "Retired United Methodist Minister, Author Admits Sex Misconduct." *The Courier-Journal*, August 3, 2005, B1, B4.

Sowell, Thomas. *Race and Economics.* New York: David McKay, 1975.

Sprague, C. Joseph. *Affirmations of a Dissenter.* Nashville: Abingdon, 2002.

Stackhouse, Max. "The Heterosexual Norm." In *Homosexuality and Christian Community*, edited by C. Seow, 133–43. Louisville: John Knox, 1996.

Stanton, Elizabeth Cady, et al., eds. *History of Woman Suffrage, Vol. 1: 1848–1861.* New York: Fowler & Wells, 1881.

Steele, Richard, with Holly Camp. "A 'No' to the Gays,." *Newsweek*, June 20, 1977, 27.

Stephens, John B. "Conflicts over Homosexuality in the United Methodist Church: Testing Theories of Conflict Analysis and Resolution." PhD diss., George Mason University, 1997.

Stone, Lora. "'Misrecognition of the Limits': Bourdieu's Religious Capital and Social Transformation." *Journal for Cultural and Religious Theory* 3 (2001) 1–37.

Strober, Myra H., and Audri Gordon Lanford. "The Feminization of Public School Teaching: Cross-Sectional Analysis, 1850–1880." *Signs: Journal of Women in Culture and Society* 11 (1986) 212–35.

Swartz, David. "Bridging the Study of Culture and Religion: Pierre Bourdieu's Political Economy of Symbolic Power." *Sociology of Religion* 57 (1996) 71–85.

———. *Culture and Power: The Sociology of Pierre Bourdieu.* Chicago: University of Chicago Press, 1997.

Thandeka. *Learning to Be White: Money, Race, and God in America.* New York: Continuum, 1999.

Thomas, James S. *Methodism's Racial Dilemma: The Story of the Central Jurisdiction.* Nashville: Abingdon, 1992.

Thomas, Jeremy N., and Daniel V. A. Olson. "Evangelical Elites' Changing Responses to Homosexuality 1960–2009." *Sociology of Religion* 73 (2012) 239–72.

Tickle, Phyllis. *The Great Emergence.* Grand Rapids: Baker, 2008.

Tooley, Mark. "Light from the Dark Continent." *Touchstone: A Journal of Mere Christianity* (September 2004) 62–63.

Troxell, Barbara B. "Ordination of Women in the United Methodist Tradition." *Methodist History* 37 (1999) 119–30.

Udis-Kessler, Amanda. *Queer Inclusion in the United Methodist Church.* New York: Routledge, 2008.

Van Geest, Fred. "Christian Denominational and Special Interest Political Action on Public Policy Issues Related to Sexual Orientation." *Sociology of Religion* 69 (2008) 335–54.

Veenvliet, Scott G. "Intrinsic Religious Orientation and Religious Teaching: Differential Judgments towards Same-Gender Sexual Behavior and Gay Men and Lesbians." *International Journal for the Psychology of Religion* 18 (2008) 53–65.

Venn, Couze. "On the Cunning of Imperialist Reason: A Questioning Note or Preamble for a Debate." *Theory, Culture and Society* 16 (1999) 59–62.

Vera, Hernan, and Andrew M. Gordon. "The Beautiful American: Science Fictions of the White Messiah in Hollywood Movies." In *White Out: The Continuing Significance of Racism,* edited by A. W. Doane and E. Bonilla-Silva, 113–26. New York: Routledge, 2003.

Verter, Bradford. "Spiritual Capital: Theorizing Religion with Bourdieu against Bourdieu." *Sociological Theory* 21 (2003) 150–74.

Wainwright, Geoffrey. "Schisms, Heresies, and the Gospel: Wesleyan Reflections on Evangelical Truth and Ecclesial Unity." In *Ancient and Postmodern Christianity: Paleo-Orthodoxy in the 21st Century,* edited by K. Tanner and C. A. Hall, 183–98. Downers Grove, IL: InterVarsity, 2002.

Walker, Alice. Preface to *In Search of Our Mother's Gardens.* New York: Harcourt, Brace, Jovanovich, 1983.

Wallace, Ruth A. "Bringing Women In: Marginality in the Churches." *Sociological Analysis* 36 (1975) 291–303.

———. *They Call Her Pastor: A New Role for Catholic Women.* Albany: State University of New York Press, 1992.

Weber, Max. *The Theory of Social and Economic Organization.* Translated by A. M. Henderson and Talcott Parsons. Glencoe, IL: Falcon's Wing, 1947.

Wellman, James K., Jr. "Introduction: The Debate over Homosexual Ordination: Subcultural Identity Theory in American Religious Organizations." *Review of Religious Research* 41 (1999) 184–206.

West, Cornel. "Christian Love and Heterosexism." In *The Cornel West Reader*, edited by C. West, 401–14. New York: Basic Civitas, 1999.

———. "Race and Social Theory." In *The Cornel West Reader*, edited by C. West, 251–65. New York: Basic Civitas, 1999.

———. *Race Matters*. Boston: Beacon, 1993.

West, Traci C. "Is a Womanist a Black Feminist? Marking the Distinctions and Defying Them." In *Deeper Shades of Purple: Womanism in Religion and Society*, edited by S. Floyd-Thomas, 291–95. New York: New York University Press, 2006.

———. "Response to Coleman." *Journal of Feminist Studies in Religion* 22 (2006) 128–34.

Westhaver, Russell. "Flaunting and Empowerment: Thinking about Circuit Parties, the Body, and Power." *Journal of Contemporary Ethnography* 35 (2006) 611–44.

Wilcox, Melissa M. *Coming Out in Christianity: Religion, Identity, and Community*. Bloomington: Indiana University Press, 2003.

Willard, Frances. *Defense of Women's Rights to Ordination in the Methodist Episcopal Church*. Edited by C. De Swarte Gifford. New York: Garland, 1987 (orig. 1889).

———. *Glimpses of Fifty Years: The Autobiography of an American Woman*. Chicago: H. J. Smith, 1889.

Williams, Delores S. "The Color of Feminism: Or Speaking the Black Woman's Tongue." *Journal of Religious Thought* 42 (1986) 42–58.

Williams, Dennis A. "Homosexuals: Anita Bryant's Crusade," *Newsweek*, April 11, 1977, 39.

Williamson, Joel. *The Crucible of Race*. New York: Oxford University Press, 1984.

Wolkomir, Michelle. "Giving It Up to God: Negotiating Femininity in Support Groups for Wives of Ex-Gay Christian Men." *Gender and Society* 18 (2004) 735–55.

Wood, James Rutland. *Where the Spirit Leads: The Evolving Views of United Methodists on Homosexuality*. Nashville: Abingdon, 2000.

Wood, James R., and Jon P. Bloch. "The Role of Church Assemblies in Building a Civil Society: The Case of the United Methodist General Conferences Debate on Homosexuality." *Sociology of Religion* 56 (1995) 121–36.

Wood, Matthew, and Christopher Bunn. "Strategy in a Religious Network: A Bourdieuian Critique of the Sociology of Spirituality." *Sociology* 43 (2009) 286–303.

Wuthnow, Robert. *The Restructuring of American Religion: Society and Faith Since World War II*. Princeton: Princeton University Press, 1988.

Yancey, George A., and Ye Jung Kim. "Racial Diversity, Gender Equality, and SES Diversity in Christian Congregations: Exploring the Connections of Racism, Sexism, and Classism in Multiracial and Nonmultiracial Churches." *Journal for the Scientific Study of Religion* 47 (2008) 103–11.

Zikmund, Barbara Brown. "The Protestant Women's Ordination Movement." *Union Seminary Quarterly Review* 57 (2003) 123–45.

Zuckerman, Phil, ed. *Du Bois on Religion*. Walnut Creek, CA: AltaMira, 2000.

Subject Index

Names Index